TOPOBIOLOGY

TOPOBIOLOGY

An Introduction to Molecular Embryology

GERALD M. EDELMAN

Basic Books, Inc., Publishers   New York

Library of Congress Cataloging-in-Publication Data

Edelman, Gerald M.
  Topobiology: an introduction to molecular embryology.

  Includes bibliographies and index.
  1. Chemical embryology.   2. Molecular biology.
I. Title.
QL963.E33   1988   574.3'3   88–47678
ISBN 0–465–08634–9

To my family

CONTENTS

PART ONE

FORM FROM PLACE

PART TWO

MOLECULAR MECHANISMS OF EPIGENESIS

PART THREE

THE MORPHOREGULATOR HYPOTHESIS: MECHANOCHEMISTRY LINKED TO DEVELOPMENTAL GENETICS

PART FOUR

DEVELOPMENT AND BEHAVIOR

LIST OF
ILLUSTRATIONS

LIST OF TABLES

PREFACE

THIS LITTLE BOOK was written to provoke interest in a body of knowledge constituting a field that I propose to call topobiology. Topobiology considers those place-dependent interactions of cell surfaces with other cell surfaces or with substrates that result in changes in cell regulation. In metazoans, such place-dependent molecular interactions can lead to regulation of the primary processes of embryological development and thus to changes in morphology.

Insofar as it is centrally concerned with developmental mechanisms, topobiology has a direct bearing upon the relationship between embryology and morphologic evolution, as well as upon the bases of behavior as determined by brain structure and function. A trio of related problems—the development of form, the evolution of form, and the morphologic and functional bases of behavior—embraces the main unsolved riddles to be confronted by modern biology as it approaches the millennium. It may seem strange that I link behavior to the other two problems, but I believe that behavior is in fact a continuing aspect of development and one that sharply affects natural selection for animal form. My main purpose in this essay is to emphasize the central significance of topobiological mechanisms to these three problems.

Topobiological mechanisms are mediated through cell surfaces and movement but at the same time are genetically determined. They therefore link developmental genetics to the mechanochemical events affecting surfaces and movement at several levels of organization, ranging in a coordinated fashion from the gene to the cell, to cell collectives, and back to the gene. Topobiology is concerned not only with place but also with time as marked by epigenetic events—changes in cellular states resulting from previous states and interactions that have occurred at particular places during growth and development. This observation provides some justification for the subtitle of this book: only when a molecular explanation of place-dependent epigenetic changes is at hand will molecular embryology come into its own.

A case will be made here that the models and mechanisms of cell differentiation studied by current molecular biology are insufficient to explain such epigenetic events. My thesis is that surface interactions mediated by molecules of a very specific type that I call morphoregulatory molecules provide a sufficient basis for epigenesis. Expression of such molecules leads to changes in cell shape and movement, to cell associations with other cells, and to new forms of regulation of gene expression. One of the chief tasks of molecular embryology is to describe how various chemical signals alter the expression and function of morphoregulatory molecules.

Although this essay reviews a large variety of facts, it is concerned mainly with a theoretical analysis. One of the goals of that analysis is to show that a true understanding of topobiology can come only from a wide-ranging view that links development, evolutionary ecology, and behavior. If the curiosity of students is aroused by this approach to the subject, or if my fellow researchers are stimulated to new ideas by the theories I propose here, I will feel that I have achieved my aim. Naturally, I would be pleased if some of the models and predictions I put forth turn out to be true. True or not, they will, I hope, provoke discussion and prompt new experimental searches.

A few words about size and thoroughness: I have resolved that this book should be readable by trained biologists in one weekend and by general scientific readers in two, and thus have been forced to gloss over several vast fields. Moreover, in focusing narrowly upon morphoregulatory molecules in chapter 7, I have had to discuss a fair number of details that in themselves are somewhat tedious but that are necessary to understand the main argument. Even worse, by the time this appears, much more of central significance to that argument will be known but will not be included. I attempt to make amends for these unavoidable inhomogeneities by suggesting some references (but not all) that should help guide interested persons into related fields and give them the opportunity to review other opinions. At the end of each chapter, readers will find references by individuals in the order that they are mentioned in the text as well as additional references that I thought would be useful.

This book is intended to be a provocative introduction, not a review, and for this reason it is no place for the reader to seek either a balanced list of primary references or a balanced account of embryology itself. I hope that my failure to mention so many key contributors is not taken amiss: the bibliographies of the large works and reviews mentioned in the references are certainly more representative for those readers seeking scholarly citations and, in addition to their primary value, they should be consulted for this purpose. I am grateful to Susan Hassler, editor of The Neurosciences Institute, for bringing some of these works to my attention, as well as for her expert editorial help. I also wish to thank Dr. Kathryn L. Crossin, who provided consistent and important scientific criticism and editing during the preparation of this manuscript. Finally, my goal has not been to provide a thorough or descriptively adequate view of morphology; instead, the morphologic examples presented are intended only to illustrate principles. Consistent with my wish to interest a diverse audience, I have attempted to explain certain specialized issues for those readers who are not experts, and thus I have in some cases simplified these issues. This elementary approach will, I hope, be recognized by experts as a necessary bridge to matters that are far from elementary.

New York, 1987

PART ONE

FORM FROM PLACE

1

Animate Form

WHEN I was a high school student, I came across Erwin
Schrödinger's *What Is Life?* I still remember my exultant reaction—a combination of adolescent pride in feeling able to understand ideas considered beyond a young person's means, and a
genuine intellectual thrill engendered by the problems that
Schrödinger addressed. Upon rereading the book, it appears to
me that its major value was to provoke interest in a central
problem of biology. Schrödinger's question—What is life?—was
mainly, although not exclusively, related to the molecular basis
of heredity.

The issue has now been resolved, and many of the questions
asked in that classic little book have been answered: the molecular basis of heredity rests in the structure of DNA and in the
genetic code. This view resolves the ancient and paradoxical
problem of preformation that asserted that a replica of an organism was contained in the sperm or egg. Rather than preformation, with its endless regress, there is a set of rules for translating
the structure of the code into proteins that share in forming the
phenotype—the aggregate of interactive structures and functions that constitute an organism of a species upon which natural
selection acts. This side of biology, once obscure, is now in the
light.

One might say, "That's that; the whole issue is resolved." But,
as usual in fundamental matters, a mystery remains. This mystery

is embedded in the problem of morphologic evolution, the process that gives animals and their organs their functional shapes
and that yields the most exquisite product of all, the human
brain. The properties conferred by these shapes determine the
phenotype, and it is the phenotype upon which natural selection
acts. We can convey the character of this problem by asking a
pair of linked questions. (1) How does the one-dimensional genetic code specify a three-dimensional animal? We will call this
the developmental genetic question. (2) How is the proposed
answer to the developmental genetic question reconciled with
relatively rapid changes in form occurring in relatively short
evolutionary times? We will call this the evolutionary question.

This pair of questions sets the frame for the subject of this book.
From the historical point of view, these questions are related to
an ancient notion called epigenesis, proposed as an alternative to
preformation in order to account for animal form and function.
Epigeneticists countered the proposals of preformationists with
the idea that form arose during development from the environment acting upon living material. It is my thesis here that, although the notion of preformation was transformed by the finding of a genetic code, an understanding of that code does not
suffice to answer our two main questions. Unlike the ancient
thesis of preformation, the antithetical problem of epigenesis has
been neither disposed of nor resolved.

Truth often lives on the outskirts of ancient controversies and
moves to the center of town only when both thesis and antithesis
are transformed. In focusing upon the possible transformation of
the idea of epigenesis in modern terms, I will be considering
what might be called the other side of biology, that part of developmental biology dedicated to the understanding of animal form
and to the related subject of morphologic evolution—how genes
can define animal shape, pattern, and phenotypic function in
developmental and evolutionary time. I will develop the hypothesis that morphogenesis and morphologic evolution depend
upon a special set of molecular regulatory mechanisms mediated
by the cell surface as it interacts at particular places in the
embryo with other surfaces, both cellular and noncellular.
These morphoregulatory mechanisms link the mechanochemical

events that affect cell shape, division, and motion to particular patterns of gene expression. They do so by means of sets of cell surface molecules that mediate one form or another of cell adhesion, and that interact directly and indirectly with the cytoskeleton, the complex structure in cells that governs their shape and motion.

In confronting the critical issue of place-dependent molecular interactions at the cell surface, a field I call topobiology, I hope mainly to sharpen the formulation of the developmental genetic and evolutionary questions. I cannot hope to emulate Schrödinger: the problems this book surveys are in one sense not as vast as the one embodied in the question "What is life?" But the number and complexity of the subjects that must be addressed are larger than those he considered in his book. Moreover, as a molecular biologist, I am more opinionated about my subject, and less qualified for philosophical musing than a thinker such as Schrödinger, who was looking from the outside in. If this lack of aesthetic distance is a defect, I hope at least to convince the reader that the time has come to sharpen the issues of morphologic evolution and developmental genetics in molecular terms. I suggest that the present framework of molecular biology must be extended to answer the developmental genetic and evolutionary questions, and in later chapters I propose a larger theoretical framework within which the ultimate answers may be cast. Only when these answers are available can we consider that Schrödinger's question has been satisfactorily answered.

That question "What is life?" is both important and ambiguous. In its primary meaning, it may be taken to be equivalent to asking, "What distinguishes animate from inanimate objects?" This question is essentially the one asked by Schrödinger and, as I mentioned, is now answerable: animate objects are self-replicating systems containing a genetic code that undergoes mutation and whose variant individuals undergo natural selection. Another way of putting this is to say that animate systems have three characteristics that allow them to evolve. They have (1) heredity, (2) a basis of variation in their hereditary material, and (3) populations consisting of variant individuals undergoing competition and differential reproduction in a changing environment, that is, natural selection occurring on the basis of differences in fitness of these individuals. On the average, the more adapted will tend to survive, leave more progeny, and thus have the functional components of their hereditary material more frequently represented in the population in ensuing generations.

This picture is in effect a snapshot of the grand theory that informs all of modern biology. In addition to Darwin's great contribution (the idea of natural selection), two modern developments have served to extend and deepen this view. The first was the so-called modern synthesis, in which the findings of Mendelian genetics (the theory of heredity) were put together with the idea of natural selection. This synthesis was spurred by a number of scientists in the 1940s, and it successfully incorporated into Darwin's theory Mendel's findings of the segregation and independent assortment of particulate units of inheritance. By the time of the synthesis, the idea had emerged that these units were definite entities called genes, although their chemical nature had not yet been firmly established. The major conclusion of the modern synthesis can be succinctly stated: the results of natural selection acting on the individuals in a population are reflected in a change in the frequencies of different genes in that population. In the main, however, selection acts not on the genes but on the individuals whose phenotypic traits are governed by the genes. But what is the chemical nature of genes? And how do genes actually replicate and govern traits?

The determination in detail of the chemical nature of the gene that provided the answers to these questions was the second development that enriched the Darwinian view. The hereditary material was found by Avery and his associates in 1944 to be a special chemical called DNA. The structure of DNA subsequently proposed by Watson and Crick provided a basis for understanding how self-replication could occur and later for the idea of a genetic code. The working out of this code by a number of laboratories and the knowledge that it determined the sequence of amino acids in proteins tied the pattern inherited in the genes (the genotype) to certain functional aspects of an organism in a species (the phenotype). This tie is through the following series: the code determines amino acid sequence; amino acid sequence determines the three-dimensional folding and shape of each protein molecule; three-dimensional shape determines protein function by assuring the molecular complementarity that is the basis for all biochemically significant reactions. The collection of all such structure-function relations is called the phenotype, and it is the phenotype upon which natural selection acts. Notice that the structure-function relations must extend upward from the molecular scale to affect the function of the whole animal.

This picture of evolutionary change resulting from natural selection acting upon phenotypes determined by the particular sequences of code words embodied in genes—code words that could be changed by mutations, thus altering protein function—could be taken as an answer to Schrödinger's question. But it turns out that while, in effect, this triumph of molecular biology answers the question about the chemical nature of the gene and how hereditary traits are *transmitted*, it does not fully answer the question of how genes determine traits.

To put it another way, the achievement of molecular genetics distinguishes the animate from the inanimate but does not necessarily account satisfactorily for all of the interesting or essential functional properties of animate objects that constitute life. As we will see, for example, it is very difficult to account for the forms, patterns, or shapes of complex animals simply by extrapolating from the rules governing the shapes of proteins. It is just these animal patterns, however, that give rise to overall function and behavior, ultimately providing the basis for such remarkable events as the evolution of the human brain and consciousness. It is in this sense that the question "What is life?" is ambiguously framed—in addition to the animate-inanimate distinction, we would certainly wish to know how such important phenotypic traits as morphology and brain function can be satisfactorily accounted for both in molecular genetic and in evolutionary terms.

The answer to this aspect of Schrödinger's question lies in the field of developmental biology. Darwin himself was quite aware of the importance of developmental biology and morphology to evolution and natural selection. In the absence of a proper genetic theory and of the molecular details, however, a satisfactory answer to the issue of morphologic evolution was not forthcoming in his day. We are still left with the problem of showing how the morphologic structures and patterns governing behavior in an animal species arise as a result of development, and we must link their developmental appearance to the properties of certain key genes. In other words, we must explain in detail how development is regulated to give form and how changes in frequencies of certain genes are related to such regulation. This is the outstanding problem posed jointly by the developmental genetic and the evolutionary questions.

The rest of this book is devoted to a short account of those aspects of molecular, developmental, and evolutionary biology that bear upon possible answers to these two questions. My main theme is that topobiological interactions at cell surfaces involving particular kinds of protein molecules provide a major clue to the answers. But before we engage that theme, we must consider further why the present knowledge of the code, of protein synthesis, and of protein shape is insufficient to answer the developmental genetic and evolutionary questions.

SELECTED REFERENCES

Schrödinger, E. 1945. *What is life? The physical aspect of the living cell.* Cambridge: Cambridge University Press; New York: Macmillan.

Mayr, E. 1982. *The growth of biological thought: Diversity, evolution, and inheritance.* Cambridge: Harvard University Press.

Mayr, E., and W. B. Provine. 1980. *The evolutionary synthesis: Perspectives on the unification of biology.* Cambridge: Harvard University Press.

Darwin, C. 1859. *On the origin of species by means of natural selection; or, The preservation of favoured races in the struggle for life.* London: Murray.

Thompson, D. W. 1942. *On growth and form.* Cambridge: Cambridge University Press.

Avery, O. T., C. M. MacLeod, and M. McCarty. 1944. Studies on the chemical nature of the substance inducing transformation of pneumococcal types. *J. Exp. Med.* 79:137–58.

Watson, J. D., and F. H. C. Crick. 1953. Molecular structure of nucleic acids: A structure for deoxyribose nucleic acid. *Nature* 171:737–38.

Judson, H. F. 1980. *The eighth day of creation.* New York: Simon & Schuster.

Raff, R. A., and T. C. Kaufman. 1983. *Embryos, genes, and evolution.* New York: Macmillan.

2

Code, Scale, and Place

THE GENETIC CODE serves as a means of storing heritable changes reflecting selection events that occurred in populations of individuals having phenotypic traits that conferred fitness. Because it is embedded in molecules of DNA, the "memory" of a coding sequence is stabilized as a covalent string, and the stability at ordinary temperatures of the covalent bonds in these molecules is sufficient to keep the appropriate sequence of code words together. Replacements of bases in code words can and do occur as mutations, however, and such mutations provide a basis of variability that alters the phenotype. At the same time, the structures of DNA and of the enzymatic apparatus for its replication and repair guarantee that the code sequences can be copied faithfully and passed on to daughter cells. The mutations that are passed on can, among other things, change the sequence of particular proteins and thus alter their shape and function.

It is important to notice, however, that while alterations in protein structure can give rise to enormous changes in the functioning of an animal or in particular traits, they do not *necessarily* form a *direct* basis for changes in shape at the scale of the animal or its organs or appendages. Such changes in shape and in animal size are under genetic control, but, within limits, they show continuous variation reflecting the complex workings of many genes.

We may ask, What is the difference between a discrete genetic change that converts normal hemoglobin to sickle-cell hemoglobin, with morbid consequences, and a genetic change that alters the shape and size of the whole animal (or even of its nose)? To address this question more fully, we will have to review some salient aspects of embryonic development and morphologic evolution in the next several chapters. But first, it may be valuable to address certain aspects of animal size, functional scale, and cell numbers that put very strong constraints on the means by which genetically introduced changes in the shape of proteins can alter the shapes of animals. The problem we are concerned with may be considered the fundamental problem of topobiology: How are cells of different types ordered in time or place during development to give species-specific tissue pattern and animal form?

An animal such as a mouse or a man is made of a large number of cells—in the case of a man, approximately 10^{12} cells. There are approximately two hundred different kinds of cells (each kind representing a different group of expressed proteins specified in an individual's collection of genes, or its genome). Cells are linked together in tissues composed of various collections of the cell types characteristic of each tissue, and the pattern of these tissues (and, to a large degree, their eventual function) is determined mainly during embryonic development. The form of the animal that ensues is characteristic of a species and is subject within limits to continuous variation.

Could the shape of proteins or, rather, a collection of proteins of different shapes account *directly* for animal shape by assembly? At first glance, it might seem that this is entirely feasible, for viruses capable of self-replication and also the shaping of *parts* of cells (such as ribosomes) are themselves so governed. The same and different proteins can form supramolecular assemblies of defined shape and function. Why could this process not be directly adapted to put together cells and tissues?

The first difficulty that this suggestion faces is one of scale and complexity: the scale factors for developmental growth and regulation can range over many orders of magnitude (see table 2.1). Cells are much bigger than proteins and are made up of many different kinds of molecules in addition to proteins. Moreover, we know that it is the linkage of cells into pattern, not the linkage of proteins only, that yields animal form. This difficulty

TABLE 2.1

*Some Matters of Scale and Complexity**

Process	Scale Factor
Growth	
Fertilized egg (1 cell)	
Mature organism (10^{11} cells)	10^{11}
Differentiation	
Egg (1 type)	
Tissue cells (≈ 200 types)	10^2
Control Loops	
Molecular 10^{-6} cm (100 Å)	1
(direct complementarity over distances of the order of 10 Å)	
Cellular 10^{-3} cm (10 μ)	10^3
(contact, diffusion)	
Organisms 1 cm to 10^3 cm (1 m)	10^9 (overall)
(circulatory, hormonal)	
Developmentally Significant Numbers and Distances	
Range of motion, cells, and epithelia	10^{-1} cm to 1 cm
Number of cells in an inducing collective	10^2 to 10^5
(10^{-1} cm to 10^{-2} cm in size)	
Types of cell surface molecules	10^4
Number of synapses in human brain	10^{15} to 10^{16}
Number of genes (mammalian)	10^5

*This table is designed to give only an approximate notion of the increase of cell numbers with time, of the range of distance over which signals must act, and of the degree of complexity of genetic or phenotypic systems.

might be circumvented by taking notice of the fact that inserted into the plasma membrane of cells are different proteins, some of which could link cells *in a particular order* to make assemblies of just the right shape. In other words, cell surface proteins could act as *addresses* providing a topobiological code for the type, position, and sequence of linked cells, yielding tissues and form.

While it is certainly conceivable that evolution could have given rise to a large number of combinatorially different addressing protein sequences that might guarantee cell recognition, this proposed solution encounters several obstacles, including how the right address protein is expressed on the right cell at the right time, the number of proteins (and structural genes) that are necessary, and how statistical events at a higher scale (such as fluc-

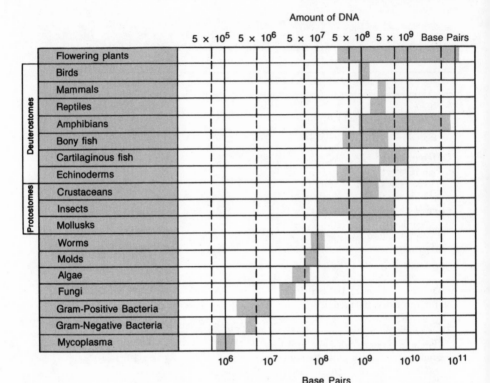

Figure 2.1

DNA content of the haploid genome is not closely related to the morphologic complexity of the species. Genome size does increase through the prokaryotes and the protostomes but extends over a wide range for the deuterostomes. The range of DNA values within a phylum is indicated by the shaded area. *(From B. J. Lewin, 1987,* GENES III, *New York: Wiley. Based on data compiled by R. J. Britten and E. H. Davidson, 1969, Gene regulation for higher cells: A theory,* Science *165:349–57.)*

tuations in cell death and cell movement) could be compensated for by any cell recognition code. It is perhaps relevant at this point to indicate that the DNA content of the haploid genome is not closely related to the morphological complexity of various species (see figure 2.1).

We will deal at length with all of these issues in the ensuing chapters. Here I wish to take up the central question of how in any case the right proteins are expressed by the right cells at the right place and time. The word *right,* of course, means "in such a way as to guarantee that the genetic instructions for the recognition proteins are realized appropriately to give rise to an individual animal in a species with a shape that ensures some degree of fitness."

There is a major obstacle to providing the answer by a direct genetic explanation. Genes do not store the information on the position in space or time of a given cell during the development of an individual animal. Nor is it possible to ensure in general that the mechanisms governing the expression of genes for recognition proteins can work so precisely as to read the exact location of a cell or its descendants in a lineage except under very limited circumstances. These circumstances are that the number of cells in an animal is very small (i.e., hundreds, not millions) and that a given cell, in making attachments to other cells, has very few choices. In certain animals, limiting conditions close to these are met (e.g., the microscopic roundworm, *Caenorhabditis elegans*). But in general, during the development of complex animals and organs, these conditions are not met.

Cell addressing faces another major topobiological difficulty. This results from the fact that, in forming the same tissues in a species, cells can *move* in patterns that show statistical variation in cell order and association (although that variation is not completely random). These patterns also show statistical variation in both the number and the position of cells that *die*. In some tissues—for example, the nervous system—up to 70 percent of the cells in a given area may die before the tissue is shaped. Although the same tissue is formed in two different animals of a species, there is no evidence to support the idea that the same cells die in the same sequence in these tissues. Even if a set of recognition molecules could establish some ordered connection among cells to give shape, variations in cell movement or in cell death would almost certainly disturb that order. To maintain it would require constant readjustment *at the level of individual cells* of the position, cell address, and relative expression of each type of surface recognition protein. Inasmuch as genes cannot directly store or specify the place of a cell at a given time, an individual cell would have to be able to read, at scale, instructions for place or for restoration of relative position by some additional chemical mechanisms. Such mechanisms have been proposed and will be reviewed briefly here and at greater length in the next chapter.

Before mentioning them, however, let us consider what characterizes the kinds of changes we have been speaking about. All of them are epigenetic changes—changes that can occur only if earlier changes occur *first* as a result of cooperative cell interactions that are to some extent historical. In other words, to make a tissue that has a shape, cells must first be made in sufficient number by cell division, they must move together or stay together after division by being linked in a certain pattern, and certain cells must die. Above all, the order of such events entails the expression of certain genes and not of others, and a reversal or alteration of that order would result in great changes in tissue composition or shape.

If we were to look at such events in terms of the genes expressed during their unfolding, two characteristics would become apparent. The first has been called by Stebbins an epigenetic sequence: during development, the expression of genes is followed by the expression of *apparently* unrelated genes in time scales that are long as compared with those in which control of intracellular events occurs. The second characteristic is that, at a given time, lists of the genes expressed in the same tissues of any two animals of a species would be orderly and would in general be the same. Indeed, from earlier tissues to later ones, a bifurcating scheme of gene expression would emerge, expressing both a lineage and an apparent differentiation scheme. The control loops over which such genes must exert their effects can themselves range over a very wide scale (table 2.1).

Given these properties and the difficulties posed by the other aforementioned matters of scale, one might imagine several sets of solutions to the fundamental topobiological problem of how cells of different types are ordered in time and place to give a pattern. Three kinds of proposals have been advanced to account for cellular behavior to yield pattern. (Of course, many other proposals exist, but most can be considered as similar to one or another of these three kinds.) The first rests on an ingenious suggestion of Turing (the originator of Turing's theorem and of the universal Turing machine, which forms the ground of computer science). Models based on his suggestions are called reaction-diffusion (RD) models, for reasons that will become clear when we describe his proposal. For now, let us say that his analysis shows that certain chemical reactions coupled in particular ways can create spatial pattern out of initially unordered, diffusing chemical components. The second idea was put forth by Wolpert and is called positional information (PI). Briefly, the notion is that a cell can read chemical signals already present in a spatial prepattern and thus alter or confirm its address. The third idea is that cells can alter their movements by long-range effects of stretch and compression propagated through matrix proteins spanning many cell diameters and that the cell movements themselves lead to such patterning effects. This idea, proposed by Oster and his colleagues, I call strict mechanical pattern propagation (SMPP).

All of these important ideas and the models in which they are embedded are ingenious, but each is either incomplete or faces a number of different difficulties when confronted with various developmental, genetic, and evolutionary observations. To show that this is so, we will have to review some classic and recent findings in the fields of developmental biology, morphologic evolution, and cell biology. We can then take up these models for pattern in more detail and suggest an alternative hypothesis aimed at resolving the linked problems posed by the developmental genetic and evolutionary questions.

SELECTED REFERENCES

Haldane, J. B. S. 1928. *Possible worlds.* New York: Harper.

Wessells, N. K. 1977. *Tissue interactions and development.* Menlo Park, Calif.: W. A. Benjamin.

Stebbins, G. L. 1968. Integration of development and evolutionary progress. In *Population biology and evolution,* ed. R. C. Lewontin, 17–36. Syracuse: Syracuse University Press.

Sperry, R. W. 1963. Chemoaffinity in the orderly growth of nerve fiber patterns and connections. *Proc. Natl. Acad. Sci. USA* 50:703–10.

Edelman, G. M. 1984. Cell surface modulation and marker multiplicity in neural patterning. *Trends Neurosci.* 7:78–84.

Turing, A. M. 1952. The chemical basis of morphogenesis. *Philos. Trans. R. Soc. Lond. (Biol.)* 237:37–72.

Wolpert, L. 1971. Positional information and pattern formation. *Curr. Top. Dev. Biol.* 6:183–224.

Oster, G. F., J. D. Murray, and A. K. Harris. 1984. Mechanical aspects of mesenchymal morphogenesis. *J. Embryol. Exp. Morphol.* 78:83–125.

3

Development

MOST PEOPLE who have witnessed the events of animal embryonic development leading to the emergence of form and of tissue detail are deeply impressed by the regularity and complexity of the process. At the same time that there is growth and increase in cell numbers, there is the emergence of shape revealing a body plan with an axis—a head and a tail end—and, at a finer scale in different places, different patterns of increasing histological complexity. What governs and integrates these events? It is tempting to suggest that the governance is at the level of cells, particularly because a major generality emerging from cell dynamics appears and reappears in development: the formation of tightly linked sheets of cells called epithelia and of loosely packed cells that are called mesenchyme. At certain places, one may see epithelia convert or transform to mesenchyme and vice versa. Furthermore, with the passage of time, it is the cells composing each that change shape, express different gene products, and differentiate to become characteristic of particular locations and organs.

It is important to recognize, however, that it cannot simply be the composition of different populations of cells that governs morphogenesis; if one analyzed the cells making up the structures of an arm and a leg, they would constitute very similar populations and their different types would appear at more or less similar times. Yet an arm and a leg are located in different places, and they are quite different in shape. The differences in position and gross shape result from the sequential (and historical) interaction of a number of different processes acting either as driving forces or as regulatory elements in shaping overall form or tissue pattern.

These cellular processes are the so-called *primary processes of development* (figure 3.1): cell division, cell motion, and cell death (driving force processes); and cell adhesion and differentiation (regulatory processes). Each of these processes results from the activity of different complex molecular systems under different control. The primary processes interact with each other to different extents during different stages of development. Although they are dissociable to some extent, as the embryologist Needham pointed out fifty years ago, they combine in a number of ways that are dependent at one stage and independent at an-

Figure 3.1

Cartoons of primary processes. The "driving force" processes—cell division, cell motion, and cell death—are regulated by adhesion and differentiation events. The key event is milieu-dependent differentiation or embryonic induction, which occurs not between single cells but between different cell collectives. (From G. M. Edelman, 1987, Neural Darwinism: The theory of neuronal group selection, *New York: Basic Books.)*

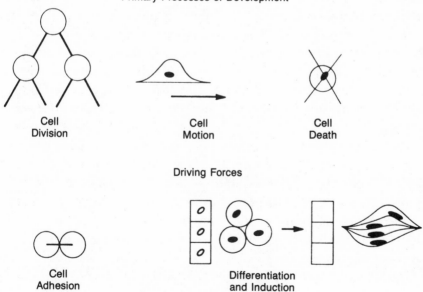

Primary Processes of Development

Cell Division   Cell Motion   Cell Death

Driving Forces

Cell Adhesion   Differentiation and Induction

Regulatory Processes

other. I have termed the first three "driving force processes" because, at the level of forming tissues, they are responsible for changes in the number of cells in a particular region and because, singly or together with adhesion, they contribute dynamically to changes in the mechanical properties of the embryo. The remaining two processes I have termed "regulatory" because they result in changes in the interaction of cells: adhesion linking cells to each other or to substrates, and differentiation (or differential gene expression) resulting in the alteration of cell characters, including those contributing to the other primary processes. Much of the subject of topobiology has to do with the place-dependent relation between the regulatory processes of adhesion and differentiation that results from partially irreversible interactions of cell surfaces with each other or with substrates. The place and time of mutual cell signaling by cells in groups are regulated to a large extent by these two primary processes.

The kind of differentiation seen in much embryonic development is dependent in a special way upon primary-process interaction, and for this reason it has been called embryonic induction. In embryonic induction, cells of different histories are brought together by morphogenetic movements, resulting in milieu-dependent gene expression or differentiation. This may be reciprocal or asymmetric. In the latter case, it affects mainly one cell population, yielding the terminology "inducer" and "induced tissue." It appears likely that induction involves signaling from the cell surface to the nucleus of the induced cells in a tissue. Induction occurs in general not between single cells but rather between cells in groups, or cell collectives, as we will call such groups.

The *timing* of induction is largely determined by the developmental stage of the responding tissue, but its *location* depends largely upon that of the inducing tissue. The competence of cells to be induced is of restricted duration and so, to a lesser degree, is the ability of the inducing tissue to affect induction. Although looking at a cell alone does not reveal its topobiological potency, its position is critical—so-called vegetal cells induce cells of the equitorial region to form mesoderm. The dorsal mesoderm will become notochord and muscle, and the equitorial cells contacting the vegetal cells on the ventral side will form blood and mesenchyme. The end result of this critical topobiological process is generally an irreversible differentiation, but as we will discuss later, when we consider the so-called regulative aspects of development for a given tissue, this is true only after certain periods of time have elapsed.

Induction is a complex, drawn-out, and sequential process with several steps, and the transactions between two inducing cell collectives may involve both negative and positive signals, enhancing or suppressing differentiation. Induction may be *instructive*, when the inducer tissue is specifically required and can force a responding tissue to a given fate, or *permissive*, when the nature of a response is determined mainly by the responding tissue and when many tissues or agents can serve as inducers. Several permissive inductions appear to require actual cell contact (e.g., kidney tubule induction by mesenchyme; the cornea by the lens), whereas instructive inductions (e.g., the lens by the optic vesicle) are apparently carried out by diffusible factors.

It is not known whether there are many chemically different inductive signals or just a few signals with the responses having continuously variable thresholds. The search for such signals and the determination of whether cells must actually contact each other at a given site for these signals to be effective has been particularly frustrating, and in many cases it appears that induction is degenerate: many different substances can induce. Despite the absence of specific knowledge of the chemical nature of inducing signals, the evidence that such sequential epigenetic signaling occurs is undeniable. One way of revealing this is to consider the process of gastrulation, the formation of three germ layers prior to or coincident with the folding of an embryo into a structure consisting of a tube within a tube.

After fertilization of the egg, a remarkable set of cell divisions occurs, leading either to a ball-shaped structure (the blastula), as seen, for example, in the frog, or to a disk-shaped structure (the blastoderm), as seen in the chick (figure 3.2). As development continues, a set of morphogenetic movements occurs in both cases, resulting in the formation of the primary germ layers—ectoderm, mesoderm, and endoderm—from which a variety of structures will subsequently be derived. This process of gastrula-

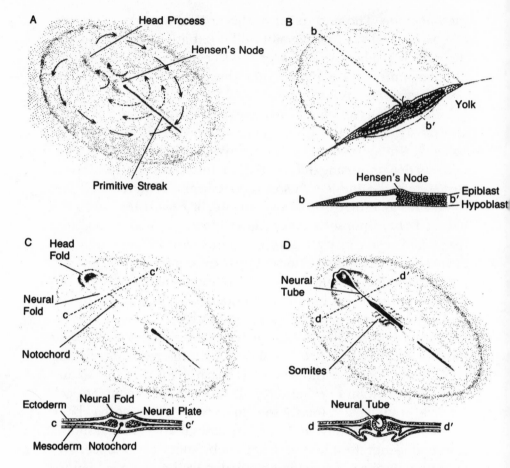

Figure 3.2

Key morphogenetic events in the early development of the chick embryo are gastrulation (A,B) and neurulation (C,D). In late gastrulation, cells from the top layer of the blastoderm converge toward the central groove (solid arrows), called the primitive streak; movements of the mesoblast (middle layer) cells are shown by broken arrows (A). A cross section (B) shows these cells spreading out to form what will become the mesoblast and ultimately the mesoderm. The sagittal section (b-b') is alongside the primitive streak. In primary (neural) induction, a key event, interactions between mesoderm and endoderm result in the formation of the neural plate (C). The plate folds to form the neural tube; soon afterward mesodermal cells segregate to form the segmented precursors called somites (D). (From G. M. Edelman, 1984, Cell-adhesion molecules: A molecular basis for animal form, Scientific American *250:102–21.)*

tion has a number of important characteristics. (1) Only cells *in certain places* in the blastula or blastoderm migrate through collectives of other cells to produce layers. (2) At these and other places, a central event is epithelial-mesenchymal transformation, the conversion of tightly linked sheets of cells forming epithelia to loosely apposed cells of mesenchyme. (3) Regardless of the initial geometry (roughly a sphere or a disk), the movement of cells or epithelia in various species results in a set of layers of epithelia or mesenchyme that interact with each other *usually in a pairwise fashion.* The difference in initial geometry implies that the movement patterns must be quite different in different species, and this in fact turns out to be so. In birds, cells ingress in a region of the blastoderm called the primitive streak. In frogs, the equivalent region of the blastula is called the blastopore, and the movements of gastrulation are remarkably complex, as we will see in chapter 4. (4) Interaction of epithelial sheets with each other or with mesenchyme (e.g., the chordamesoderm and the overlying ecto-dermal epithelium) results in an exchange of inductive signals leading to milieu-dependent differentiation. In the example just cited, the result is the emergence of a specialized region, the neural plate. (5) Cells in epithelia *in particular locations* can maintain for some time the ability to induce other epithelia in characteristic fashion. The most famous is the so-called organizer of Spemann, a region in the dorsal lip of the blastopore that can, if transplanted to another portion of the gastrulating embryo, begin the induction of a second neural plate and a new embryo. (6) In these induction processes, cells in inducing collectives maintain their capacity to induce for a certain time, and cells that respond to inducing signals have a competence to respond that depends upon their previous history of location and exposure as well as upon their current location. After a cell responds in terms of its competence, it can become determined to a particular fate (cen-tral nervous system neuron, bone, and so forth). (7) Although *place* matters, there is nothing sacrosanct about the *layer* of origin of a cell—*within a certain time frame,* for instance, cells can be moved from mesoderm to ectoderm and behave as ectodermal cells. Thus, within a time frame, a cell's competence depends upon its location, its previous history of locations, and the proximity of its neighbors in a collective. There is no indication that a cell's *exact* position in this collective is critical, but its fate can be determined by *how many* cells of similar history are located close by. A cell's fate thus depends upon its competence and upon its neighborhood. Similar factors and signals can be applied recursively to influence a cell, with different consequences that depend upon that cell's previous history.

Gastrulation is one of the key events of development, and it serves as a model of early inductive processes. After it is complete, inductive events of greater or lesser complexity ensue at a variety of locations in the embryo to give rise to a series of specialized organs and tissues. While they differ in detail, particularly in terms of the history and competence of the cells involved, principles very similar to those observed in gastrulation can be seen to apply at a variety of secondary sites of induction (heart, liver, feather germs, and so on).

Clearly, the present and past *locations* of a cell or group of cells place a major constraint on cellular competence and fate. How far back can we push this conclusion? Does it, for example, go back to the egg itself? Here we come to a famous debate concerning whether development is regulative or mosaic. We have, in fact, already been discussing regulative development, development in which cells of different history are brought together by morphogenetic movements resulting in mutual inductive events. Such development can compensate for or regulate fates within certain time frames as a result of cellular interactions. Of key significance is the idea that inductive events are not tied to regulation by a single cell but rather are mediated by cells in collectives interacting across borders in particular neighborhoods. In some cases, the fate of a collective can be regulated by the entire collection of cells in the embryo. We have touched upon these properties in mentioning the differences between the competence and the fate of cells. Given a certain competence, a cell's fate can be changed by its relocation to interact with different neighbors, provided that this relocation occurs in a certain time frame. After a certain time, however, the cells may become determined and are then committed to a particular differentiation pathway and fate. At this point, they are unresponsive and no longer regulate their fate to neighborhood change.

The contrasting notion to regulation is mosaicism, implying a pattern of differentiation determined or fixed early by a defined set of cell locations. This idea arose as a result of certain classic experiments in embryology. It was observed that very early in development a given cell (or blastomere) is committed to give rise only to certain parts of the organism and that the dividing egg is a mosaic of such cells. While this is true to some extent in certain organisms, it has been shown that in others very early cells at certain cleavage stages could be regulated depending on the presence or absence of neighbors in one plane, whereas if they were isolated with neighbors from an orthogonal plane they could not. Thus, there are different degrees of mosaicism and regulation at different stages in different species, and this trade-off depends upon location. The main conclusion is that the response to location of a cell depends upon when it contacts certain neighbors in a historical process. Except perhaps at the very earliest cleavage stages, however, the *exact* address of a single cell is not the key determinant. Only the relative position of a cell in a collective within a certain time frame is important.

But what about the egg itself? It has no neighboring cells of an identical type, and thus one might argue that the topobiological factors we have been discussing do not enter into those asymmetries of the egg that lead to a certain degree of mosaicism. The egg has built into it a series of polarities, altering the cytoplasmic environment and the succession of gene expression events that follow fertilization. These asymmetries are already maternally determined. Insofar, however, as the egg is the result of complex differentiation events in the ovary, followed by a variety of environmental interactions either in fallopian tubes or by alterations in the external environment of an egg mass (such as in the frog), it is reasonable to hypothesize that these polar asymmetries are also determined by locale-dependent interactions of the egg surface within a series of cellular and noncellular environments. We conclude that gametogenesis is also subject to topobiological constraints that, to a large extent, must reflect surface interactions.

Now let us consider a number of factors that contribute to the regulative processes of development, and relate them to the matters of scale discussed in the preceding chapter. We mentioned that genes cannot store the information concerning the place of a cell at a certain time of development. Moreover, the driving force primary processes are not necessarily exactly or determinately controlled. While it is true, for example, that early cell divisions can be quite precise, variations do occur. This stochastic factor is much more prominent in cell motion and cell death. In both of these cases, what cell moves or dies in a particular order in a certain neighborhood is, in general, a statistical matter.

These observations have provided us with a basis for a hypothesis on the evolutionary selection of regulative properties of cells in a neighborhood: while the location of a cell within a particular *collective* in a certain period of time is important, its *exact* location in that collective does not in general appear to be critical. As long as there is a sufficient number of cells of similar histories, the death of a particular cell would not alter the fate of adjoining cells. A similar relaxation of constraints applies to the motion of cells in a mesenchyme: their exact order, rank, or file is not a major determining variable in inductive processes.

It is a fact, nonetheless, that local constraints do increase with time until, in general, cells at a particular location are determined. A number of fundamental questions relating these determinative events to pattern and histology will be considered in the next chapter. Before taking up this central question of pattern formation, we may attempt a few brief generalizations based on our observations about inductive events—generalizations related to scale, movement, and the statistics of primary processes. One way of doing this, admittedly crude, is to consider the relative average path length of a cell during movement patterns of migration (mesenchyme) or folding (epithelium) on a scale referred to the size of the whole embryo at each stage considered (figure 3.3). At early stages, cells may contact a variety of others in their trajectory: prospective lens cells contact endodermal cells and mesodermal cells before interacting with their final inductors, the ectodermal cells of the optic vesicle. For such migrations leading to solid tissues, the average relative path length (and thus the locations and types of cells encountered) will in general decrease with time and as determination increases. For fluid tissues (blood and lymph), the reverse will occur. For cells in folding epithelia, the path length will decrease sharply after early embryogenesis

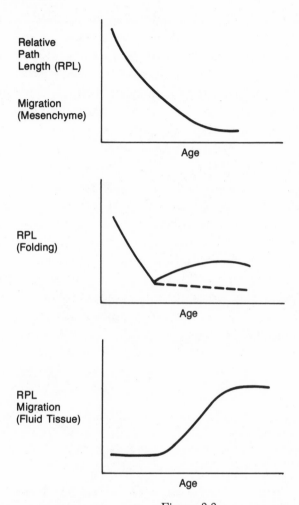

Figure 3.3
*Some fanciful diagrams of average relative paths (path length/overall organism length)
of different types of developmental movements at different stages in solid and fluid
tissues. No attempt has been made to relate these figures quantitatively; in any case, the
relative path depends directly upon the actual distance of movement and inversely upon
the organism length.*

and slowly increase to some plateau as a result of growth of the
formed structures. These various trajectories of movement govern and are governed by inductive signals.

Given the need to relate the mechanics of development to
these critical regulatory signals across several levels of scale (see
table 2.1), two points seem obvious. (1) There is a distinct evolutionary advantage in having regulative processes concerned with
cell locations in neighborhoods and also with what we may call

the trajectory of cells. Small errors and statistical fluctuations will tend to be smoothed, provided that the cells' *general* location in a trajectory or collective is sufficient to yield form under regulation. Indeed, given the statistical features of primary processes, any strict requirement for a precise cell address would be lethal. (2) The pathways of induction and determination involve a historical series of milieu-dependent gene expressions that are coupled to those mechanical and mechanochemical events that actually govern the achievement of form and pattern. At any one time, there is an interplay between the place, scale, and size of bordering collectives, and various inductive molecular signals not only maintain the pattern so far established but also transform it into a new pattern. This brings us to the central problem of morphogenesis—pattern formation—and at the same time to a critical reexamination of the developmental genetic question, for it is obvious, given the consistent morphologic differentiation within various animal species, that developmental pattern formation is under genetic control.

SELECTED REFERENCES

Weiss, P. 1939. *Principles of development.* New York: Henry Holt.

Needham, J. 1933. On the dissociability of the fundamental process in ontogenesis. *Biol. Rev.* 8:180–223.

Spemann, H. 1938. *Embryonic development and induction.* New Haven: Yale University Press.

Hamburger, V. 1988. *The heritage of experimental embryology: Hans Spemann and the organizer.* New York: Oxford University Press.

Jacobson, A. G. 1966. Inductive processes in embryonic development. *Science* 152:25–35.

Slack, J. M. W. 1983. *From egg to embryo: Determinative events in early development.* Cambridge: Cambridge University Press.

Nieuwkoop, P. D., A. G. Johnen, and B. Albers. 1985. *The epigenetic nature of early chordate development: Inductive interaction and competence.* Cambridge: Cambridge University Press.

Gerhart, J. 1980. Mechanisms regulating pattern formation in the amphibian egg and early embryo. In *Biological regulation and development,* ed. R. Goldberger, 133–316. New York: Plenum.

Gurdon, J. B. 1987. Embryonic induction—Molecular prospects. *Development* 99:285–306

See also the reference to Raff and Kaufman in chapter 1.

4

Pattern

AS WE MENTIONED in the last chapter, not only do embryonic cells of a particular history have to be within certain collectives that exchange signals at particular times, but their ordering in place and time must lead to a functioning pattern. A given pattern (which involves gene expression) is specific to a species and thus must have resulted in phenotypic functions that underwent natural selection. From species to species, the patterns change, and we must therefore not only account for how the code can specify three-dimensional animals of one species but also show how genetic changes can occur that lead to adaptively advantageous patterns in related species.

Before considering possible molecular mechanisms of epigenesis that underlie these processes, we must briefly review the problem of pattern formation in relation to developmental genetics in this chapter and then take up the central puzzle of modern biology, morphologic evolution, in the next. Knowledge of the cellular mechanisms of pattern formation is more extensive in studies of vertebrate species, whereas knowledge of the genetic control of pattern is most developed in studies of invertebrate species. For this reason, we will have to take an eclectic approach both in our descriptions and in presenting various models of pattern formation. Although a thread of evolutionary homology actually exists to justify this procedure of using model systems from widely divergent species to create a cogent picture, it is barely sufficient, and therefore the use of several such systems to frame our argument must be considered a stopgap.

To begin with, we must construct some working definitions. These are pragmatic, not universal, but this limitation should not alter the course of the argument. By *pattern formation,* we mean the processes by which ordered arrangements of cells or their products are attained. Some workers prefer to distinguish pattern formation from morphogenesis, largely because they adhere to an hypothesis about how preexisting patterns of molecules guide morphogenesis. While noting this, we may for the present put it to one side; we will discuss and criticize such mechanisms later on.

Rather than argue the case for prepattern, it may be more useful to qualify patterns in terms of their scale, order, production, and plasticity, as well as their relation to various degrees of cellular differentiation (table 4.1). For example, if one observes the overall form of individuals in a particular animal species, one certainly sees a describable ordered arrangement of body parts. While that order may be recognizably constant even at different stages of growth in certain species, the relative proportions of parts may differ with time. In some cases the underlying order is obvious, but in others it is not. In many instances, for example, a basic alteration of patterned proportions may be attributable to so-called allometric growth. In animals, proportions can change nonisometrically or allometrically with scale. This latter form of change noted by D'Arcy Thompson was descriptively formalized by Snell and by Huxley in the equation $y = ax^b$, where y is a variable of interest, x is body size, b is the slope of a line produced in a logarithmic plot, and a is the intercept at unity. Allometric growth can result in remarkable changes in shape, as is seen, for example, among different insect castes within a given eusocial species. Despite these manifest changes, it is clear that all such castes share an underlying body pattern.

If, within a species, we go down in scale to sizes smaller than main body parts, we can see certain regional differences in pattern—some periodic, for example, metameric organization, and some unique, for example, cephalization or specialization of organs. One step down in scale, we may see extraordinary local patterns in tissues and organs reflecting histological organization.

TABLE 4.1

Patterns at Different Scales

Different Levels of Body Plan	Examples or Types
Overall Shape	
Symmetry	Fivefold, bilateral, sagittal, etc.
Polarity	Cephalization
Metamerism	Periodic repeats
Appendages	Four or six or more
Organs and Appendages	
	Symmetry and asymmetry
	Periodicity
	Branching structures
Tissues	
	Periodic
	Layers
	Stripes
	Blobs
	Aperiodic
	Cortex
	Medulla
Cells	
	Shapes
	Round
	Spindle
	Stellate
	Pyramidal
	Etc.

A further step down, and we may discern cellular and intracellular patterns reflecting supramolecular assemblies and organelles. It is important to understand how these various patterns at different scales (table 4.1) relate to each other.

If we look at certain appendages and decorations (pigment, hair, feathers, and so on), we will see a remarkable combination of varieties of pattern, in which certain themes such as spots, blobs, or stripes at the two-dimensional level can be combined with overall growth and shape to yield different overall distributions of shape at different locales. An example is the alteration of hexagonal feather patterns to chevron-like patterns as a result of the overall shape change of a body part.

A static classification of the kind we have been discussing is only minimally useful, however; what we wish to know is how pattern ranging from that in a single cell to that of a given phenotype is dynamically *produced*. This entails a description of the spatial and temporal order of patterns, the hierarchy of types of patterns as they succeed each other, the nature and mixture of the driving forces that lead to order in space and time and to succession, and, finally, the manner in which the entire process of pattern formation can be maintained under genetic control susceptible to evolutionary change.

This is a tall order. Nonetheless, we may make a beginning by trying to discern the driving forces leading to pattern, by examining the transformation of one pattern into another, by searching for evidence of signals between cells and tissues engaged in pattern formation, and by considering how any of these might be susceptible to genetic control. If we are willing to use examples from widely different species, we can cite evidence bearing on each of these issues. With these examples in hand, we can evaluate how well certain proposed cellular models of pattern formation, including the RD, PI, and SMPP models mentioned in chapter 2, stand up to criteria based on the evidence.

We will discuss two main examples of pattern formation found in vertebrate species—gastrulation and neurulation to form the body plan, as was initially described in the preceding chapter, and the elaboration of a periodic skin appendage, the feather. These examples should serve to indicate how interacting cells in both primary and secondary induction must somehow link mechanical and mechanochemical events to the production of inducing signals under genetic control. But in the vertebrates, not much is known about that control, and to illustrate the intricacy of control events we will therefore use as a model system an invertebrate example—*Drosophila melanogaster*—a species in which developmentally important genes have been identified but for which very little is known about the molecular regulation of cellular mechanochemical events actually leading to shape. Given the reciprocal deficiencies of the available information, we will have to synthesize a picture by using pertinent evidence from these widely separated vertebrate and invertebrate taxa.

Let us take up the vertebrate example of gastrulation at the point where we left off in the preceding chapter and draw four general conclusions related to pattern. The first conclusion is that, at the cellular level, there are three main driving forces for pattern formation. These are the primary processes of cell division, cell motion, and cell death. Note that, while each is under complex control of intracellular and extracellular molecular interactions that are not fully understood, they all are essentially "blind." That is, if dissociated from their environment and one another, these processes may lead to some kind of pattern at a given scale, but in general that pattern is not the kind one sees in orderly development of a phenotype. At the scale of cells or groups of cells, each primary process can lead to mechanical changes—division by accretion of daughter cells, movement as a result of migration or folding of tissue sheets, and death by selective removal of cells or tissue regions.

A second salient conclusion is that, in gastrulation, one sees a conversion from loosely associated cells (migratory or stationary), called mesenchyme, to linked cells in sheets with a definite structure and cellular polarity, called epithelia. Such epithelial-mesenchymal transformations are a major feature of embryonic patterning. They can occur in both directions and are often associated with alterations in substrate molecules that can form a complex assembly underlying epithelia, known as a basement membrane. Epithelial-mesenchymal transformations can lead to segmentation events as seen in somites, condensations as seen in feathers, or cell migrations as seen for neural crest derivatives.

Third, it has been observed that when cells migrate they generally do so either on basement membranes or substrate molecules present in various combinations, or on other cells. Cells change form when they migrate. As we have already noted, in earlier stages of development, cell movements referred to the actual scale of the overall embryo tend to occur over larger relative distances and traverse a larger number of locales containing cells of different histories than they do subsequently.

This leads to our fourth conclusion—that, as the relative scale of such movements diminishes (see figure 3.2), the entire process of movement and division is increasingly accompanied by local differentiation and determination. At such later stages, foldings and branchings of tissue sheets (particularly in solid tissues) are more prominent than large-scale cell migrations, and increasing numbers of different cell types appear. This generally means that a larger number of borders defining different cell collectives appear in a given space and that concomitantly a larger number of different genes are expressed. Thus regional differentiation arises as a result of both border formation and histological differentiation.

At all stages and levels at which these principles apply to pattern formation, we see polarity at different scales (the largest being cephalization), as well as periodicity (which is not universal but is prominent in certain structures; see table 4.1). In a given species, these various properties emerge in a quite definite order, and the regulation in varying proportions of cell division, movement, and death clearly provides a dynamic scaffold leading to particular forms.

To illustrate these various events and properties, let us use a second example of patterned induction in avian development. This example is the feather—an internally periodic skin appendage induced in definite periodic patterns over different regions of a bird's skin. Each feather has a structure that is both periodic and hierarchical (figure 4.1). The feather illustrates the sequence of later induction events (called "secondary inductions" to distinguish them from "primary induction" by the organizer already described in the preceding chapter). It also exemplifies the successive interactions of induction with other primary processes and histogenetic events to yield a basic functional unit. Furthermore, a study of the feather shows how different kinds of symmetry can be achieved by altering the differential contributions of each of these various primary processes. We can best see this by comparing the development of a nestling or downy feather, which is radially symmetrical, with that of an adult feather, which has bilateral symmetry. Feathers have undergone many different shape changes during the evolution of different bird species, and they are excellent subjects for studies of the relation of development to evolution.

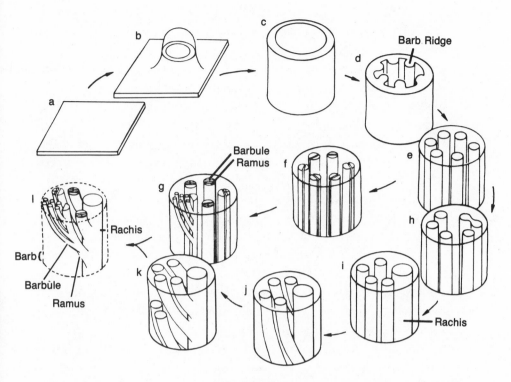

Figure 4.1

Steps in the development of the highly ramified structure of the feather from a simple epidermal sheet. The epidermal sheet (a) evaginates to form a bud (b) and then a filament consisting of a cylinder of epidermis with a dermal core. The simple hollow cylinder shown in section in c develops ridges of epithelium (d) called barb ridges. These ridges are in turn subdivided (f,g,l) to form the barbs and barbules that are the substance of the mature feather. The barb ridges also fuse in some places with adjacent ridges (h, i, j, k) to form the branched pattern characteristic of the feather. (From C.-M. Chuong and G. M. Edelman, 1985, Expression of cell-adhesion molecules in embryonic induction: I. Morphogenesis of nestling feathers, J. Cell Biol. 101:1009–26.)

Feathers arise in the following fashion (figure 4.1). After formation of the early skin (periderm and ectoderm), cells from somites migrate as mesenchyme, reaching a layer subjacent and contiguous to the skin. These mesodermal cells then induce a series of placodes (cell collectives in the epidermis that contain elongated cells), each of which will be part of a distinctive feather germ. The mesodermal cells subjacent to each placode undergo condensation and are arranged in a hexagonal pattern. It is clear from experiments on hybrid exchanges of cells from different germ layers between species having morphologically distinct feathers, such as chicken and duck, that the mesoderm is the initial inductor for the ectoderm. In the dorsal feather field of a chick, placodes form first in the midline and then laterally in a hexagonal array.

Following this initial induction, a series of cell divisions and mechanical movements form a feather follicle and filament in which a second mesodermal-ectodermal induction is important (figure 4.1, c). Then a basement membrane is formed, separating a central mesodermally derived pulp from a cylindrical shell of cells of ectodermal origin. These ectodermal cells are the source of all further structures of the feather. Cell division in the cylinder leads to the formation of so-called barb ridges, which fold and then separate as rods to be inserted into several fused ridges that will become the feather shaft or rachis (figure 4.1, d–k). Within each ridge, a similar rearrangement occurs to produce a smaller set of structures that will become barbules (figure 4.1, g).

Separating the barb ridges is an alternately disposed set of cells called marginal plates, and at a smaller scale separating barbule cells in an alternating manner is a set of axial plates. As histodifferentiation occurs, the cells in these marginal and axial plates die and those in barb ridge and barbule derivatives express keratins, the molecules guaranteeing the rigidity of the final structure. As a result, an alternating arrangement of *borders* between cell collectives becomes the source of *edges* in the final formed feather.

This remarkable sequence of events illustrates a number of key processes: (1) the formation of periodic structures having one type of symmetry as a result of induction between two germ layer derivatives, (2) mechanical events of cell and sheet motion, (3) periodic border formation in epithelia derived from one germ layer, and (4) correlation of histogenetic fate (keratin expression, death) with such border formation in a precise fashion. We will describe the molecular influences governing each of these processes in a later chapter, but first let us consider how pattern-forming events yielding such structures in the embryo might be genetically regulated.

Although a fair amount is known about the molecular and cellular contribution to pattern formation in certain vertebrate species, little is known about the genetic contribution—a contribution we know to be paramount simply by examining the consistent differences in feathers of different bird species. Before considering various models that propose to explain how particular cellular primary processes leading to such pattern formation are regulated, let us mention briefly a body of evidence that strongly indicates that the phenotypic regulation of pattern is in fact by *particular kinds of genes.* For this, we must turn to the results of experiments on developmentally significant genes in *Drosophila* as a model system. Because this species can be genetically manipulated and mutants can be selected with comparative ease, it has proven to be a major source of information on the genetic control of developmental pattern. One of the most important features in *Drosophila* development is the segmented or metameric pattern forming an early basis for the body plan. As we will see, although the structure and evolutionary history of this species are remote from those of vertebrates, there are remarkable homologies in certain developmentally important genes or in DNA sequences across these widely disparate taxa.

Let us begin from the beginning, just after fertilization. In *Drosophila* development (figure 4.2), a fertilized egg undergoes syncytial nuclear divisions, and most nuclei move to the cortex of the egg; a few at the posterior pole of the egg become cells that are precursors to the germ line cells in the germ band. Following thirteen rounds of nuclear division, 6,000 or so nuclei become cells and undergo gastrulation with a characteristic series of invaginations. After folding, leading to approximation of the germ band cells to the head, a series of segments are formed: lobed head segments, three thoracic segments, eight abdominal segments, and a caudal region. Genetic analysis has identified a series of mutants at discrete loci that result in morphologic alterations: *gap locus* mutations, deleting groups of segments; *pair rule locus* mutations, deleting alternate segmental units; and *segment polarity* mutations, leading to an altered pattern within each segment.

Among the most striking sets of developmentally important gene loci are those in which mutations alter the actual identity of segments or of pairs of segments. These so-called homeotic mutants result in the formation of structures in one part of the

I

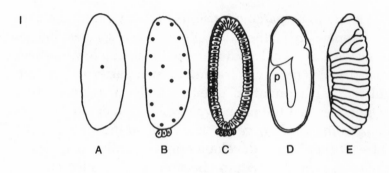

A   B   C   D   E

II   Gap   Pair Rule   Segment Polarity

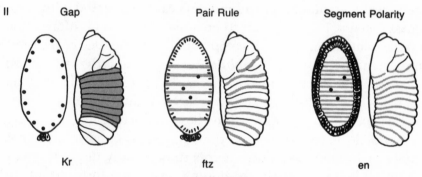

Kr   ftz   en

Figure 4.2

Drosophila *development and gene loci controlling segmentation. I. Stages in early* Drosophila *development.* A: *A fertilized egg, showing the asymmetries evident in the shape
of an oocyte (ventral is to the right; anterior is up).* B: *After a series of syncytial nuclear
divisions, most of the nuclei move to the cortex of the egg. A few nuclei at the posterior
pole are formed into cells, some of which will become the germ line precursor cells.* C:
*After a total of thirteen rounds of nuclear division, the approximately 6,000 resulting
nuclei are formed into cells. Immediately thereafter, gastrulation begins with a series of
invaginations.* D: *Gastrulation and germ band elongation produce an embryo with the
most-posterior precursor cells moved so that they lie behind the developing head region
(P = posterior end of germ band). While the germ band is extended, the segments first
appear.* E: *After the germ band shortens (by about ten hours), the lobed head segments,
three thoracic segments, eight abdominal segments, and the caudal regions are visible.
II. Classes of segmentation loci: patterns of gene expression and deletion phenotypes. The
diagrams show one example from each of the three classes of segmentation genes. Krüp-
pel* (Kr) *is a "gap" locus; null mutant Kr embryos lack thoracic and anterior abdominal
segments (gray). The initial pattern of Kr transcripts is a belt near the middle of the
embryo (gray shading). Kr RNA is first detected before cells form, as shown. Fushi tarazu*
(ftz) *is an example of a pair rule gene. Mutations in ftz cause deletions of alternate
segmental boundaries, as indicated (gray areas). Shortly before cellularization, ftz RNA
and protein products are observed in seven stripes (gray), the most posterior of which is
wider than the others. The engrailed* (en) *gene is required in the posterior of each segment
(gray areas). The en gene is an example of the segment polarity or polarity reversal class
of loci. The en striped pattern is first seen after cells have formed. There are fourteen
(later fifteen) en stripes, about twice the number observed in pair rule gene mutants.*
*(Modified from M. P. Scott and P. H. O'Farrell, 1986, Spatial programming of gene
expression in early* Drosophila *embryogenesis,* Annu. Rev. Cell Biol. 2:49–80.)

embryo that are normally appropriate to another part of it. This suggests that the wild type functions of homeotic loci are concerned with the developmental pathways affecting the *fate* of particular groups of cells. A large number of these genes are located in two clusters, the bithorax complex (BX-C) and the antennopedia complex (ANT-C). To yield a normal fly, the appropriate combinations of homeotic genes must be expressed at appropriate positions at appropriate times. If that expression is deferred, a fly may, for example, develop a leg where an antenna should be. In some fashion, homeotic genes act as selectors for developmental sequences.

Molecular biological analyses have resulted in the isolation of DNAs corresponding to a variety of segmentation and homeotic genes. An examination of their properties has revealed several important features. First, several of the segmentation gene products appear to be DNA-binding proteins, suggestive of some regulatory role. Second, the RNA transcripts of these various genes appear at their known sites of function; for example, in segmentation-related genes, the transcript patterns appear in stripes corresponding to the segmentation disorders to which the genes are related. Third, some of the genes have a highly conserved sequence, the homeobox sequence, which encodes a protein structure with homology to certain bacterial DNA-binding proteins. The homeobox sequence is seen in a variety of species, including vertebrates, although its functional significance in these species has not yet been defined. Fourth, segmentation genes can control the expression of other segmentation genes and may also play a part in regulating homeotic gene expression. This suggests that there may be a complex regulatory cascade that controls the expression of all of these developmentally important genes.

These observations lead to the important conclusion that *a network of distinctly different genes* is crucial in controlling the sequences of development. Furthermore, this interactive network is topobiologically constrained, that is, it is expressed in a fashion concordant with place and morphology. Unfortunately, however, although there is some evidence about the reaction of cells to place and position in *Drosophila,* much less is known than is known in vertebrates about the cellular primary processes and the molecules that mediate mechanochemical events leading to actual tissues. Clearly, for a complete explanation, we need knowledge both of developmentally significant genes and of their relation to morphoregulatory molecules at the cell surface. In later chapters, we will consider such morphoregulatory molecules in connection with the establishment of pattern in vertebrates and attempt to link them with the genetic evidence from invertebrates such as *Drosophila* in a model that gives a provisional answer to the developmental genetic and evolutionary questions.

At this point, we have considered enough phenomenological information from both vertebrate and invertebrate development to review in greater detail some of the models that have been proposed to account for pattern formation. Each of these models differs from the others in scope and emphasis; all are important in focusing attention upon fundamental matters. None explicitly attempts to deal in detail with *both* the developmental genetic and the evolutionary questions. The majority deal with chemical events as they might be transformed into higher-order cellular pattern, but some deal only with genetic regulation without specifying detailed mechanisms of the transformation of mechanochemical events into actual pattern. It is important to reiterate that any adequate model must face two problems: (1) a topobiological one, in relating events at different scales (molecular, cellular, tissue, organic) to tissue locale and fate, and (2) an epigenetic one, in relating cell interaction at a position to gene expression occurring in such a way as to result in pattern even in the face of stochastic events affecting cell division, movement, and death.

Let us begin our examination of types of pattern models by emphasizing again the issue raised in chapter 2 concerning the direct interactions at equilibrium of protein gene products. At the scale of viruses, it is sufficient that proteins interact in a complementary fashion stoichiometrically to give rise to supramolecular assemblies and shape. Clearly, this mode of assembly, which could conceivably take place at thermodynamic equilibrium, or at least close to it, is inapplicable to metazoan cell assembly. The units of assembly and control are in this instance the cells themselves, and, in general, their interactions are far from equilibrium, are kinetically constrained, and, given the movement paths of cells as they relate to competence and fate, are in some sense historical.

Among the earliest attempts to translate from the molecular level to the level of cell patterning was that proposed by Turing in a classic paper, "The Chemical Basis of Morphogenesis." He demonstrated that, provided certain boundary conditions were met, randomly diffusing substances X and Y being produced under certain kinetic and flow conditions could become segregated and ordered in a spatial pattern. If X is considered as an excitatory substance and Y as an inhibitory one, simultaneous equations of the form

$$\frac{\partial X}{\partial t} = k_1 X + k_2 Y + D_X \nabla^2 X \tag{1}$$

$$\frac{\partial Y}{\partial t} = k_3 X + k_4 Y + D_Y \nabla^2 Y, \tag{2}$$

where the k's are kinetic constants and the Laplacians refer to diffusion terms, could be solved under appropriate boundary conditions leading to a spatial accumulation of X and Y in separate regions. Subsequent refinements of such reaction-diffusion (RD) equations have led to the proposal of a variety of models as the basis both of animal form and of various patterning events (readers who wish to pursue further the connection between the mathematics, physics, and biology may refer to the book by Meinhart).

Without denying that such ideas may apply in certain cases such as butterfly wings, in which pigment distribution is developed after most of the cellular primary processes have come to a steady state, there are a number of reasons why RD models alone are inadequate to explain morphogenesis. One reason is the requirement that a pattern of synthesized molecules must *precede* the formation of cellular pattern, at least locally. The stabilization of such a chemical pattern in the face of higher-order convective and stochastic cellular primary processes would be more than somewhat precarious. The idea of a continuous chemical pattern providing a basis for form without detailing how cells move, link to form epithelia, and express genes is inadequate. The need for long-range scaling of continuous chemical prepatterns and the difficulties in linking such patterns to gene control and later histogenetic expression are also embarrassments: to work according to RD models, cells would have to "read" a particular concentration gradient subject to many disturbances in three-dimensional space and then alter a large number of parallel and serial expressions of gene products and surface molecules in a precise way.

Another model attempting to solve this topobiological dilemma is Wolpert's proposal of positional information (PI). According to this idea, each cell does not respond to a gradient but rather responds in a threshold manner to its specific *position* at a given time within a given chemical condition. The proposal of PI was originally put forth to explain pattern formation in the developing vertebrate limb. This idea had the advantage of being able to be linked rather more directly to cellular primary processes such as cell division, but it, too, required some preexisting pattern of chemical information at certain locales, and it was posed at a single-cell level. While it is true that the information no longer needed to be in the form of a chemical gradient but could be on neighboring cells, no notion was provided of how this could be related in detail either to genetic control or to specific cell surface properties.

Perhaps the most stringent of models related to ordering at a cellular level was the chemoaffinity hypothesis of Sperry, proposed to explain how detailed neuronal maps could be organized in the optic tectum during development. This organization occurs in such a fashion as to map visual space onto the tectum via synapses from optic nerve fibers arising in the retina (see figure 10.3). According to this idea, down almost to the level of the individual neurons, there were chemical markers that would specify the attachment and synapse formation of the appropriate retinal fibers. This would require the evolution of complementary surface molecules having a large number of specificities as well as of genetic controls for expression and cytodifferentiation of such markers that would have to operate at a very refined scale. Recent experiments have suggested, however, that the achievement of tectal map order occurs dynamically and in several stages, the last of which is determined by the coordinate synaptic activity of retinal fibers. It is difficult to envision how large numbers of chemoaffinity markers could be evolved or be genetically controlled to account for such dynamic events.

The models discussed so far have involved chemical patterns derived in various ways. In a detailed mathematical model that emphasizes cellular mechanical interactions, Oster and his colleagues have shown how patterns may arise by motion, tension, and process extension in cells of the limb bud. This strict mechanical pattern propagation (SMPP) model does not depend upon prepattern and is closely tuned to primary processes of embryogenesis, but it relies *only* upon cell substrate interactions, ignores cell-cell adhesion at the molecular level, and has no reference to elements of genetic control or inductive signaling. It is therefore difficult to connect the SMPP model to genetic variation. Furthermore, it does not clearly distinguish among the various effects of local cell-cell adhesion interactions or consider the role of inductive processes on morphogenesis.

A model that is almost opposite in orientation to the RD, PI, and SMPP models has been proposed by Scott and O'Farrell to account for the data obtained on the spatial programming of gene expression in *Drosophila* embryogenesis. Its emphasis is exclusively upon the process of gene regulation and expression and not upon the mediators and regulators of cell movement, division, epithelial-mesenchymal transformation, or the mechanochemistry of pattern formation itself.

This model is a digital gene regulator (DGR) model, so-called because it is based on a series of *discrete* subdivisions of cell populations by local interactions of genes. It explicitly excludes the definition of cell position by the cell's interpreting a gradient distributed in an analog fashion. The fundamental idea of the DGR model is that pattern formation is controlled by the local discrete expression of a number of regulatory gene products (regulators), and the model assumes a series of *sequential* subdivisions of the embryo. Control of the expression of these regulatory products involves a cascade that occurs sequentially but is *com-*

binatorial. Certain combinations of regulators will lead to the expression of other regulators as a function of cephalocaudal position in the embryo, but a particular induced regulator "down stream" (e.g., from head to tail in segments) may be specified by *more than one combination* of inducing regulators. Each cell nonetheless is distinguished from its neighbors by a particular combination of regulators, and induction occurs by reading out the existing prepattern of regulators. To create finer pattern elements, it is proposed, the induction step is combined with a subdivision step (presumably epigenetic) in which the regulators that are at first evenly distributed in a region are nonuniformly segregated. If, for example, two regulators are expressed in each spatial unit (say, a presumptive segment) and one is suppressed in the neighborhood of an anterior adjoining unit while the other is suppressed in the neighborhood of a posterior adjoining unit, three zones would be created: one expressing one regulator, one expressing both, and the third expressing the other regulator. Reiteration or recursion of this process in time in smaller and smaller regions could refine pattern. If certain regulators of this type persisted from early steps and affected later events in some regions, they could be used to switch homeotic genes.

This DRG model addresses the means by which regulatory cascades of genes interact to give pattern, but it is abstract and noncommittal in dealing with how collectives of cells form actual patterns, borders, sheets, and then elicit the appropriate signals to give the proposed epigenetic subdivision. Although it does rely upon local cell interactions and could use mitotic cell lineages for segment subdivision, it is actually less a model of morphogenesis itself than a "metamodel" for certain control steps in morphogenesis.

This very brief critical survey of a number of ingenious models serves to point out what is required if we are to explain morphogenesis. While no single model is complete or adequate, each touches upon important aspects of the problem of defining locale by epigenetic events, a problem that is the essence of topobiology. All models explicitly or tacitly incorporate the idea that the cell surface is a central ingredient in this definition of locale, but each differs in the attention it pays to the means of linkage of the gene-controlled primary processes of development with the mechanically controlled primary processes. Such linkage assures signaling across borders of cell collectives to induce the next step of gene expression as a function of history, thus yielding form. Our survey of model types points up the clear need for an hypothesis that relates the control of regulatory genes in cascades with the actual mechanochemical processes leading to form and pattern at each stage.

To develop this hypothesis, we must review a series of developmentally important molecular families that we will designate morphoregulatory molecules. Such molecules are concerned with the formation of cell sheets and mesenchyme, with substrate formation, with the regulation of movement, and with the chemical communication between and among cells. Even if we had an adequate model to link the properties of these molecules to the genetic control of development, however, we would face a serious challenge—that of explaining *why* a particular sequence of molecular events happened in a given species. To deal with this problem of ultimate causes, one must first consider how *any* morphogenetic model or developmental hypothesis can be linked to morphologic evolution and then examine whether developmental events themselves act as a constraint on this evolutionary process. We will explore these issues in the next chapter, before presenting an extensive account of morphoregulatory molecules and their relation to topobiology.

SELECTED REFERENCES

Alexander, R. M. 1971. *Size and shape.* London: Edward Arnold.
Schmidt-Nielsen, K. 1984. *Scaling: Why is animal size so important?* Cambridge: Cambridge University Press.
Bonner, J. T. 1965. *Size and cycle.* Princeton: Princeton University Press.
Huxley, J. S. 1932. *Problems of relative growth.* London: MacVeagh.
Willmer, E. M. 1970. *Cytology and evolution,* 2d ed. New York: Academic.
Wolpert, L. 1982. Pattern formation and change. In *Evolution and development,* Dahlem Konferenzen, Life Sciences Research Report 22, ed. J. T. Bonner, 169–88. Berlin: Springer-Verlag.

Turing, A. M. 1952. The chemical basis of morphogenesis. *Philos. Trans. R. Soc. Lond. (Biol.)* 237:37–72.

Meinhart, H. 1982. *Models of biological pattern formation.* London and New York: Academic.

Sengel, P. 1976. *Morphogenesis of skin.* Cambridge: Cambridge University Press.

Oster, G. F., and E. O. Wilson. 1978. *Caste and ecology in the social insects,* Monographs in Population Biology, vol. 12. Princeton: Princeton University Press.

Garcia-Bellido, A. 1975. *Genetic control of wing disc development in Drosophila.* Ciba Foundation Symposium 29, 161–82. Amsterdam: Elsevier.

Scott, M. P., and P. H. O'Farrell. 1986. Spatial programming of gene expression in early *Drosophila* embryogenesis. *Annu. Rev. Cell Biol.* 2:49–80.

Nüsslein-Volhard, C., H. G. Frohnhöfer, and R. Lehmann. 1987. Determination of anteroposterior polarity in *Drosophila. Science* 238:1675–81.

Davidson, E. H. 1986. *Gene activity in early development,* 3d ed. Orlando: Academic.

John, B., and G. L. G. Miklos. 1988. *The eukaryote genome in development and evolution.* London: Allen & Unwin.

Murray, J. D. 1981. A prepattern formation mechanism for animal coat markings. *J. Theoret. Biol.* 88:161–99.

See also references to D'Arcy Thompson, to Raff and Kaufman, to Mayr and Provine in chapter 1, and to Sperry, Wolpert, and Oster et al. in chapter 2.

5

Morphologic Evolution

DARWIN recognized that an understanding of morphology and embryology was essential to a satisfactory explanation of the workings of natural selection. He made the explicit point that "community in embryonic structure reveals community in descent." The relation between these issues forms the background for some of the greatest unsolved problems of modern biology, those of morphologic evolution. These problems include (1) explaining the origin of a finite number of body plans (*Baupläne*) without subsequent addition of any new ones since the Precambrian period, (2) explaining how relatively large changes in shape can occur in relatively short periods of evolutionary time, (3) understanding the bases of allometry and body size, and (4) accounting for the origins and relations of the complex structure of body parts and their functions in terms of evolutionary fitness. No explanation in terms of genetics alone is adequate to this composite task.

To see why this is so, we may summarize a particularly clear analysis put forth by Lewontin. He points out that the adequate measure of natural selection for adaptive advantage and fitness is gene frequency in a population. That is, in a given taxon over some period of time, certain genes will increase in frequency in the genotype as a result of the advantages their combined action confers upon the species. This is the measure used in population genetic analysis to indicate the occurrence of evolution. But evolution and natural selection do not in general act directly to select

for genes. Rather, they select upon the phenotype, acting upon
those forms and functions in a breeding population that increase
fitness or inclusive fitness. It is the species that evolves by means
of such selection, a process which in turn changes gene frequencies in the population. As a result, we need transformation rules
that will relate alterations in a "genotype space" to those in a
"phenotype space."

   In a clever diagram, figure 5.1, Lewontin points out that at
least four such transformation rules are required. The first (T_1)
connects events and morphologic patterns in embryonic development to those properties in the "mature" animal that confer
advantage. The second (T_2) is chiefly related to the ecological
interactions of mature animals in interspecies and intraspecies

Figure 5.1
Diagram illustrating sets of transformation rules (T_1-T_4) *that must be understood to*
relate phenotypic selection to changes in gene frequency. (From E. Sober, 1984, The
nature of selection: Evolutionary theory in philosophical focus, *Cambridge: MIT Press.*
Adapted from R. Lewontin, 1974, The genetic basis of evolutionary change, *New York:*
Columbia University Press.)

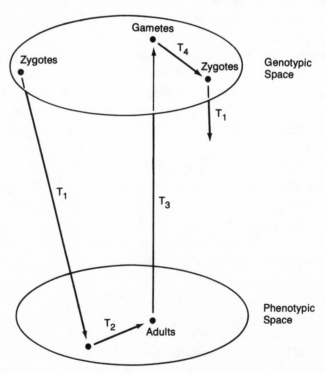

competition. The third (T_3) is related to processes of gamete formation that enhance fertilization, egg properties, recombination, and other such traits. The fourth (T_4) is concerned with zygote formation and with properties that are related to the assortment of genes reflected, for example, in the Hardy-Weinberg law.

Although there is much to be learned about each of these rules, the one about which least is known and about which controversy rages most is T_1. Curiously, however, this arena, concerned with the relation of developmental genetics to evolution, has had the least effect upon evolutionary theory in modern times, and particularly upon the modern synthesis that linked Mendelian genetics to Darwinian evolution in so impressive a manner in the 1930s and 1940s. This is a great paradox, for in some sense the understanding of T_1 is the most important of all evolutionary problems; without it, the modern synthesis is certainly incomplete.

It is worth considering why this has been true, both for the historical lessons it provides and for the current wisdom it may impart. To understand the issue, we must briefly examine some classic views on the relation between ontogeny and phylogeny. This will help us recognize that neither a purely morphological level of analysis nor a purely genetic one will provide a satisfactory picture. What seems to be required is a set of *molecular mechanisms* related to the *dynamics of control of morphogenesis,* mechanisms that can be linked to developmental genetics through defined gene products having mechanochemical functions in pattern formation and leading eventually to changes in fitness. At the same time, one must understand how much of the evolved pattern of a given species was determined by its relation to the external world $(T_2,$ see figure 5.1) and how much by coordination of developmental processes within T_1.

In the nineteenth century, the dominant idea linking development to evolution was embodied in Haeckel's biogenetic law— "Ontogeny is a recapitulation of phylogeny." This idea engendered much argument but generally held sway until the emergence of analytic methods of embryology embodied in His and Roux's *Entwicklungsmechanik* and the rediscovery of Mendelian genetics by De Vries in 1901, after which it simply melted away. One reason for its passing was the revelation that many developmental processes postulated in descriptive embryology on the basis of homology simply were not found to be as described. The history of this subject has been amusingly and penetratingly told by Gould in his book *Ontogeny and Phylogeny*. Thus it appeared that the earlier ideas of von Baer (who discovered, among other remarkable things, the mammalian egg, the notochord, and neural folds as precursors of the nervous system) were more nearly correct. In his laws of development, von Baer stated that, whereas earlier stages of various taxa resembled one another, as development progressed, each species developed in its own specialized and idiosyncratic pattern. Nonetheless, even this notion, while perhaps somewhat closer to the truth, obviously had to be based on gross or microscopic *morphologic* observations and not on a description of the dynamics of cellular processes as regulated by molecules under the control of complex genetic regulatory rules.

Adequate answers to the two central questions on which this book focuses would provide such a dynamic description. This description would be in molecular terms and would relate inductive signal paths in development to higher-order cellular structures and to phenotypic selection, which would result in a further modification of signal paths in the genetic webs concerned with developmental selection. In any particular instance—say, an account of development within an evolutionarily related set of species—this would be a mechanistic description of T_1, and it would provide a secure basis for developing a further understanding of the evolution of various morphologies.

But even with such a description, which we will try to outline in hypothetical terms in later chapters, it is necessary to be aware that morphologic evolution comprises a much larger set of problems. Although we will certainly not attempt to investigate them all in this book, some of them should be mentioned so that the proposed answer to the developmental question is placed in the proper framework. This is a very rich framework. It includes many higher-level interactions between species and environment, as well as between species and species (coevolution). We wish to ask how developmental processes affect evolution and also how developmental processes themselves evolve. An answer to these questions will bear strongly on the matters of macroevolution (evolution of taxa above the species level) and on the apportionment of phenotypic diversity. That a particular apportionment cannot solely be a question of mutation and adaptation has been trenchantly expressed by Gould and Lewontin in a well-known essay that attacks the excessive and vacuous use of the idea of adaptation alone to explain structures. As Gould and Lewontin have pointed out, a close consideration of these matters will show that they cannot be accounted for by any simple notion of "adaptationism"—selection *exclusively* by adaptation in a population—even though such selection certainly plays a role in morphologic change.

The main point is that while possible epigenetic matches among developmental processes constrain evolutionary paths in a given species, their *actual* sequences, timing, and control result from their success in phenotypic function, and that is determined by the events of natural selection. Thus the *particular* form of an animal in a species is the *combined* result of the two factors: developmental regulation and natural selection affecting developmental dynamics.

With this statement in mind, let us identify some of the outstanding problems of morphologic evolution. A list summarizing the problems in the form of questions is collected in table 5.1. A glance at it shows that only the last of the questions related to T_1 is directly pertinent to our task. The implications of an adequate description of T_1 cannot be fully appreciated, however, without an awareness of certain higher-level interactions at the level of ecology and historical accident. Conversely, a better understanding of T_1 would clarify the answers to many of the previous questions on the list. We will therefore touch upon these questions before proceeding to consider the last one on the list, which is our central concern.

A major morphologic problem is that posed by the existence of various body plans. Assemblages of homologous architectural and structural features, including certain developmental properties, are usually considered the bases for body plans. Great arguments still prevail among evolutionists about how higher taxa

TABLE 5.1

Some Unsolved Problems of Morphologic Evolution

---

1. How can we account for the types and numbers of basic body plans (*Baupläne*) in the Precambrian and early Cambrian (650–570 M.Y.B.P.)?
2. Do such body plans arise in a variety of fashions, that is, do *Baupläne* arise in a single step or by piecemeal changes or in both ways?
3. How can we account for the relatively great increase in the number of species in higher taxa that has occurred since the formation of these *Baupläne?*
4. What are the relative contributions of gene change during evolution and of ecological opportunity in these processes? How much is microevolutionary and how much macroevolutionary?
5. What is the origin of complexity in evolution, and how does it relate to the developmental issue of body form?
6.* What role do developmental constraints play in all of these processes? More specifically, what is a reasonable molecular dynamic basis for (T_1) affecting such constraints (see figure 5.1), and how can it be directly related to the action of a web of regulatory genes of the kind described in such models as the DGR model (see chapter 4)?

---

*It is this problem that is attacked directly in this book. As the text indicates, the others are more appropriately the province of evolutionary studies proper.

sharing a given body plan have arisen. Some of these arguments concern the distinction between microevolutionary processes, which act upon species exhibiting genetic recombination and also relatively short generation times, and macroevolutionary processes, in which selection is at taxonomic levels of species and above and is relatively slow. In general, microevolution will dominate because of the speed of its processes in maintaining genetic heterogeneity in populations, whereas the slower macroevolutionary processes will tend to fix traits and eliminate heterogeneity over longer time periods.

Most explanations proposed to answer the first four questions in our list (table 5.1) suggest that body plans emerged as a result of a combination of microevolutionary events similar to those that gave rise to new species—changing ecological opportunities, isolation in small populations, and genetic drift. But these explanations do not take T_1 explicitly into account. It is clear that the evolution of basic morphologic forms is related to developmental dynamics: given the rapid alterations of various environmental barriers and conditions, developmental factors might have played a large role in determining whether new plans could be assembled relatively rapidly (i.e., in less than 10^6 years). As Gould has pointed out, it is likely that changes resulting in heterochrony (alterations of tissues and form by mutations leading to changes in the relative rates of development of different body parts) are required to explain the emergence of different body plans.

To explain why most body plans have evolved early—no new ones have emerged since the Precambrian period—several suggestions have been put forth. The first is that any early novelties arising by genetic drift and leading to new body plans are relatively poorly adapted and need a relatively large open adaptive space to become fixed or established. Presumably, novel types found little interference or competition in the late Precambrian period, since few metazoans existed to compete. But successful movement into somewhat different ecological conditions might require a new body plan for an adaptive radiation to be successful. This might be so either for radiation or for occupation of a space emptied by extinction. After a significant amount of coevolution had occurred, however, the existence of increased competition would tend to reduce the likelihood of the introduction of a new plan, which might in general be expected initially to have reduced fitness. Another reason for the failure of the emergence of new plans may be that major alterations in earlier genomes (required for plan changes) had less drastic effects upon the continuity of developmental events than would be the case for later genomes, when development required more integrative capabilities.

Given the existence of a particular set of body plans, how do we in general account for the increase of complexity during evolution (question 5, table 5.1)? One proposed answer by Stebbins is that evolution selects against both complexity and simplicity but as a rule is more likely to select more against simplicity. Ceteris paribus, evolution is more likely to modify an already existing structure; once a particular functional arrangement has been achieved, frequent replacement by convergence of an equivalent functional structure is unlikely. Another suggestion relates directly to topobiology: given the evolution of multicellularity in metazoans, the limits imposed by size and differentiation in unicellular organisms are to some extent mitigated or transcended with the creation of a richer *milieu intérieur* (circulatory systems,

duplication of organs, hormonal and neural control). By these
homeostatic means, multiple parallel changes in pattern are less
immediately constrained by the environment. Stebbins has proposed that in any given case of adaptive organization to a new
environmental factor to which several kinds of response may be
possible, the adaptation chosen is one that requires the smallest
mutational readjustment of the *existing* developmental pattern
(Stebbins's hypothesis of selective inertia). This would tend to
select against the simplification or elimination of developmental
stages and would lead, albeit slowly, to increasing complexity.

All of the explanations proffered above to account for morphologic evolution must obviously be considered to be tentative.
They do suggest, however, that strict unitarian and reductionist
views of natural selection that ignore development or that emphasize a strong opposition between microevolutionary and macroevolutionary processes are inadequate.

In considering these issues, we find one theme that is of great
significance for our present purposes: developmental integration
is a major factor in all issues of morphologic evolution. *The internal environment during development can exert as great a selective force on newly appearing mutations as the external environment.* We therefore need a satisfactory model that will answer
both the developmental and the evolutionary questions. This
model must account for the evolution of complex functional morphologic systems by showing how molecular regulatory means
can connect cell interactions in development to gene regulation
leading to changes in fitness. Without such a detailed account of
T_1, population genetics is incomplete, and so is the evolutionary
synthesis. An adequate explanatory model must be able to deal
not only with the emergence of different body plans but also with
the previously discussed issues of size change, allometry, and
continuous genetic variation involving polygenic effects as well
as the pleiotropic effects of single genes. All of these phenomena
involve highly nonlinear changes during development, and such
changes, being epigenetic, would in general be expected to be
highly context dependent. We will show this to be the case in
later chapters, particularly when we consider the evolution and
development of the brain in relation to the function of bones and
muscles.

At this point, it is not my purpose to propose a means by which a satisfactory molecular set of rules for T_1 can be integrated into an answer to the evolutionary question. For that we must first describe morphoregulatory molecules, which we will do in the next part of this book. Here, it is important to emphasize the matter of developmental constraint on evolutionary paths (question 6, table 5.1). One conclusion related to developmental constraint has already been made abundantly clear by our account so far—genes control the phenotype *indirectly,* not directly: the overall phenotypic pattern, including adult morphology and life history, is not controlled directly even by genetic fine tuning, as important as that is. Epigenesis is just as important as genetics, and at best *genes specify local rules, not global pattern.* Above all, developmental events intervene between genotypic and phenotypic space (figure 5.1). Given that not all developmental paths for T_1 are equally accessible, the number of phenotypes actually formed would be expected to be small compared with all those that might conceivably be produced to be acted upon by natural selection. Existing developmental paths thus can sharply constrain evolutionary possibilities. Nonetheless, when successful alteration of relative developmental timing (or heterochrony) does occur as a result of genetic change, certain developmental processes can be radically altered and uncoupled from each other without loss of function or without lethal effects.

Recognition of the existence of such developmental constraints does not vitiate this contrasting idea that developmental paths can nevertheless be highly degenerate—often the *same* kind of structure can be produced from a *variety of different* epigenetic sequences, as is seen, for example, in gastrulation events among different vertebrates. This concept of degeneracy—invoked at the gene regulator level in the DGR model (see chapter 4) and at the tissue level in the nervous system (see chapter 10) has many important consequences for the understanding of structure-function relations. To some extent, the existence of degeneracy relaxes the stringency of developmental constraints and, together with the regulative aspects of development, provides the necessary "leeway" for evolutionary changes that would otherwise lead to blind ends or lethality. In other words, in contrast to the present considerations in which the developmental constraints *on evolu-*

tion have been emphasized, degeneracy implies a certain relaxation of constraint *during development,* opening certain evolutionary possibilities in a given set of phenotypes.

What kinds of genetic control allow both constraint and degeneracy, and does their coexistence require the action of many genes? We know that, in the formation of the phenotype, thousands of genes may be involved. The critical question is, How many genes are required *specifically* to determine key aspects of a given form? The number may not be large. The application of modern genetic techniques has led to the suggestion that developmental change in evolution is guided mainly by regulatory genes rather than by structural genes. This could certainly reduce the number of genes required. Furthermore, it has become increasingly clear, as we saw in the last chapter, that regulatory gene sequences are embedded in a context-dependent web and that not all regulatory genes need be specifically involved in *developmental* events. The question may be rephrased once more: *Which* regulatory genes are particularly significant for morphogenetic events? In relating the evolution of form to developmental genetics, we must ask whether there exist *special* families or complexes of genes controlling the expression of morphoregulatory molecules that may be essential in linking the code to pattern formation. Such genes would govern products that are not directly critical for the life or detailed cytological specialization of a cell but that are nonetheless absolutely critical for morphogenesis and for morphologic evolution. If such gene complexes do exist, a major issue to be understood is their timing of expression and their modes of interaction with other genes that *are* critical to the cell's survival. Differences in the timing of the developmental appearance of ancestral traits have been invoked as a major basis of morphological changes. Identification of complexes of morphoregulatory genes would open the possibility of explaining such heterochrony (and therefore a good deal of morphologic evolution) at the molecular level.

In this chapter, I have ranged widely and somewhat superficially over several large issues in an attempt to sketch in the idea that no explanation of development (even one complete at the molecular level) is sufficient to account for morphology. Instead, we must consider the evolution of animal form in terms of its mutual interaction with development. This entails a view of evolution as a process of phenotypic transformation resulting largely from *genetically mediated change in developmental dynamics that is itself altered throughout phylogeny.* The task that this recognition imposes is to relate these developmental dynamics (and the selection of their control parameters by evolution) to *particular molecular processes* linking cells in development in regulative collectives. We must ask whether these molecular processes are few in number, how they apply differently in different contexts, whether they are degenerate, and whether, as a result of the genetic and epigenetic rules governing them, development is reversible or irreversible. Only when these matters are resolved at the molecular level will it be possible to provide a satisfactory answer to the evolutionary question.

With this end in mind, we must now look in greater detail at certain chemical and genetic processes that are important in the formation of cell collectives as a function of place. We must also examine key mechanisms of control at the cell membrane. Both tasks entail a description of certain recently discovered properties of cell surfaces and of the adhesion and junctional molecules that function at these surfaces.

SELECTED REFERENCES

Lewontin, R. C. 1974. *The genetic basis of evolutionary change.* New York: Columbia University Press.

His, W. 1874. *Unsere Körperform und das physiologische Problem ihrer Entstehung.* Leipzig: Vogel.

Roux, W. 1986. The problems, methods, and scope of developmental mechanics. In *Defining biology: Lectures from the 1890s,* ed. J. Maienschein, 107–48. Cambridge: Harvard University Press.

de Beer, G. R. 1940. *Embryos and ancestors.* Oxford: Clarendon Press.

Bonner, J. T., ed. 1982. *Evolution and development,* Dahlem Konferenzen, Life Sciences Research Report 22. Berlin: Springer-Verlag.

Edelman, G. M., and J. A. Gally. 1970. Arrangement and evolution of eukaryotic genes. In *The neurosciences: Second study program,* ed. F. O. Schmitt, 962–72. New York: Rockefeller University Press.

Gould, S. J. 1977. *Ontogeny and phylogeny.* Cambridge: Harvard University Press.

Gould, S. J., and R. C. Lewontin. 1979. The spandrels of San Marco and the Panglossian paradigm: A critique of the adaptionist programme. *Proc. R. Soc. Lond. (Biol.)* 205:581–98.

Raup, D. M., and D. Jablonski. 1986. *Patterns and processes in the history of life,* Dahlem Konferenzen, Life Sciences Research Report 36. Berlin: Springer-Verlag.

Arthur, W. 1984. *Mechanisms of morphological evolution: A combined genetic, developmental and ecological approach.* Chichester and New York: Wiley.

Alberch, P. 1980. Ontogenesis and morphological diversification. *Am. Zool.* 20:653–67.

———. 1982. The generative and regulatory roles of development. In *Environmental adaptation and evolution,* ed. D. Mossakowski and G. Roth, 19–36. Stuttgart: Gustav Fischer.

———. 1989. Orderly monsters: Evidence for internal constraint in development and evolution. In *The construction of organisms: Opportunity and constraint in the evolution of organic form,* ed. R. D. K. Thomas and W. E. Reif. Chicago: University of Chicago Press (in press).

Frazzetta, T. H. 1975. *Complex adaptations in evolving populations.* Sunderland, Mass.: Sinauer Associates.

Maynard Smith, J., R. Burian, S. Kaufman, P. Alberch, J. Campbell, B. Goodwin, R. Lande, D. M. Raup, and L. Wolpert. 1985. Developmental constraints and evolution. *Q. Rev. Biol.* 60:265–87.

Raff, R. A., and E. C. Raff, eds. 1987. *Development as an evolutionary process.* New York: Alan R. Liss.

Williams, G. C. 1966. *Adaptation and natural selection.* Princeton: Princeton University Press.

See also references to Raff and Kaufman and to Mayr and Provine in chapter 1, as well as those to Sperry, Turing, Wolpert, Stebbins, and Oster et al. in chapter 2.

PART TWO

MOLECULAR MECHANISMS OF EPIGENESIS

6

Mechanochemistry and Cellular Driving Forces

W E MAY SUMMARIZE our account of form arising from place through epigenesis as follows. Evolutionary emergence of cell-cell adhesion and signaling by way of cell surfaces resulted in new place-dependent mechanisms for the control of gene expression. This gave rise to multicellular forms and developmental variants with different body plans and to the divergence of phenotypes with different sequences of primary processes in development. Concomitantly, there was a further elaboration of multilevel signal pathways involving signals exchanged between cell collectives in development. The release of and response to these signals depended on the actual formation of these collectives, which, because of the geometry and numbers of their cells, necessarily contribute to pattern and overall shape.

Such developmental divergences and elaborations put a strong constraint on macroevolutionary processes: developmental events leading to form can be reconciled with only a small subset of signals out of all sets possible. In other words, not all of the dynamic interactions between mechanochemically controlled cellular processes and the regulatory signals to developmentally important genes can be reconciled with continuation of the developmental process and function and therefore with fitness. At the same time, natural selection acting upon functioning morphologic arrangements is responsible for the particular surviving developmental sequences that lead to a given morphology in any single species.

One of the most striking features of morphogenesis in different species is the differing contribution that each of the driving force processes makes at different stages of development. These differences in the sequences of primary processes coordinated by activation of developmentally important genes are just what one would expect to give rise to different morphologies.

We need a topobiological analysis of these events—that is, an analysis of the coordination of primary processes by cells as a function of place in development, recognizing the influence of natural selection in favoring certain phenotypes over others. In order to understand the dynamics of such developmental and evolutionary constraints, we must consider the actual developmental mechanisms at both cellular and molecular levels. To do so, we will describe the cell surface as a nexus of interaction and control affecting both cell shape and cell interactions. We will then take up those primary processes of development that act as driving forces to produce form (see figure 3.1). These include cell and tissue motion, cell division, and cell death. Many of the events that result in cell motion and division are mechanochemical—they use cellular metabolism to drive interactions of cytoskeletal molecules that result in cell motion and changes in cell shape as well as in cytokinesis. Although we will not describe the molecular events affecting the cytoskeleton in detail, we will describe their results. Following that description we can, in the next chapter, consider the molecules that are involved in forming cell collectives and that lead to morphology by altering mechanochemical responses.

The Cell Surface

It is obvious that the cell surface must play a key role in the molecular transactions concerned with cell-cell interactions, cell substrate interactions, signaling, and the determination of place in an epigenetic developmental sequence. The surface presents an array of different receptors to the outside environment, possesses a number of mechanisms (such as endocytotic processes) for incorporating portions of the environment, and acts as an important two-dimensional interface that governs and is governed by cell shape, cell motion, and cell division. To understand the developmental significance of these functions, we must review briefly the structure and dynamic interactions of cell membranes, surfaces, and cell cortical regions (figure 6.1).

Discoveries over the last fifteen years indicate that the cell membrane is a fluid bilayer that can undergo various local phase transitions. In this bilayer are inserted a variety of molecules, mainly glycolipids and glycoproteins in varying proportions in different cells. In general, these molecules turn over. For example, proteins are synthesized as a result of the expression of different messenger RNAs and, after the processing of signal sequences at vesicle interfaces and glycosylation at the Golgi apparatus, are inserted into the plasma membrane. They may in turn be taken up and recirculated or destroyed by various endocytotic events involving coated pits and vesicles, and lysosomes. Thus the constitution of the cell surface depends upon differential gene expression, posttranslational processing, and turnover events, all of which may be susceptible to local environmental signals. Various classes of proteins may be found in the fluid bilayer, differing in their signaling function, their mode of attachment to the bilayer, and their role in facilitating direct intercellular communication. Although some of these glycoproteins may not bind small molecules or other proteins, we will adopt the convention of calling them cell surface receptors.

Cell surface receptors may be extrinsic proteins (attached to the membrane surface by way of other molecules) or intrinsic proteins (attached via a membrane-spanning region, generally hydrophobic in nature). Obviously, the nature of the cell surface will depend upon the types and specificities of receptors, the variety of their ligands, their mode of attachment, and the absolute and relative numbers of each per cell, as well as upon the local surface density of each type at a particular part of the cell.

A

B

Type I Forces
(outside)

protein-protein
protein-carbohydrate
carbohydrate-carbohydrate

NH₂

Type II Forces
(bilayer)

IMP

protein-protein
protein-lipid
lipid-lipid

COOH

Type III Forces
(cytoplasm)

protein-protein
interactions via
submembranous
assemblies

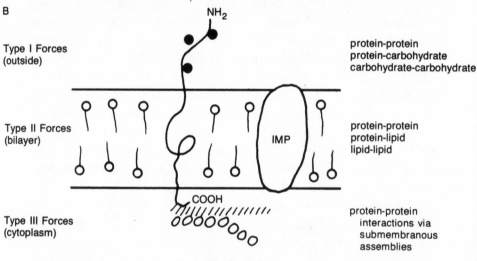

Figure 6.1

*Cell surface and cytoskeleton. A: Diagram illustrating transmembrane interactions of
receptors with cytoskeletal elements in cell cortex. (Some typical cytoskeletal proteins and
their presumed functions are listed in table 6.1.) Note that by means of these interactions,
a two-way path is opened for binding events on the outside to affect molecular interactions on the inside and for alterations of the cytoskeleton to affect the distribution and
function of cell surface receptors as well as intracellular signal paths. This diagram is
only figurative and is not completely accurate in scale or receptor density. B: Forces and
interactions affecting a single transmembrane receptor. (B is from G. M. Edelman, 1976,
Cell surface modulation in cell recognition and cell growth,* Science *192:218–26.)*

Alterations in numbers and modes of its attachment can lead to differences in mobility of a receptor in the plane of the membrane. This mobility will in turn be affected by intracytoplasmic interactions at the cell cortex of the cytoplasmic domains of intrinsic proteins. In general, these interactions are with components of the cytoskeleton (see figure 6.1 and table 6.1), a complex multiprotein assembly that influences the nature of the cortex, altering cell shape and movement. Early studies have indicated that such interactions of surface proteins not only govern their mobility but also act as a transmembrane path whereby binding reactions leading to clustering of receptors can alter cell shape and movement, as well as responses to mitogenic signals by means of second messengers. Thus the exterior interactions of cell surface components can act globally through a transmembrane path to modulate cell responses, and alterations in cytoskeletal elements can affect primary processes such as cell division. Reciprocally interactive surface modulating assemblies that consist of receptors interacting with the cytoskeleton can act as mechanochemical transducers affecting shape, movement, and biochemical response to various external and cytoplasmic signals. As we will see, such global cell surface modulation resulting from the reciprocal interactions between receptors and cytoskeleton and of receptors with cells and substrates is likely to be a major means of coordinating cell responses in development.

Given this elementary background on the dynamics and potential control functions of the cell surface, we may briefly survey a variety of cellular and molecular events that provide a mechanical basis at the microscopic level for different responses of cells to place at different times. These range from cytoskeletal and cytoplasmic rearrangements affecting gene expression to cell migration, tissue folding, cell division, and cell death. Each has a potential influence on morphogenesis through microscopic mechanics and at the same time can play a conjugate regulatory role in altering inductive signals and the epigenetic sequences that involve differential gene expression. Following the style I adopted in part one of this book, I will provide one or more key examples of these events, which together may be considered to form major components of a cellular grammar of development.

TABLE 6.1

Some Tubule and Filament Proteins Contributing to the Cytoskeleton

Microtubules (28 nm diameter)—lend rigidity, affect cell shape, and help mediate cytokinesis during cell division

Protein	Function
Tubulins	Basic building block for microtubules
MAPs* and τ proteins	Involved in polymerization and cross-linkage to other filaments
Dynein	Flagellar "motor"
Kinesin	"Motor" for transport along microtubules

Microfilaments (8 nm diameter)—involved in motility, alteration of cell shape, and cell surface protein constraint through membrane interaction

Protein	Function
Actin	The basic microfilament subunit protein
Vinculin	Binds ends of actin filaments to membrane
Talin	Links to transmembrane proteins and receptors
α-Actinin	Binding of actin filament to membrane; cross-linkage of filaments
Spectrin (fodrin, filamin)	Submembranous anchor point to membrane
Gelsolin (villin)	Nucleates the polymerization of F-actin; cleaves actin filaments into fragments
Profilin	Binds to monomers of actin; retards polymerization
Fimbrin	Cross-links adjacent filaments to form parallel fibers
Myosin	Generates tension in microfilament arrays; involved in movements of filaments
Tropomyosin	Regulates binding of actin to myosin

Intermediate filaments (10 nm diameter)

Protein	Function
Vimentin	
Desmin	All lend structural rigidity to cell
Cytokeratins	
Neurofilament proteins	Lend structural rigidity to axons; (?) role in transport
Glial fibrillary acidic protein	Contributes to cell shape

*MAPs, microtubule-associated proteins.

THE CYTOSKELETON, CELL SHAPE, AND CYTOPLASMIC REARRANGEMENTS

The cytoskeleton is a complex intracellular array of interactive proteins that influences how the cortex of the cell interacts with the surface. It mediates cell movement, process extension, and endocytotic events and also governs cell shape. It consists of a large variety of proteins (see table 6.1) that are disposed differently in the cytoplasm. Several, such as fodrin and vinculin, are generally found at the cortex. Others, such as microtubular proteins (and associated proteins), actin, and intermediate filament proteins, are also disposed in various patterns in the cytoplasm and by their structure and associations can alter cell shape, rigidity, and mobility. The interactions of this complex array of proteins are highly dynamic and are associated with changes in cell shape and movement, particularly the extension of lamellipodia mediated by actin and myosin interactions. Accompanying such mechanochemical rearrangements are remarkable changes in the cell cortex and surface receptors that play a key role in morphogenesis.

One of the earliest types of cell cortical rearrangement that can critically affect development is a shift in the cytoplasmic components of the fertilized egg prior to cleavage, already alluded to in chapter 3. This shift of the endoplasm relative to the egg surface that is based on cytoskeletal interactions has been shown to affect the displacement of determinants of axial structural development in the frog embryo. In the egg of *Xenopus,* for example, maternal influences (presumably topobiological) have already led to a localization of cytoplasmic materials—a primary polarity. The so-called animal hemisphere (see figure 6.2) contains various organelles and melanin granules and the spindle and chromosomes. The vegetal hemisphere has fewer organelles and contains yolk platelets and germ plasm granules. This polar organization is topographically related to the ultimate fate of tissues in the embryo (figure 6.2). Sperm entry determines a meridian that will be the prospective ventral midline, and the opposite meridian will be the site of most of the

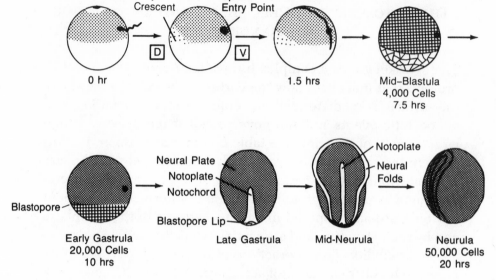

Figure 6.2

Schematic development of Xenopus *egg from fertilization through neurulation. The animal sphere is up* (dark), *and the vegetal sphere* (unpigmented) *is down. The sperm happens to have entered on the right, and after the first cell cycle a gray crescent forms at the equator at a point roughly opposite that of sperm entry. The dorsal midline will be on the meridian bisecting the crescent. The blastopore forms in gastrulation. The late gastrula is shown rotated 90° toward the reader to illustrate the formation of the blastopore lip and the onset of neurulation. (Modified from J. Gerhart and R. Keller, 1986, Region-specific cell activities in amphibian gastrulation, Annu. Rev. Cell Biol. 2:201–29; and A. G. Jacobson, G. M. Odell, and G. F. Oster, 1985, The cortical tractor model for epithelial folding: Application to the neural plate, in Molecular determinants of animal form, ed. G. M. Edelman, 143–66, New York: Alan R. Liss.)*

origins of the vertebrate structures determining the axis of the embryo.

The major reorganization of the endoplasm during the first postfertilization cell cycle leads to the appearance of the gray crescent at the equator opposite the sperm entry point. This in turn leads to a difference in the ability of various regions of this now bilaterally symmetric egg to form various dorsoventral structures.

As we mentioned, the cortical-cytoplasmic rotation that underlies this major morphologic differentiation is determined by cytoskeletal components in the egg. Alteration of the cytoskeleton by low temperature, high pressure, and the drug nocodazole, all of which dissociate microtubules, inhibits rotation and leads to the formation of a cylindrically symmetric embryo that lacks a vertebrate body axis. Gerhart and his coworkers have shown that such deficient embryos can make ventral structures (ciliated epidermis, red blood cells, a malformed gut) but cannot make key dorsal structures. Thus cortical rotation leads to *regional* cytoplasmic differences, probably by local activation of maternal components and messages.

This set of events depends upon egg structures that must have been determined by maternal interactions during oogenesis as well as upon local surface interactions (e.g., the sperm entry upon fertilization) after maturation of the egg. After this, most of the polarity-determining inductive events depend mainly upon cell-cell interactions of cells of the dividing egg. These are in turn determined by a set of morphogenetic movements that also require cytoskeletal rearrangements, but in a different fashion, one mainly involving primary processes: various forms of cell and tissue motion, cell-cell and cell-substrate adhesion, cell division, and death, can all alter the shape of the embryo and its local inductive history. Instead of cytoplasmic asymmetries, asymmetries of cell populations are involved in these events. Let us turn to a brief survey of such events, the molecular basis of which constitutes a kind of mechanochemistry influencing the mechanics and therefore the form of cell collectives.

EPITHELIAL-MESENCHYMAL TRANSFORMATION AND CELL MIGRATION

One of the most striking processes in embryonic development is the conversion of contiguous cells linked in sheets known as epithelia to the loosely associated migratory cells known as mesenchyme. This transformation, which can occur in either direction, is a prominent feature of embryogenesis at various stages. We have already considered the formation of primary mesenchyme in the primitive streak of the chick embryo during gastrulation (chapters 3 and 4). The mesenchyme can condense into mesodermal epithelial structures, which can in turn give rise to secondary mesenchyme; this process is seen, for example, when somites form the so-called sclerotome. A similar process is seen in ectodermal derivatives when neural crest cells disperse, migrate, and recondense into epithelia, leading to ganglion formation. The relative amount of mesenchyme in all layers during development increases in the evolution from primitive chordates to land animals having bony endoskeletons.

The properties and mechanical characteristics of epithelial cells and mesenchymal cells are strikingly different (see figure 6.3). Epithelial sheets are apically sealed structures with a free surface, and they interact at their basal surface with molecules of the so-called extracellular matrix (ECM), often present in the form of a basement membrane. In general, epithelial cells are cuboidal, squamous, or stratified. Mesenchymal cells are generally elongated, have only minimal contacts with each other, and have surfaces that are not strongly polarized, as are those of epithelia. Although epithelia can produce some ECM, the mesenchymal cells produce the bulk of it. We will see in the next chapter that the polarity of epithelia depends in part on cell adhesion molecules (CAMs).

Clearly, epithelial-mesenchymal transformations are sensitive to time and place of development. The key question that arises concerns the nature of the topobiological signals mediating such transformations. There is evidence to suggest that these signals act at the cell surface and that they are related to the chemical nature of the components in the ECM at a given locus. Hay has, for example, shown that epithelial cells of the cornea produce a matrix component called collagen type IV. When closely surrounded by a gel of collagen type I (another molecular species of this ECM protein), such cells will mitose, change shape, migrate into the gel, and produce collagen type I rather than type IV. This alteration is blocked by agents that disrupt the actin components of the cytoskeleton. Another indication that cell surface contacts provide or sustain appropriate signals governing the cortex is the fact that two different ECM molecules—laminin or collagen—when coupled to beads will bind mainly to the basal surface of epithelia and result in reorganization of only that actin which is present in the basal cell cortex. As we will see when we

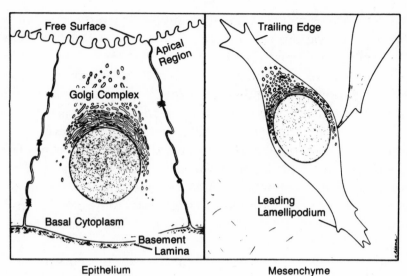

Epithelium   Mesenchyme

Characteristics of Epithelial and Mesenchymal States

Characteristic	Epithelia	Mesenchyme
Linked in contiguous sheets	+	−
Polar with outer free surface, apical Golgi apposition	+	−
Juxtalumenal tight junctions	+	−
Lateral gap junctions and desmosomes	+	−
		(or a very few)
Basal surface on extracellular matrix	+	−
Bipolar and stellate shape	−	+
Migratory	−	+
Vimentin, type I collagen, fibronectin (can produce fibroblasts with type II collagen)	−	+
Cytokeratin, laminin, type IV collagen	+	−

Figure 6.3

Diagram and table showing the major differences between an epithelial cell (left) and a mesenchymal cell (right). The epithelial cell sits on top of a basement membrane, under which connective tissue fibrils assemble. The mesenchymal cell resides in the extracellular matrix (ECM) and, if it is migrating, has a trailing edge containing the Golgi complex. In the epithelial cell, the Golgi complex is usually in the apical cytoplasm, the free surface is specialized for dealing with the outside world, and the basal surface is specialized to connect to the underlying ECM; the lateral surfaces form numerous junctions with adjacent epithelial cells. Only occasional junctions are seen between mesenchymal cells. Some characteristics of each state are summarized in the table below the figure; the molecules listed in the table will be considered in the next chapter. (After E. D. Hay, 1981, Collagen and embryonic development, in Cell biology of extracellular matrix, ed. E. D. Hay, 379–409, New York: Plenum.)

consider various morphoregulatory molecules in more detail in later sections, various cell surface receptors for such ECM molecules, called integrins, have been identified.

As a result of epithelial-mesenchymal transformation, two kinds of motion can arise that differ to some degree in scale. The first involves the obvious cell migration that can take place after conversion to mesenchyme, as well as its cessation following condensation of mesenchyme into rounded epithelial masses. The second (discussed in detail in the next section) is the folding, invagination, or evagination of whole tissue sheets to form various structures, including tubes. In both cases, new cellular environments are created, leading to the possibility that different inductive signals will be released.

When epithelial-mesenchymal transformation occurs, the cell surface changes in its molecular composition (figure 6.3, *bottom*); we will review the details in later sections. This suggests that such transformation involves an alteration in gene transcription or translation under the influence of modulation at the cell surface, with subsequent effects on the cytoskeleton. Thus the intriguing issues related to epithelial-mesenchymal conversion are (1) what particular epigenetic events yield appropriate signals for the transformation and (2) whether migrating mesenchymal cells follow local topobiological cues provided by certain ECM molecules that guide their actual paths or whether their migration is mainly a permissive one, constrained by cellular barriers and basement membranes in a purely mechanical fashion.

The available data suggest that place-dependent syntheses of particular ECM molecules may trigger the epithelial-mesenchymal transformation, but it is not known what conditions the sequence of such syntheses in the embryo. Moreover, as we will see later, before epithelial-mesenchymal transformation can take place, at least one permissive step must occur to release epithelial contacts made by means of cell adhesion molecules (CAMs). Whatever the case, epithelial-mesenchymal transformation frequently underlies many pattern-forming inductive events in the embryo. Similarly, condensation of mesenchyme into epithelia and the folding of epithelial sheets, to which we now turn, can also alter the place, history, and contact of cells in collectives, producing new inductive signals while yielding form.

EPITHELIAL FOLDING

Epithelial sheets constitute the external and internal boundaries of organisms. Such sheets can remain as connected entities while folding, invaginating, and deforming to produce a variety of three-dimensional structures. Although the apical seal (see figure 6.3) of such epithelia is maintained during these processes, it is by no means certain that cells in epithelia may not exchange places, at least locally. Indeed, there is evidence that, to a limited extent, they do. It is of special interest that the linkage of cells into epithelia provides a means for converting mechanochemical cell activity into particular kinds of larger-scale mechanical motion and reordering, with important consequences for form and inductive signaling.

A variety of successive embryonic events in different species depends upon the movement of epithelial sheets. These events include gastrulation and epiboly (the movement of the ectodermal sheet) in frog embryos. During gastrulation, these embryos show a particularly complex process of movement. This includes convergent extension of cells, neurulation (the rolling up of the neural tube), and the formation of various placodes (specialized epidermal structures giving rise to structures as varied as eyes, ears, ganglia, and feathers). Two examples of these events nicely illustrate the possible mechanisms of epithelial folding and will be discussed here. They are, in order of complexity, neurulation in the chicken and so-called convergent extension to form the gastrula in the frog.

The mechanism of neurulation has been extensively studied by Jacobson, who has pointed out that the neural plate consists of two domains of cells: a notoplate and the neural plate proper. The notoplate, which overlies the notochord (see figure 6.4) and underlies the neural plate, elongates and narrows during neurulation, and its constituent cells change places in this process. In contrast, this cellular exchange is much less prominent in the epithelial cells of the neural plate, which do, however, shrink their apical surfaces as the neural plate rolls up and as both domains elongate.

Two models have been proposed by Jacobson and his colleagues to account for this dramatic and precise folding of the neural tube. In the first, it is suggested that adhesive and contractile events are coupled to give this mechanical change. It is proposed that notoplate cells are less adhesive than those of the neural plate proper and they attempt to invade this more highly adhesive domain. Because this cannot occur, the notoplate–neural plate boundary extends, lengthening the midline. This causes the neural plate to buckle into a tube, much as a sheet of rubber, when stretched at two nodal points, will tend to buckle into a tube.

A second model, which is more recent and more detailed (figure 6.4), explains the mechanics of folding by invoking the properties of the cell cortex described earlier (see figure 6.1). This so-called cortical tractor model is based on a set of ideas arising from an analysis of moving cells, but it is applied in this instance to cells forming an epithelial sheet. Moving cells, in this model, show a cortical flow of plasmalemma and actin-myosin complexes from leading to trailing surfaces. Adhesion molecules and junc-

Figure 6.4

Epithelial folding according to the cortical tractor model of Jacobson, Odell, and Oster. A: Schematic of the cortical tractor mechanism. The actomyosin in the cortex flows as indicated by the arrows, and cell-cell adhesion structures are dragged along by the flow of the cortex. B: Diagram of a section of the neural epithelium. Each cell undergoes the cortical tractor motion (arrows). In this case, the cells are active basally. C: (Upper figures) Apical view of four epithelial cells as they change neighbors. (Lower figure) Lateral view of the cortical tractor mechanism showing cell B interdigitating between cells A and C. Cell B is laterally and basally active. D: Diagram (top view, looking down on the cell apices) illustrating how interdigitation of cells can elongate the boundary at the neural plate–notoplate interface. E: Vertically arranged diagrams (left) illustrate how events are interpreted to occur at the epidermis–neural plate boundary. Neural plate cells tractor on the bottoms of the epidermal cells, pulling them into a fold, and at the same time stretching the neural plate cells until their apical surfaces are points, or even become released. Neural plate cells interdigitate along the boundary (not shown) to elongate the neural folds, and their tractoring produces a rolling moment toward the midline and lifts the folds up out of the plane. The corresponding drawings vertically arranged (right) are tracings of cells from cross sections of newt neurulae at stages 15, 16, and 17, and the actual cell shapes can be compared with the diagrams on the left. (From A. G. Jacobson, G. M. Odell, and G. F. Oster, 1985, The cortical tractor model for epithelial folding: Application to the neural plate, in Molecular determinants of animal form, ed. G. M. Edelman, 143–66, New York: Alan R. Liss.)

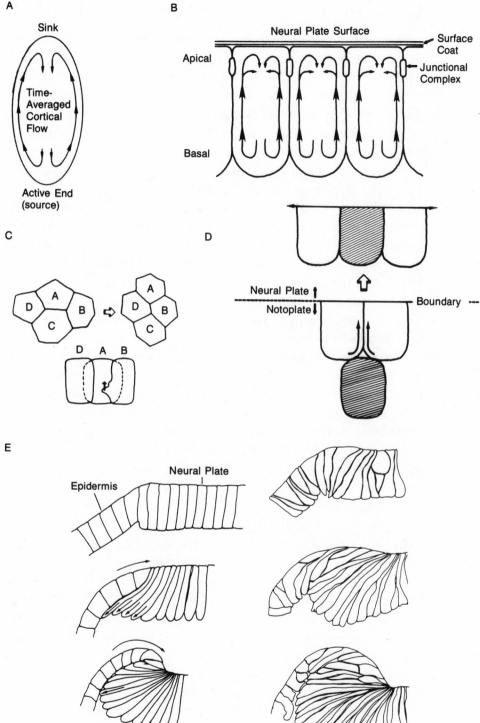

Sink

Time-Averaged Cortical Flow

Active End (source)

tional molecules are assumed to be inserted at the leading edge and to follow the flow unless they are stabilized by contacts with other cells or substratum. The model proposes that epithelia carry out the same processes but that, because their boundaries are attached at their apical regions, the flow will tend to concentrate cellular microfilament bundles (parts of the cytoskeleton) at the apical region, leading to contraction at the cell apex.

In such a dynamic epithelium, there would be no relative motion if each cell had the same intensity and frequency of flow from the basal region to the apex. If certain cells show greater flow, however, their basal and lateral surfaces can extend lamellipodia between other cells in the sheet, and such lamellipodia can be swept apically to the surface of the sheet by the tractor, leading to the positioning of that cell between its neighbors (figure 6.4, *C*). Inasmuch as new cell junctions are inserted at the same time they are recycled, the apical seal is not broken by this local switching of position.

This model has been used to explain neurulation (Figure 6.4, *D*) as follows. If the rate of tractoring in the apical junctions is slightly less than that of the basal junctions of the neural plate cells, this will elongate these cells, as is actually observed. At the same time, notoplate cells are supposed to have their basal faces *inactivated* by contact with notochord cells below; their apical surfaces, which have an ECM coat, are *normally* inactive. This results in the presence of active cortical tractors only on the lateral faces of notoplate cells. Such cells will exchange neighbors randomly in a local fashion. But if notoplate cells stick more to overlying neural plate cells than to each other, and if contact with a neural plate cell inhibits the activity of the contacting face by contact inhibition, the tractoring will be restricted to notoplate cell faces that do *not* touch the neural plate. The net result will be an elongation of the notoplate–neural plate boundary by interdigitation. This process will lead to elongation of the notoplate, as we mentioned earlier.

Furthermore, the boundary between the neural plate and epidermis (figure 6.4, *E*) will add another inhomogeneity, leading to the folding of the neural tube. Epidermal cells are assumed to have basal and apical surfaces that are inactive, whereas the adjacent neural plate cells are basally active. The faces of these tractoring cells adhere to epidermal cells, and that causes them to crawl beneath these epidermal cells. As their adherent faces become inactivated, they tractor more neural plate cells after them, crowding these cells into folds. The tethered apices of the neural plate cells plus the tractoring will buckle the epidermal sheet into an arch; at the same time, the neural plate cells will stretch and constrict their apical surfaces.

According to this model, notoplate extension and the cortical tractoring described above are *both* necessary to cause the sheet to be completely rolled into a neural tube. This suggests that the mechanochemical and mechanical causes of such structural changes are both complex and multiple. Nonetheless, it is important to note that the cellular mechanisms behind them are *local* and are based on the interplay between cell motility and cell tethering by adhesion.

An even more complex set of epithelial foldings accompanies gastrulation in the frog egg. We have already considered the effects of polar displacement of the endoplasm of such eggs. Keller has studied in detail the region-specific activities of cells leading to gastrulation. This constitutes a complex of activities in five regions (figure 6.5). (1) *Animal cap* cells show an isotropic expansion to cover almost half of the gastrula surface, a process called epiboly. (2) In the *vegetal hemispheres,* bottle cells contract their apices (facing the midline) and elongate basally; these cells form the vegetal pole. As contraction occurs, a blastoporal pigment line is formed. (3) Between this line and the animal cap, a *marginal zone* of cells forms. The vegetal half of this zone involutes, turning inside out and coming to form the epithelial roof of the so-called archenteron cavity. The rest of the marginal zone is noninvoluting. Cells of both parts of the marginal zone show convergence toward the dorsal midline while extending in the animal-vegetal direction. As Keller has shown, *this convergent extension is the key to gastrulation movements.* (4) Inside the blastocoel, *deep* cells migrate and spread over the wall and roof. (5) *Vegetal base* cells (large yolk cells) extend to the blastocoel floor, ultimately forming the floor of the archenteron.

Inductive interactions of animal and vegetal cells are responsi-

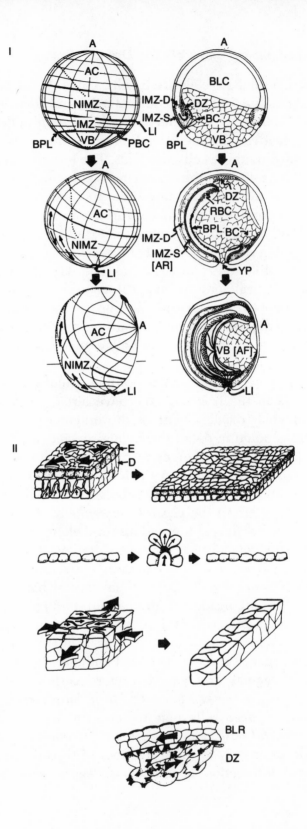

ble for establishing these five main functional regions. Prospective endodermal cells of the vegetal base of the blastula cause adjacent animal cells to form a marginal zone, leading to convergent extension, spreading migration, and bottle cell formation instead of epiboly. Epiboly itself, however, appears to develop autonomously in uninduced animal cap regions.

What mechanochemical events cause these complex structural changes? It is assumed (figure 6.4, *B*) that epiboly results from cell intercalation and spreading of cells of the animal cap. Although little is known of this process, it may resemble events (already discussed in the cortical tractor model) whereby notoplate cells intercalate. In this case, however, the cells expand and flatten, and the marginal zone may also tend to pull the animal cap downward.

Convergent extension of the circumblastoporal region is also autonomous and is the cause of the spreading of the marginal zone toward the blastopore, involution of this zone, and blastoporal closure. Convergent extension involves intercalation of deep cells of the involuting marginal zone to bring about a larger, narrower array (figure 6.5, II). During this process, cytoplasmic flow has been observed, and cortical tractoring may thus be a major mechanism. Indeed, the convergent extension of the dorsal noninvoluting marginal zone assists in blastoporal closure, and

Figure 6.5

I: Xenopus *development is shown at the early gastrula* (top panel), *late gastrula* (middle panel), *and neurula* (bottom panel) *stages (see figure 6.2). Figures on the left represent whole egg; those on the right are sagittal sections through the egg. Morphogenetic movements are shown from a midsagittal viewpoint. Embryos are arbitrarily oriented to have the prospective dorsal midline on the left (in the visual plane of the page) and the prospective ventral midline on the right.* Arrows indicate the direction of movement (A, *animal pole; AC, animal cap; AF, archenteron floor; AR, archenteron roof; BC, bottle cells; BLC, blastocoel; BPL, blastopore pigment line; DZ, deep zone; IMZ, involuting marginal zone; IMZ-D, IMZ deep layer; IMZ-S, IMZ superficial layer; LI, limit of involution; NIMZ, noninvoluting marginal zone; PBC, prospective bottle cells; RBC, respread bottle cells; VB, vegetal base; YP, yolk plug).* II: The four major cellular processes in Xenopus *gastrulation are illustrated: cell intercalation and cell spreading during epiboly of the animal cap* (top); *formation of bottle cells and their subsequent respreading* (top center); *cell intercalation during convergent extension of the involuting and noninvoluting marginal zones* (bottom center); *traction of the stream of involuting deep zone cells on the roof of the blastocoel* (bottom). Arrows *indicate direction of cell movements or tissue displacements (BLR, blastocoel roof; E, superficial epithelial cells; D, deep nonepithelial cells; DZ, deep zone cells). (Modified from J. Gerhart and R. Keller, 1986, Region-specific cell activities in amphibian gastrulation,* Annu. Rev. Cell Biol. *2:201–29.)*

this zone is the origin of the notoplate. Bottle cells do not drive gastrulation, as does the convergent extension of the marginal zone, but they probably orient the initial involution, possibly by the kind of tractoring discussed previously.

As the description of this complex coordinated process shows, cell migration, surface protrusion, and apical contraction are thus all basic to gastrulation. Individual cells of early gastrulae are not preprogrammed but follow their paths as a result of their *local interactions* with cells in their neighborhood. Interference with these interactions, or with components of the ECM by antibodies, or alteration of cytoskeletal elements by cytochalasin leads to failure of gastrulation.

Aside from the extraordinary coordinative aspects of the process of gastrulation, its most striking feature is topobiological. As Gerhart and Keller point out, "ultimate cell fate is determined by the gastrulation processes that place the cell in its ultimate *position*" (italics mine). Early gastrulation is epigenetic: the gastrula is just enough determined to set up the next stage and so on. By this means a given stage provides the context for its ensuing stage in a position-dependent manner. The ensuing inductions can occur as a result either of mesenchymal interactions or of the interpositions caused by epithelial folding. Cell migration and sheet folding are thus two major driving forces for events that lead to animal form.

CELL DIVISION AND CELL DEATH

Aside from migrations, condensations, and epithelial foldings, all of which involve movement, there are two other major primary processes of development that can act as driving forces to change the mechanochemical interactions of cells. These are cell division and cell death. We will consider these complex processes here from a quite restricted but important point of view: they can be dissociated to some degree, as Needham first pointed out; they can occur simultaneously with or independently from those of motion; they can be tightly programmed in lineage-dependent animals or be stochastic, as in complex vertebrate development;

and they can contribute to the mechanics of the developing embryo in a number of subtle ways that go beyond the sheer increase or decrease of cell mass.

Obviously, the regulation of early cell division and egg cleavage plays a key role in setting up later regions with different epigenetic influences. An examination of different embryogenetic patterns in different species shows a striking difference in the timing and extent of cell division at different stages and areas as compared with morphogenetic movements. This can be seen by comparing frog development and mouse development (table 6.2). In the frog, there is an early rapid proliferation to 4,000 cells

TABLE 6.2

Differences in the Timing and Relative Contribution of Two Primary Processes (Proliferation, Movement) in Early Events of Development of Different Species

Frog—Early rapid proliferation to 4,000 cells with utilization of maternal message followed by production of new messenger RNA; cleavage not a major part of gastrulation (see Gerhart and Keller 1986).

Precleavage	*Cleavage*	*Gastrulation*
Shift of endoplasm relative to surface	At 32-cell stage, subequatorial dorsal vegetal blastomeres are necessary and sufficient for axis formation (endoderm precursor)	Autonomous and independent of prospective chordamesoderm
	Dorsal axial mesoderm does not specify differentiation of any special cell type but new transcription	Induction of neural plate by dorsal strip of mesoderm

Mouse (mammals)—Combine a phase of rapid cell proliferation with the tissue arrangements of gastrulation (see Snow 1985).

	Cleavage	*Gastrulation*
	At 8–16 cells, blastocyst redistribution is followed by compaction; at 16–32 cells (2½–5 days), inner cell mass shows tissue-specific proteins; doubling time 10 hours	600 cells (6½ days); beginning of tissue lineages and concomitant large proliferation; doubling time 5 hours

or so before the production of much autonomous messenger RNA. During epiboly and gastrulation, during which the movements we have just described predominate, division certainly continues but is not prominent. In the mouse, there is, by contrast, an early production of up to 600 cells at a doubling time of ten hours, but then much more rapid cell proliferation is concomitant with the tissue rearrangements of gastrulation, leading to the body plan. In this period, the doubling time decreases from ten to about five hours.

It is clear from such facts and our previous discussion that the dependency on different modes of oogenesis, the development of amniotic embryos, and the various stages of mechanochemical interactions leading to different morphologies in an epigenetic fashion resulted from the evolution of different synchronies and heterochronies among the primary processes in different species. As cell division occurs, it obviously provides new cells to an area but can also be centrally important to histogenetic processes following early inductions. We will see this in later chapters when we discuss some striking examples in the nervous system and in skin appendages.

Although cell divisions are regulated epigenetically, it must be stressed that, in general, morphogenesis does not depend upon an *exact* number or sequence of divisions, at least not in the later stages of development of complex embryos such as those we have been considering. To some extent, division is stochastic, and overall regulation called "catch-up growth" can occur in cases where fewer divisions occur initially. These findings are in contrast to those in simpler animals with smaller numbers of cells, where much stricter lineage control can be seen. The main point is that control of cell division contributes to the regulative aspect of embryonic development in complex animals and that a certain trade-off with other primary processes can occur, provided that epigenetic sequences allow for an exchange between appropriate inducing cell collectives.

A strongly stochastic but nevertheless place-dependent property is seen for cell death as well. Cell death can be a major topobiological shaping force in morphogenesis at a variety of sites: the development of phalanges, the fusion of the palatal arch, the ultimate shaping of epidermal appendages such as the feather, and, particularly, the sculpting of the nervous system. Failure of cell death to occur at certain sites can lead to teratological disorders: in the hands and feet, to paddle-shaped extremities or fused phalanges; in the head, to cleft palate.

At some locations in the nervous system, up to 70 percent of the cells in a region contributing to histogenesis may die before a final neuroanatomical network is fixed. Studies of mutants in the formation of neural connections suggest that much of this cell death is contingent and location dependent and, to some extent, stochastic. Combined with the variability of cell division and movement, this implies that particular cells in particular positions of a normal fetus were not preprogrammed exactly for their fate. Rather, groups of cells obey topobiological principles related to local interactions with other groups of cells at particular places and times of development. How can stochastic events of primary processes such as death, division, and movement be coordinated at these loci? We take this question up in the following section.

GLOBAL CELL SURFACE MODULATION AND THE COORDINATION OF PRIMARY PROCESSES

Evolution and natural selection of the phenotype govern not only the mix of different driving force primary processes at a given stage and site in a species but also their coordination to give rise to functioning structures. This brings us to a key question of topobiology. Given that evolution determined an adaptive mix of primary processes, what developmental events at a given time are responsible for the coordination of these processes in a site-dependent fashion? In general, cells that move extensively do not divide and vice versa. Moreover, cells in epithelial sheets generally reach a steady state in total number and divide only to increase cell numbers in specific circumstances. And, obviously, death removes given cells from the game but can also trigger other processes.

It seems highly unlikely that these various processes, which are topobiologically controlled in the embryo, are regulated *only* by a local concentration or gradients of humoral factors. Not only would the large-scale changes of cell and sheet movement disturb the stability of such gradients but the stochastic elements in many primary processes would also be difficult to compensate for. Another factor seems to be required, one that reflects the position and interaction of the cell surface and that correlates the state of the cell surface and cortex with signals for movement and division.

We have seen that the surface and cortex play a prominent role in a variety of mechanochemical events and receptor interactions (see figure 6.1), and it is therefore reasonable to propose that the surface itself is an important locus of general control. The unit or element of control must be the cell at a place, and control itself must be determined by collective surface interactions with a certain number of other cells or substrates in the neighborhood.

A consistent hypothesis is that, in addition to specific changes of particular receptors, the cell surface is *globally* modulated by particular interactions of certain of its receptors with other cells or substrates in the vicinity. If such interactions altered or inhibited the cytoskeletal states connected to motion, they could also change cell shape. If, in addition, certain of these altered states blocked the cell's response to mitogenic signals, the state of a cell could be correlated with the expression of a given pri-

Figure 6.6

Global cell surface modulation. A: Diagram of free (F) and anchored (A) cell surface receptors in the plane of the lipid bilayer (compare figure 6.1). A_1 receptors interact with the cytoskeleton. When tetravalent concanavalin A (Con A) is added, the cross-linkage of receptors by binding to their sugars (see diagram of Con A in B; S is the sugar-binding site; Ca and Mn are binding sites for these metals) leads to global modulation with a sharp increase in the number of anchored (A) receptors. This decrease in receptor mobility can be detected by watching the inhibition of the patching (and therefore the capping) of free receptors by bivalent antibodies that cause their patching (C). Globally modulated cells with inhibition of lateral mobility of their receptors have altered shape, motion, and response to mitogenic signals (IMP, intramembranous particle; MF, microfilaments; MT, microtubules). (From G. M. Edelman, 1976, Cell surface modulation in cell recognition and cell growth, Science 192:218–26 [A]; J. W. Becker, G. N. Reeke, Jr., B. A. Cunningham, and G. M. Edelman, 1976, New evidence on the location of the saccharide-binding site of concanavalin A, Nature 259:406–9 [B]; J. L. Wang, G. R. Gunther, I. Yahara, B. A. Cunningham, and G. M. Edelman, 1975, Receptor-cytoplasmic interactions and lymphocyte activation, in Immune recognition, New York: Academic [C].)

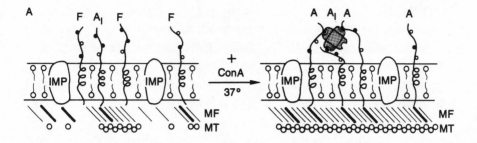

A

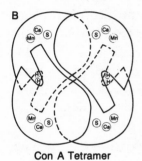

B

S = Sugar-binding Site
H = Hydrophobic Cavity
Ca = Calcium-binding Site
Mn = Manganese-binding Site

Con A Tetramer

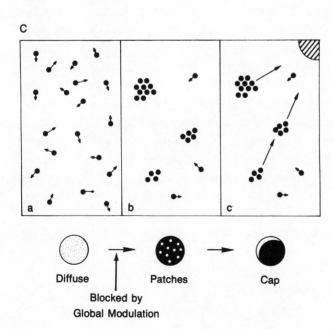

C

Diffuse → Patches → Cap

Blocked by
Global Modulation

mary process such as motion or division. Inasmuch as such events would be coordinated by interactions of surface receptors with cells or substrates in the vicinity, the state or property of the surface in response to signals in that vicinity could in turn govern cellular responses by altering cytoskeletal states. Reciprocally, alterations in these states mediated by various exterior or interior signals could affect primary processes.

Some suggestive evidence for this hypothesis of global cell surface modulation as a source of topobiological control has already accumulated (figure 6.6). The cross-linking of glycoprotein cell surface receptors by tetravalent lectins such as concanavalin A present on only a small percentage of a cell surface results in a series of modulations of the cell state. As a result, the overall lateral diffusion of various cell surface receptors is greatly diminished. Moreover, the modulated cell does not undergo normal motile shape changes, and it becomes unresponsive to mitogenic or transforming signals that it has already received. These effects can be reversed by agents such as colchicine or nocodazole that are known to disrupt the microtubules of the cytoskeleton. The reverse is also true: cell state responds to microtubular state. For example, nonconfluent cells in culture that are actively dividing can be blocked in their division by such drug treatment. In contrast, when confluent, the same cells do not spontaneously divide. When treated in this confluent state by microtubule-disrupting drugs such as colchicine, however, the cells spontaneously undergo a round of division, without the addition of growth factors.

These observations on the regulatory role of the cytoskeleton are consistent with the need to coordinate its central mechanochemical role, as seen in migration and epithelial folding. They are also consistent with our earlier observations that the composition of the ECM interacting with the surface can determine whether cells of a given type are epithelial or mesenchymal. Although the exact effect of the modulated cytoskeletal state on the signal path to the nucleus, on posttranslational events, or on migration remains to be determined, it is highly likely that specific cell surface receptors interacting reciprocally with cytoskeletal elements are parts of a control pathway governing the allocation of primary processes in development at a particular place and time. Before considering this important notion in more detail, however, let us turn to a description of the actual molecules that can have morphoregulatory functions as a result of their properties at the cell surface.

SELECTED REFERENCES

Edelman, G. M. 1976. Surface modulation in cell recognition and cell growth. *Science* 192:218–26.

Curtis, A. S. G. 1967. *The cell surface: Its molecular role in morphogenesis.* London: Logos Press.

Palade, G. E. 1985. Differentiated microdomains in cellular membranes: Current status. In *The cell in contact: Adhesions and junctions as morphogenetic determinants,* ed. G. M. Edelman and J.-P. Thiery, 9–24. New York: Wiley.

Gerhart, J., and R. Keller. 1986. Region-specific cell activities in amphibian gastrulation. *Annu. Rev. Cell Biol.* 2:201–29.

Edelman, G. M., ed. 1985. *Molecular determinants of animal form.* New York: Alan R. Liss.

Hay, E. D., ed. 1981. *Cell biology of extracellular matrix.* New York: Plenum.

Browder, L. W., ed. 1986. *Developmental biology: A comprehensive synthesis.* Vol. 2, *The cellular basis of morphogenesis.* New York: Plenum.

Jacobson, A. G. 1985. Adhesion and movement of cells may be coupled to produce neurulation. In *The cell in contact: Adhesions and junctions as morphogenetic determinants,* ed. G. M. Edelman and J.-P. Thiery, 49–65. New York: Wiley.

Jacobson, A. G., G. M. Odell, and G. F. Oster. 1985. The cortical tractor model for epithelial folding: Application to the neural plate. In *Molecular determinants of animal form,* ed. G. M. Edelman, 142–66. New York: Alan R. Liss.

Thiery, J.-P. 1984. Mechanism of cell migration in the vertebrate embryo. *Cell Differ.* 15:1–15.

Snow, M. H. L. 1985. The embryonic cell lineage of mammals and the emergence of the basic body plan. In *Molecular determinants of animal form,* ed. G. M. Edelman, 73–98. New York: Alan R. Liss.

Cowan, W. M. 1973. Neuronal death as a regulative mechanism in the control of cell number in the nervous system. In *Development and aging in the nervous system,* ed. M. Rockstein, 19–41. New York: Academic.

Bock, G., and M. O'Connor, eds. 1987. *Selective neuronal death.* Ciba Foundation Symposium 126. Chichester: Wiley.

Le Douarin, N. M. 1982. *The neural crest.* Cambridge: Cambridge University Press.

See also references to Edelman in chapter 2 and to Needham in chapter 3.

7

Morphoregulatory
Molecules

IN SEARCHING for molecules that might be candidates for topobiological regulation, one is drawn to an essential primary process, that of adhesion of cells to each other and of cells to substrates such as the ECM. Such adhesion is an obvious mechanochemical event at the cell surface, and, though dynamic, it is less a driving force process than a regulatory one. Extensive searches over the last decade have revealed that at least three families of molecules are involved in one aspect of adhesion or another. We will consider these molecular families separately and then discuss their potential structural and functional relations. We will call these molecular families cell adhesion molecules (CAMs), substrate adhesion molecules (SAMs), and cell junctional molecules (CJMs). In discussing them separately, it is important to mention that they appear in development on different schedules and at different sites, are structurally and functionally different, and differ in their contributory roles to morphogenetic events. We will emphasize CAMs and SAMs, introducing CJMs found in specialized structural assemblies such as epithelial junctions only briefly when we consider the stabilization of cellular epithelial structures. Our discussion will take us into considerable chemical detail; much of this is necessary to understand the various structural and functional distinctions among adhesion molecules as well as how they work. The reader who wishes to pass quickly over these details upon a first reading should glance at the concluding summary, read the sections on CAMs and SAMs, and then glance cursorily at the description of gap junctions.

Cell Adhesion Molecules (CAMs)

We will begin our detailed discussion of the molecular regulation of animal form with CAMs because, of the three families, most is known about their functional relations to morphogenesis. Because CAMs link cells together at their surfaces to form linked collectives from the very earliest stages of development and because the borders of such collectives are determined by CAM specificities, CAMs can be considered paradigmatic morphoregulatory molecules. By a *cell collective* we mean a group of adjacent cells with common phenotypic properties acting as a source of or a target for signals; such cells are usually linked by CAMs but in the case of mesenchyme are not so linked. All of the well-characterized CAMs are large cell surface glycoproteins; the evidence suggests that they are also intrinsic membrane proteins. The known structures of some CAMs are summarized in figure 7.1.

Although N-CAM, the neural cell adhesion molecule, is specified by a single gene located on chromosome 9 in the mouse, N-CAM fractions contain three major related polypeptide chains, each of which has three domains: an N-terminal binding domain, a polysialic acid–rich middle domain, and a cell-associated or cytoplasmic domain (figure 7.1). The large domain (ld) polypeptide differs from the small domain (sd) polypeptide in the size of its cytoplasmic domain; the small surface domain (ssd) chain has no such domain. Proceeding outward from the position of the molecule at the cell membrane to the amino terminus, these polypeptides are structurally very similar or identical. In muscle, a fourth kind of chain is found, resembling the ssd chain but with a small, unique stretch of sequence midway between the fifth domain and the membrane. One of the most exciting structural observations, which we will discuss later, is that N-CAM is homologous to members of the immunoglobulin superfamily, which

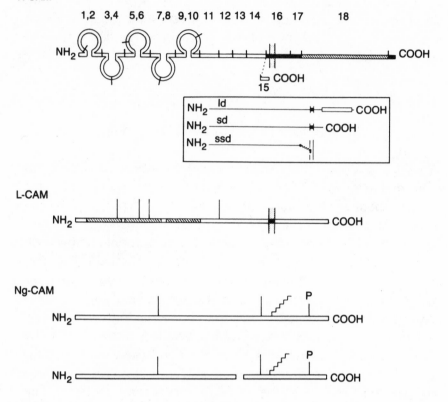

Figure 7.1

Diagrams of the linear chain structure of two primary CAMs (N-CAM and L-CAM) and of the secondary Ng-CAM. N-CAM consists of three chains (inset) that differ in the size of their cytoplasmic domains and the mode of attachment to the cell surface (see also figure 9.1). The ld (large domain) polypeptide contains approximately 250 more amino acid residues in this region than does the sd (small domain) polypeptide. A third, and the smallest, polypeptide (ssd—small surface domain) is attached to the membrane by phosphatidylinositol. The numbers above the figure indicate exons of the N-CAM locus specifying the corresponding homology domains, of which there are five. Each domain has one interchain disulfide bond forming a loop. The thick vertical bar *indicates the membrane-spanning region. Most of the carbohydrate is covalently attached in the fifth homology domain at three sites; attached to these carbohydrates is polysialic acid. The calcium-dependent L-CAM has three homology regions and four attachment sites for carbohydrate (vertical lines) but lacks polysialic acid. Its structure is completely different from that of N-CAM. Ng-CAM is shown as a major 200-kD chain. Two components (135 and 80 kD) are probably derived from a posttranslationally cleaved precursor. Each is related to the major 200-kD chain (which may be this precursor), and the smaller is arranged as shown on the basis of a known phosphorylation site. All three CAMs have different specificities. N-CAM and L-CAM show homophilic binding; Ng-CAM shows homophilic binding on neurons as well as heterophilic binding to other molecules on glial cells. (From G. M. Edelman, 1987, CAMs and Igs: Cell adhesion and the evolutionary origins of immunity,* Immunol. Rev. *100:9–43.)*

includes those molecules that mediate cell interactions in the immune response.

L-CAM (figure 7.1) also consists of an amino terminal binding region and a cell-associated region and contains several sites susceptible to proteolytic cleavage in the absence of calcium ions. Both its conformation and its binding are calcium dependent. It is found on epithelia and not on mesenchyme. Recent work indicates that N-CAM and L-CAM have completely different amino acid sequences, and thus they do not appear to be evolutionarily related.

Both N-CAM and L-CAM are primary adhesion molecules, so-called because they appear very early in development. Ng-CAM, a secondary CAM (figure 7.1), consists of a large glycoprotein (200 kD) that is posttranslationally cleaved into two components, of 135 kD and 80 kD. The evidence suggests that the amino terminal portions of the two larger chains are similar and that the 80-kD chain corresponds to the more carboxyl-terminal portion of the 200-kD chain. Besides the three well-characterized CAMs shown in figure 7.1, a number of other candidate CAMs of different specificity have been described, the most notable of which are a set of L-CAM related molecules called cadherins, described by Takeichi and his colleagues. These workers have shown that N-cadherin (the structure of which is homologous to L-CAM) has an embryonic distribution similar to that of N-CAM.

Although in most of these cases the detailed physicochemical binding properties are unknown, all of the well-characterized CAMs have different binding specificities. A given CAM does not have large numbers of variant binding specificities, however, and the CAMs studied so far are specified by one or only a few genes. It is the binding specificities of different CAMs that determine borders between different cell collectives. N-CAM is the first CAM whose binding mechanism has been worked out. Its binding is second-order homophilic, that is, N-CAM to N-CAM on an apposed cell (figure 7.2). This so-called *trans* binding is calcium ion independent, and it is highly cooperative: small changes in surface density lead to large changes in the binding rates of artificial lipid vesicles into which purified N-CAM has been inserted. This suggests that, at higher surface densities, CAMs form

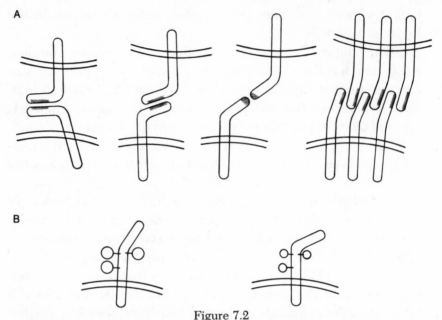

Figure 7.2

N-CAM, an example of homophilic binding that can be altered by local chemical modulation of attached carbohydrate (polysialic acid). A: Several hypothetical modes of N-CAM trans homophilic binding. From the left, N-CAM molecules on apposing cells may interact with each other in a manner similar to the pairing of domains in immunoglobulin (Ig) molecules (see figure 10.4). In this mode, interacting chains will have the same N-to-C orientation, and the binding region of one molecule (shaded) will contact the equivalent region of the bound molecule. If the binding is not strictly analogous to that of Ig domains, the interacting chains may have opposing senses, and the binding region can be more or less extensive. If the binding region (shaded) is spatially distinct from its receptor on another molecule (unshaded), oligomeric or polymeric assemblies can be formed between adherent cells. All of these possible modes of binding will be facilitated by a flexible hinge region, with the possible exception of the end-to-end mode. B: The large polysialic acid groups on embryonic N-CAM (left) may interfere by charge or excluded volume effects with cis intermolecular interactions or with the proposed flexible hinge region. The reduced amount of carbohydrate on adult N-CAM (right) is consistent with less restricted intermolecular interactions and greater molecular flexibility. This would be expected to result in faster rates of intercellular homophilic binding. (From G. M. Edelman, 1987, CAMs and Igs: Cell adhesion and the evolutionary origins of immunity, Immunol. Rev. 100:9–43.)

multivalent structures on the same cell by *cis* interaction or cytoskeletal anchoring. L-CAM and N-cadherin binding, unlike that of N-CAM and Ng-CAM, is calcium ion dependent; it has recently been found to be homophilic, by inserting DNA specifying the molecule into cells that do not ordinarily express L-CAM and showing that they bind when they do express it. In contrast, Ng-CAM, which binds neurons to neurons and neurons to glia, has a ligand different from itself on glial cells, and this binding must therefore be heterophilic. This conclusion is supported by its presence on neurons and by its absence on glia in the central nervous system. Its neuron-to-neuron binding appears to be homophilic by a separate mechanism, however.

These various observations suggest that two major means exist for altering binding behavior or forming borders between cell collectives. The first is to express a new CAM at cell surfaces having a binding specificity different from that on neighboring cells (e.g., L-CAM instead of N-CAM or vice versa). The second is to change the mode by which a particular CAM is expressed at the cell surface by mechanisms collectively known as local cell surface modulations. Unlike global modulation (see chapter 6, particularly figure 6.6), local cell surface modulation is alteration over time of the amount, distribution, or chemical properties of a *particular* kind of molecule at the cell surface. CAMs have in fact been shown to change in amount (prevalence modulation), in position or distribution (polarity modulation), or in molecular structure (chemical modulation) during development. Local cell surface modulation is an important determinant of CAM action at the cellular level, and, as we have already indicated, a variety (table 7.1) of actual and potential modulation mechanisms can operate in tissues.

The known nonlinear binding properties of CAMs at the cell surface that result from cell surface modulation are consistent with the cell-regulatory nature of cell-cell adhesion. Extensive examples of prevalence and polarity modulation will be given below, in our description of the developmental expression sequences of CAMs. An example of chemical modulation is the embryonic-to-adult (E-to-A) conversion of N-CAM (figure 7.2). E-to-A conversion is seen in brain, muscle, and skin. This is a gradual but large decrease during development in the polysialic acid content, from 30 g per 100 g polypeptide to 10 g per 100 g polypeptide; this negatively charged carbohydrate does not participate directly in binding but does modulate it. Binding experiments indicate that the E-to-A conversion is accompanied by a fourfold increase in rates of binding, as tested by the vesicle assays in vitro that we mentioned above. Several other forms of modulation have been described. One is the differential cellular expression of two different CAMs (differential prevalence). Another is

TABLE 7.1

CAM Modulation Mechanisms

Mechanism	Effect	Examples
Prevalence Change in synthesis or expression on cell surface	Increase or decrease in binding rate	N-CAM homophilic binding—a twofold increase in surface concentration leads to a thirtyfold increase in rate of binding
Differential Prevalence Change in relative expression of CAMs of different specificity on same cell	Border formation for cell collectives	CAM expression rules (see figure 7.3)
Cytoplasmic or surface domain switch Alteration in size and structure of cytoplasmic domain by RNA splicing	Selective expression of ld or sd polypeptides; (?) altered cytoskeletal interaction	Selective expression of N-CAM ld chain (see figure 7.1) in cerebellar layers
Polarity Change in location on selected cell regions	Localization of binding on particular portions of a cell	Concentration of N-CAM at motor end plate of muscles
Chemical Posttranslational change in structure	Altered binding rates; abrogation of binding	E-to-A conversion of N-CAM—a loss of two-thirds of the polysialic acid leads to a fourfold increase in binding (see figure 7.2)

the appearance of two different forms of the *same* CAM, such as the chains of N-CAM (see figure 7.1), altering how they are associated with the cell surface or cortex (cytoplasmic or surface domain switch). This latter mechanism occurs through differential splicing of RNA messages transcribed from the single gene for N-CAM.

The existence of local modulation mechanisms (table 7.1) shifts attention from the binding sites of different CAMs (each undoubtedly with a different specificity) to the functions of those parts of each molecule that are related to membrane insertion, secretion, *cis* interaction, cytoskeletal interaction, and alternative RNA splicing that yields different polypeptide forms of the same CAM. Each of these processes may have an important role in altering CAM binding, affecting the way that cell collectives change their morphology and signal their states to one another. This is all the more significant in view of the facts that the multiple bonds formed by groups of CAMs at the cell surface are nonlinear in their effects and that a cell can control the number and types of CAMs at its surface in response to local signals.

We already saw in previous chapters that cooperative topobiological interactions among the cells of a tissue and particularly inductive interactions between the cell collectives forming tissues are pivotal factors in normal development. The evidence we have discussed so far suggests that the CAMs mediating the binding between cells at a particular location *initially enable those cells to form the multicellular collectives having developmental properties different from those of a group of isolated cells.* In interpreting CAM function, one must therefore consider where, when, and on what cells the CAMs are expressed, for CAM expression in particular places is largely responsible for altering the driving force processes of movement, division, and death, which order the distribution of cells during development.

The topobiological significance of local cell surface modulation at different sites can be appreciated by considering developmental sequences of CAM expression. A systematic examination of the spatiotemporal appearance of each CAM during development shows a characteristic expression sequence (figure 7.3). In the chick blastoderm, the two primary CAMs appear together on all cells; at gastrulation, however, ingressing cells (see figure 3.2) stain much less with anti-N-CAM and anti-L-CAM. Cells in the chordamesoderm then reexpress N-CAM at neural induction, and endodermal cells reexpress L-CAM. During neural induction in the chick embryo, a remarkable transition occurs in the blastoderm: after completion of induction, the presumptive neural plate shows increased amounts of N-CAM and loses L-CAM, and reciprocally the surrounding somatic ectoderm loses N-CAM but continues to express L-CAM. Thereafter, at all sites of secondary

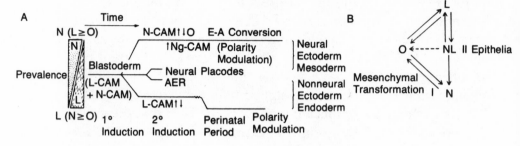

Figure 7.3

Schematic diagrams showing some CAM expression sequences and epigenetic expression rules for two primary CAMs in the chick. A: The temporal sequence of expression of CAMs during embryogenesis, starting from the stage of the blastoderm and proceeding through neural and secondary inductions. Germ layer derivatives are indicated at right. *The* vertical wedges (left) *refer to the approximate relative amounts of each CAM in the different layers or parts of the embryo, for example, the line referring to blastoderm has relatively large amounts of each CAM, whereas that for neural ectoderm has major amounts of N-CAM. After they diverge in cellular distribution, the CAMs are modulated in prevalence within various regions of inductions or actually decrease greatly when mesenchyme appears or cell migration occurs. Note that the placodes that have both CAMs echo the events seen for neural induction. Just before the appearance of glia, a secondary CAM (Ng-CAM) emerges; unlike the other two CAMs, this CAM could not be found before 3.5 days. In the perinatal period, a series of modulations occurs: E-to-A conversion for N-CAM and polar redistribution for L-CAM. B: Diagram summarizing epigenetic rules for N-CAM and L-CAM expression. Arrows refer to transitions. Mesenchyme cells derived from blastoderm express N-CAM and never reexpress L-CAM; they can lose or reduce N-CAM or reexpress it (rule I). Epithelia express N-CAM and L-CAM and can lose one or the other (rule II); mesenchymal tissues showing N-CAM do not reexpress L-CAM. This illustrates two primary CAMs; rules for other primary and secondary CAMs remain to be worked out. (Modified from G. M. Edelman, 1986, Cell adhesion molecules in the regulation of animal form and tissue pattern, Annu. Rev. Cell Biol. 2:81–116.)*

embryonic induction, N-CAM or L-CAM or both undergo a series of prevalence modulations that follow two main rules (figure 7.3, B): all epithelial-mesenchymal transformations show expression or loss of N-CAM, that is, $N \rightarrow O \rightarrow N$, where O means low or undetectable levels (rule I), and epithelial cells show other modal transitions in which one or the other CAM is lost, that is, either $NL \rightarrow L$ or $NL \rightarrow N$ (rule II). One of the striking aspects of these epigenetic sequences of primary CAM expression is the finding that, at many sites of induction, cell collectives consisting of mesenchymal condensations that have followed rule I are found in proximity to epithelial cell collectives that follow rule II. Their borders are distinguished by having a collective linked by at least one CAM of specificity different from that of the other collective.

Undoubtedly, other CAMs such as N-cadherin will also show coherent expression rules in a given species.

Primary CAMs are locally modulated not only during early
embryogenesis (particularly in the formation of cell collectives
during mesenchymal-epithelial transformation) but also during
later histogenetic events in which complex tissues consisting of
many different differentiated cell types are formed. This implies
that CAM expression can be independent of particular cytodifferentiation pathways and yet be *correlated* with particular examples of cytodifferentiation. During these events, secondary
CAMs not seen earlier also appear. This is most striking in the
nervous system, in which the CAMs alter how cells associate,
move, and send out processes to form connections, all by complex
and dynamic processes of cell surface modulation. In other tissues, sequences of these events accompanying histodifferentiation can involve the same CAMs: for example, feathers show a
series of staged morphogenetic events in which sequences of
N-CAM and L-CAM expression reflect repeated recursive application of each of their respective rules as borders between presumptive structures are being formed.

Let us use the feather to illustrate the different roles of CAMs
in early induction as well as in later morphogenesis and histogenesis. As a periodic and hierarchically organized structure (see
figure 4.1), the feather allows us to analyze the coupling of cell
collectives in detail and to relate their borders and interactions
to cytodifferentiation events within a dimensionally well-orga-
nized appendage. Feathers are induced through the formation of
dermal condensations of mesodermally derived mesenchyme
(figure 4.1, *a*); these condensations act as inductors upon ectodermal cells to form placodes (special epidermal regions with elongated cells). Such placodes and condensations are eventually hex-
agonally close packed, as feather induction proceeds in rows
from the medial to the lateral aspects of the chicken skin. Within
each induced placode, a dermal papilla is subsequently formed
by repeated inductive interactions between mesoderm and ectoderm. Later, cellular proliferation within these structures forms
barb ridges, which fuse to form a rachis or shaft; they then insert
into that structure (figure 4.1, *e–k*). This is followed by barbule
plate formation, and the barbules insert into the barbs. Such

events yield the bases for three hierarchical levels of feather branching: rachis, ramus, and barbule.

The importance of CAM function in forming cell collectives and their borders is particularly well exemplified by recent discoveries on the inductive development of feathers in embryonic chicken skin. When cell-cell interactions in cultured chick epidermis from seven-day-old embryos are partially disrupted by fragments of antibodies to L-CAM (a molecule that links epidermal cells but not dermal cells to each other), an abnormal morphologic and histological pattern develops even in the inducing mesodermal condensations that are linked by N-CAM and that contain no L-CAM (figure 7.4). Instead of hexagonal arrays of feather germs, stripes are formed. Thus perturbation of the L-CAM-linked epidermis leads to changes in the pattern of cell accumulation and cell division in the underlying dermis, *which does not express L-CAM.* In long-term cultures, scalelike structures rather than normal, filamentous structures are formed in the explanted skin perturbed by the anti-L-CAM; obviously, these structures are not true scales but abnormal arrangements.

These experiments show that alteration of the cooperative interactions among cells of one tissue as a result of perturbation of cell interactions mediated by one CAM can change the developmental pattern induced in another adjoining tissue linked by another CAM. This suggests that CAMs are part of the complex causal loop of induction, probably by changing how cells in one collective linked by a given CAM respond to signals produced in another collective, whose cells are linked by another CAM.

In these early events and in the later histodifferentiation events occurring in a feather, one observes extraordinary repetitions of CAM modulations according to the two rules mentioned earlier. Moreover, alteration in the relation of L-linked collectives of cells to N-linked collectives, either by movement and adhesion or by cell division and adhesion, is seen at various developmental stages of the feather. The early appearances of CAMs at borders can be correlated with the shapes shown in figure 7.4 (see also figure 4.1). Initially, L-linked ectodermal cells are approached in vitro by CAM-negative mesenchymal cells, which become N-CAM positive in the ectodermal vicinity (rule I). As these cells accumulate to form condensations, placodes are induced

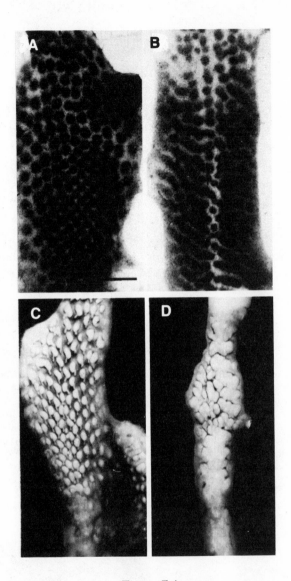

Figure 7.4

*Perturbation of structures in one inducing cell collective linked by a specific CAM after
interference with the linkage of cells by a CAM of different specificity in an adjoining
collective. Whole mounts of seven-day-old embryonic chicken skin as feather induction
occurs, maintained in culture for three days (A, B) or ten days (C, D). Those in A and
C were cultured in the presence of Fab' fragments of antibodies from unimmunized
rabbits; those in B and D were cultured in the presence of Fab' fragments of rabbit
antibodies against L-CAM. Note the breakage of hexagonal symmetry of the N-CAM–
linked mesodermal condensations viewed through the translucent epidermis (compare
A and B) and the long-term alterations of overall morphology (compare C and D). (From
W. J. Gallin, C.-M. Chuong, L. H. Finkel, and G. M. Edelman, 1986, Antibodies to L-CAM
perturb inductive interactions and alter feather pattern and structure, Proc. Natl. Acad.
Sci. USA 83:8235–39.)*

in the overlying L-linked cells. A similar couple consisting of L-linked ectodermal cell collectives adjacent to N-linked mesenchymal collectives is seen in the papilla, which forms subsequently. After N-CAM-positive mesenchymal cells are excluded by a basement membrane, the collar cells derived from the L-CAM-positive papillar ectoderm express both N-CAM and L-CAM (rule II).

After this event, further site-restricted applications of rule II lead to a remarkable periodicity of borders (figure 7.5): cells derived from papillar ectoderm by division form barb ridges and express L-CAM. At a later stage of growth, the basilar cells in the valleys between the neighboring ridges lose L-CAM and express N-CAM to form marginal plates. A similar process occurs as the ridge cells organize into L-CAM-positive barbule plates; N-CAM

Figure 7.5

CAMs in barb ridge formation during feather development, showing formation of borders between cell collectives having CAMs of different specificity (see figure 4.1 for a diagram of stages in feather development). A and B: Transverse sections of later-developing feather follicles from a newly hatched chick wing, showing alternating sequence of expression of L-CAM (A) and N-CAM (B) during adult feather histogenesis. The same sections were doubly stained with fluorescent antibodies to each CAM. Formation of the barb ridges (br) starts from the dorsal side (the side with the rachis) and progresses bilaterally toward the ventral side, making a ventrodorsal maturation gradient. Positions of the last-formed ridges are marked by curved arrows. *L-CAM stains all of the cells of the barb ridge epithelium. Bright N-CAM staining starts to appear in the valleys between pairs of the barb ridges (see panel B). N-CAM appearance starts about eight ridges away from the last formed ridge and increases in staining intensity and distribution dorsally until it reaches the rachis (rc). Ultimately, all L-CAM–bearing cellular areas will become keratinized, and all cellular areas bearing N-CAM only (marginal and axial plates) will die. (From G. M. Edelman, 1987,* Neural Darwinism: The theory of neuronal group selection, *New York: Basic Books.)*

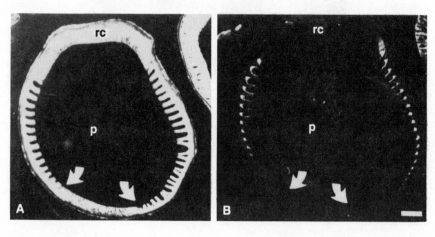

is expressed in cells between the barbule plate cells to form axial plates. The end result is a series of cellular patterns that follows rule II, in which cell collectives linked by L-CAM alternate with those expressing N-CAM at both the secondary and tertiary barbule level. After further extension of the barb ridges into rami, a dramatic correlation of CAM expression with primary processes occurs: the L-CAM-positive cells keratinize, and the N-CAM-positive cells die without keratinization, leaving spaces between barbules and yielding the characteristic feather morphology. Differing CAM expression in neighboring collectives is thus linked to cytodifferentiation events and death, as borders become edges.

In this histogenetic CAM expression sequence, ranging from induction to the finished feather itself, one observes periodic CAM modulation following primary CAM rules, periodic and successive formation of alternative L-CAM-linked and N-CAM-linked cell collectives that border each other, and the definite association of gene expression during cytodifferentiation with particular kinds of CAMs. The most specific example is the expression of genes for keratins (the substances leading to the hardening of the feather) only in L-CAM–containing cells. Throughout this histogenetic process, there is also an intimate connection between the regulatory process of adhesion and the epigenetic sequences involving different primary processes that act as driving forces. These processes include morphogenetic movement for the original mesenchymal induction, mitosis for the formation of papillar ectoderm and barb ridges, and death for the N-linked collectives in the final period of feather formation.

These various observations on the feather indicate that CAM function is important in inductive sequences, and they suggest that a series of local signals is responsible at particular sites for particular sequences of CAM expression. Given the epigenetic nature of tissue formation and the existence of defined CAM expression sequences, it is not surprising that CAM expression and modulation must depend upon local signals that themselves vary according to the state, composition, and integrity of particular interacting cell collectives. *It is the context-dependent interaction between these various signals and the CAM-linked collectives responding to these signals and emitting them that plays a major role in morphogenesis.*

Experiments on a variety of other tissues are consistent with this set of conclusions. Alteration of CAM binding by appropriate anti-CAM antibodies leads, for example, to changes in the morphology of cerebellar tissues during cell migration, to alteration of retinal structure during development, and to perturbation of retinotectal brain maps. Conversely (and just as important for understanding the meaning of local modulation), alteration in morphology can lead to changes in *expression* of the same CAM with different responses at different structural levels of a connected set of tissues. A good example is shown in nerve-muscle interactions. In developed striated muscle, N-CAM is present at the neuromuscular junction but is absent from the rest of the surface of the myofibril. After the nerve supplying the muscle is cut, the molecule appears diffusely at the cell surface and in the cytoplasm of the muscle cell. These experiments indicate that early events related to regeneration can be accompanied by altered CAM modulation. More recent experiments show that the crushing or cutting of a nerve has widespread effects, ranging from altered CAM expression in motor neurons of the spinal cord (on the affected side) to modulatory changes in N-CAM and Ng-CAM within the Schwann cells, the peripheral glial cells that are local to the lesion and that participate in regeneration.

We may summarize our overall description of the developmental role of CAMs by saying that CAMs regulate morphology and are regulated by it: *disruption of their binding alters morphology, and disruption of morphology alters regulation of CAM expression.* This is an important set of conclusions, and in part three we will attempt to connect the mechanochemical role of CAMs to developmental genetic events. At this point, we will emphasize that CAMs obviously play a major topobiological role in development: their structure, function, and location at the cell surface, their modulation at quite distinct locations in quite reproducible patterns, and their connection with signaling sequences and differentiation during induction and histogenesis amply justify the claim that CAMs are central morphoregulatory molecules.

As important as these considerations are, however, it must not be assumed that CAMs are the only such molecules. At least two other families of proteins play essential topobiological roles, and their molecular structure and the regulatory loops controlling their expression differ significantly from those of CAMs. Let us briefly consider such molecules, beginning with substrate adhesion molecules, or SAMs.

SUBSTRATE ADHESION MOLECULES (SAMs)

Although they can bind to cells by means of particular receptors, SAMs are usually found as components of the extracellular matrix (ECM). The ECM is material produced by a variety of cells consisting of various glycoproteins, collagens, elastins, and proteoglycans, and it provides the substrate upon which epithelia rest or mesenchymal cells migrate (see figure 6.3). The matrix can exist in two major states (basement membrane and matrix proper) in which both physical structure and molecular composition can vary. This is consistent with the idea that the ECM provides place-dependent attachment sites for cells and thus can influence morphology by altering movement and surface signaling.

Epithelia are the first tissues formed in an embryo, and they sit on the form of ECM known as the basement membrane, a structure deposited in a polar fashion around epithelial and endothelial cells. (In some differentiated tissues—fat cells, muscle, and Schwann cells—the basement membrane surrounds the cells on all sides.) The basement membrane (figure 7.6) is about 100 nm thick, and electron microscopy indicates that it consists of three zones: (1) a central lamina densa made up of a compact sheet of collagen (usually of so-called type IV), (2) a less dense zone in closer proximity to the cell, the lamina rara externa, and (3) a less dense zone on the other side of the lamina densa nearer regions of connective tissue, called the lamina interna. Both lamina interna and externa have layers of proteoglycan granules attached by filaments to underlying collagen fibrils (lamina interna) or to cells (lamina externa).

In certain other regions, the ECM exists not as basement membrane but as a true matrix containing similar families of molecules, though of different detailed composition (we discussed

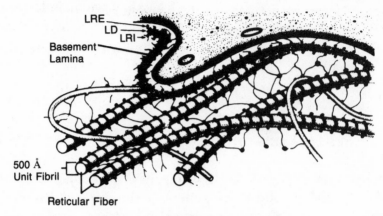

Figure 7.6

A diagram of basement membrane consisting of laminae densa, interna, and externa in association with basal portion of an epithelial cell (compare with figure 6.3). Collagen IV fibrils are approximately 50 nm in diameter but can be associated in bundles called reticular fibers. The type IV collagen forms a chicken wire–like network that may be important in basement membrane assembly, which consists of the attachment of glycoproteins (laminin, fibronectin, etc.) and proteoglycans in the extracellular domain. The diagram depicts relations of proteoglycans, collagen fibrils, and basement lamina in the tissues (see table 7.1 and figure 7.7 for more-detailed descriptions of these molecules). At the top, the drawing includes part of the basal cytoplasm of an epithelial cell. The outermost layer of the basal lamina, the lamina rara externa (LRE), is attached to the epithelial cell by small filaments presumably composed of glycoprotein. The LRE and LRI (lamina rara interna) each contains a layer of proteoglycan granules. The lamina densa (LD) contains collagen and possibly other glycoproteins. Collagen fibrils associated with the basement lamina are small (50 nm in diameter) and may form small bundles called reticular fibers that stain with silver salts. The fibrils are covered with proteoglycan granules and are connected by ruthenium red-staining filaments that may consist of hyaluronic acid. Collagen fibers are larger than reticular fibers; they contain less proteoglycan and a greater variety of unit collagen fibrils (50–1,500 nm in diameter). (From E. D. Hay, D. L. Hasty, and K. L. Kiehnau, 1978, Fine structure of the collagens and their relation to glycosaminoglycans (GAG), in Collagen-platelet interaction, *ed. H. Gastpar, K. Kuhn, and R. Marx, 129–51, Stuttgart: Schattauer.)*

some aspects of this in the preceding chapter). It is through such ECM that the mesenchymal cells derived from epithelia move. When later more histodifferentiated states are achieved, the term *connective tissue* is applied to the collagen fibrils and ECM molecules around members of the fibroblast family (osteoblasts, chondroblasts, fibroblasts). In such tissues, the collagen fibers contain a greater variety of fibrils (500–1,500 Å in diameter) and less proteoglycan than do the reticular fibers of basement membranes (see figure 7.6).

From this brief survey, it can be seen that, whatever its state, the

ECM is a very complex structure. Indeed, if we include various subvarieties of molecules, there may be as many as fifty different kinds making up a particular ECM. In general, the major components are those we have mentioned: various forms of collagens, various glycoproteins having different binding sites and structures (e.g., laminin, fibronectin, and cytotactin), and proteoglycans of various types. Because there are many different kinds of these molecules and because they are large and may interact in a variety of ways both with one another and with cells in different environments, we must adopt a preliminary classification. This is all the more necessary because the matrix proteins may bind to cell surface receptors and act as SAMs. A classification of ECM molecules is presented in table 7.2, and some diagrams of characteristic types can be seen in figure 7.7. *A major point is that because they are released by cells, the kind of adhesion mediated by these ECM molecules as well as its control and consequences must differ from that mediated by CAMs, which are intrinsic membrane proteins regulated directly by the cells they bind.*

We already saw in chapter 6 that the matrix can influence the epithelial-mesenchymal transformation. We have also noted the correspondence between the existence of interstitial spaces and matrix (as well as the distribution of mesenchyme), and the correspondence between the existence of a basement membrane and epithelia. The ECM functions we mentioned are (1) the promotion or inhibition of migration (e.g., fibronectin, cytotactin), (2) the indirect mediation of adhesion, (3) the stabilization of morphology (basement membrane), and (4) the reorganization of the cytoskeleton (fibronectin, laminin, proteoglycan), a modulatory factor that can alter cell shape and, by *global* modulation, possibly affect both protein synthesis and growth control. In accord with this idea, it has been shown that cell proliferation is stimulated by ECM components such as fibronectin and that responses to growth factors are altered by the presence of such matrix components. Similar effects on protein synthesis, RNA metabolism, and cellular differentiation have been observed.

In the attempt to understand the functions of the various extracellular molecules, it is particularly important to determine the nature of their cell surface receptors. Analyses of such receptors

TABLE 7.2

Extracellular Matrix Components and the SAM Complex

Component	Subtypes	Location	Subunits	Structures, Chemical Properties, and Functions
Collagens*	Interstitial type I	Skin, bone, tendon, cornea	α1(I), α2(I) chains in 2:1 ratio	20–100 nm diameter
	type II	Cartilage, notochord, vitreous body, corneal stroma	$[\alpha 1(II)]_3$	
	type III	Loose connective tissue, blood vessel walls, dermis; not in bone, tendon, or cornea	$[\alpha 1(III)]_3$	50-nm collagen fibrils
	type IV	Basement membranes	$[\alpha 1(IV)]_3$	
	type V	Placenta, basement membranes	α1(V)α2(V)α3(V)	
Glycoproteins	Laminin	ECM and basement membranes	Multidomain structure, 1,000-kD, A,B_1,B_2 chains	Heparin binding domain; type IV collagen binding domain; cell binding domain
	Entactin (? Nidogen—a proteolytic fragment)	Endodermal matrix (basement membrane)		
	Fibronectin	In or on cell matrix, early fibroblasts, myoblasts, chondrocytes, endothelial cells; found in many basement membranes; found in plasma	450 kD; ss-linked dimer of 220-kD chains	Adhesion and migration; collagen and heparin binding domains; cell surface binding domains

*This list is partial; other types and variants continue to be discovered.

TABLE 7.2 (Continued)

Component	Subtypes	Location	Subunits	Structures, Chemical Properties, and Functions
Glycoproteins (cont'd)	Chondronectin	Serum and cartilage	180 kD	Binds chondrocytes to collagen III
	Cytotactin	Appears in cephalocaudal sequences in early embryos, neural crest path, glia (not neurons), smooth muscle, along basement membranes	200 kD, 220 kD; six subunits linked in a hexabrachion	Affects (slows) migration of neural and other cells; binds to a chondroitin sulfate proteoglycan and also to fibronectin
*Proteoglycans (and hyaluronic acid)**	Chondroitin/dermatan sulfate	Cartilage	400-kD core; O-linked and N-linked oligosaccharides, two N-terminal globular domains, one C-terminal globular domain	
	Small interstitial keratan sulfate	Cornea	N-linked oligosaccharide	
	Interstitial dermatan sulfate	Connective tissue	40-kD core; O-linked and N-linked oligosaccharides	

*Hyaluronic acid is often found associated with certain proteoglycans.

TABLE 7.2 (Continued)

Component	Subtypes	Location	Subunits	Structures, Chemical Properties, and Functions
Proteoglycans (and hyaluronic acid) (cont'd)	Basement membrane	EHS tumor Glomeruli	400 kD 20 kD	
	Cell surface-associated (intrinsic)	Melanoma cells (chondroitin/dermatan sulfate)	240-kD core	
		Ovarian granulosa cells (heparan sulfate)	250-kD core	Organization of microfilaments in focal plaques
		Mammary epithelial cells (hybrid of heparan sulfate and chondroitin/ dermatan sulfate)	55 kD	
	Hepatocyte	Liver	30 kD	
	Fibroblast	Skin	Two ss-linked chains of 90 kD (modified transferrin receptor)	
	Small serine-rich	Mast cells, yolk sac	10-kD core; serine glycine repeats	

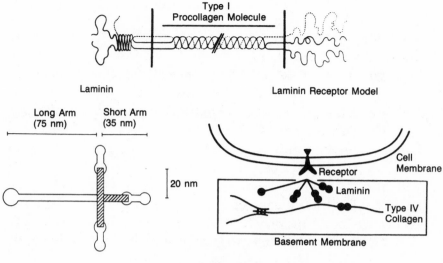

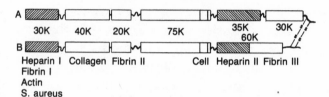

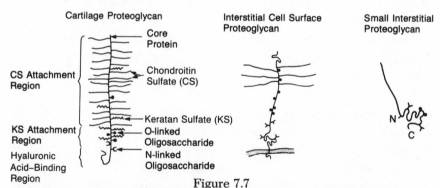

Figure 7.7

Some diagrams of typical ECM molecules (see table 7.2 for more details of structure and function). (Sources: T. F. Linsenmayer, 1981, Collagen, in Cell biology of extracellular matrix, ed. E. D. Hay, 5–37, New York: Plenum; V.C. Hascall and G. K. Hascall, 1981, Proteoglycans, in Cell biology of extracellular matrix, ed. E. D. Hay, 39–63, New York: Plenum; V. C. Hascall, 1986, introd. to Functions of the proteoglycans, Ciba Foundation Symposium 124, 1–8, New York: Wiley; L. A. Liotta, U. M. Wewer, C. N. Rao, and G. Bryant, 1985, Laminin receptor, in The cell in contact: Adhesions and junctions as morphogenetic determinants, ed. G. M. Edelman and J.-P Thiery, 333–44, New York: Wiley; K. M. Yamada, 1981, Fibronectin and other structural proteins, in Cell biology of extracellular matrix, ed. E. D. Hay, 95–114, New York: Plenum; K. M. Yamada, M. J. Humphries, T. Hasegawa, E. Hasegawa, K. Olden, W.-T. Chen, and S. K. Akiyama, 1985, Fibronectin: Molecular approaches to analyzing cell interactions with the extracellular matrix, in The cell in contact: Adhesions and junctions as morphogenetic determinants, ed. G. M. Edelman and J.-P. Thiery, 303–32, New York: Wiley.)

are not as advanced as those of ECM molecules themselves, but knowledge is accumulating rapidly. An intrinsic membrane protein with a molecular weight of 70 kD that is a receptor for laminin has been found, and there are 20–100,000 receptors per cell. Free laminin that is bound to the receptor is internalized by the cell. This receptor may mediate interactions of cells with basement membranes by way of the laminin they contain. Another cell surface receptor for fibronectin with a molecular weight of 140 kD has been isolated. This receptor can be localized at cell substrate contact sites and has a wide distribution in embryogenesis. This may be similar or identical to a surface protein, CSAT, that binds to both laminin and fibronectin. Recently, as described by Hynes and by Ruoslahti and his colleagues, a whole family of receptors (integrins) for a variety of molecules has been identified (see figure 7.8 for a list of some of these receptors). These molecules are significant mainly because of their potential to transfer signals to the cells that express them, signals that vary in bound and unbound states, and they reflect the interaction of these receptors with different SAMs.

It is important to realize that the interaction of free ECM molecules with cell surface receptors is in principle quite different from that of CAMs. An ECM protein in local excess may saturate cell receptors and inhibit or alter its own function. On the other hand, at smaller numbers or in the absence of free molecules, the cell will be attached via the ECM molecule to the substrate. Thus cell substrate adhesion will depend upon the kinds of molecules, the number of free molecules, the availability and types of cell surface receptors, and the number of binding sites. This is in sharp contrast to the homophilic binding of integral CAMs, which, though still complex, is more direct.

Since particular kinds of receptors can bind more than one ECM molecule (e.g., in the chicken, CSAT binds laminin and fibronectin) and since ECM molecules can have more than one kind of binding site for cells or for other substrate molecules that themselves can bind to other cell surface receptors or molecules, a rich modulatory network (figure 7.8) of matrix proteins can be important in linking cells and substrates and in affecting movement and other functions, as we already mentioned in the

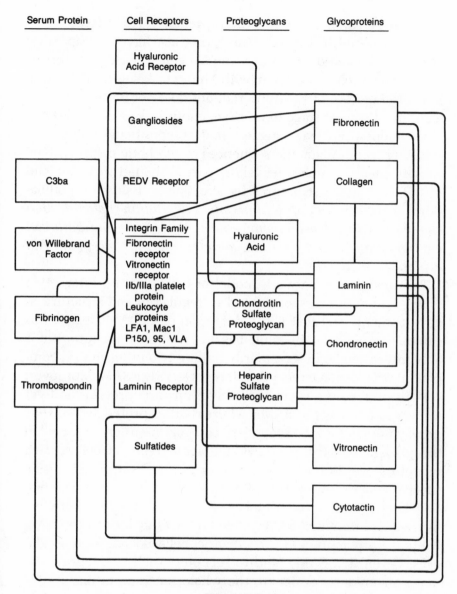

Figure 7.8

Network of ECM proteins, SAMs, and serum proteins capable of interacting with one another and with cell surface receptors. Lines in the diagram indicate possible interactions based on binding sites; actual interactions form subsets that differ in protein type and amount at different embryonic sites. One would expect the modulatory effects of such interactions to reflect the chemistry and structure of the part of the network that is involved at each morphogenetic site. The interactions form the basis for the idea of SAM modulatory networks (see chapter 8), which can, by altered combinations of interactions, lead to different forms of global and local cell surface modulation.

preceding chapter. Because ECM proteins tend to be large multi-subunit and multivalent structures, they also have the capability of cross-linking and "patching" mobile cell surface receptors or of altering their association with the cytoskeleton. This combinatorial picture of ECM interactions does not imply that each locus in a tissue or stage of embryogenesis lacks a defined structure. It does, however, suggest that compositional differences resulting from epigenetic sequences of synthetic or proteolytic activity affecting molecules taking part in the network can lead to different tissue structures by affecting cell surface modulations. *This concept of a dynamic modulation network that changes during development, epigenetically altering both cell environment and cell response, complements the concept of CAM expression sequences.*

The modulation network model of cell substrate interaction raises a number of issues related to regulation and structure in development. The first is the definition of a SAM. Clearly, this can be complex: if a molecule has no cell surface receptor but is only intermediate in secondarily linking two other matrix components that do have receptors, it is not strictly a SAM. Moreover, certain proteoglycans are themselves intrinsic proteins and yet can presumably act as SAMs, whereas other proteoglycans may or may not fall into the secondary category mentioned above. In the present paucity of knowledge about types of cell surface receptors, we do not know whether every ECM protein has a specific cell-associated receptor or shows cell-binding capabilities. Under these circumstances, we must distinguish between defined and potential SAMs. Defined SAMs include fibronectin, laminin, cytotactin, and the intrinsic, cell-associated proteoglycans. Given that SAMs bind to receptors such as integrins, we may conveniently designate the whole set of molecules (SAMs linked to receptors on cells) the "SAM complex" (see table 7.2).

Another issue brought up by the modulation network model has already been hinted at: the structure and properties of the matrix will depend upon both the number and the types of matrix molecules produced by a given cell or set of cells at a certain stage and place. If a given sequence of SAM expression in turn affects a cell at a given location by global cell surface modulation, there can be an epigenetic regulation of primary cellular properties (motion, division, protein synthesis, proteolysis) by the matrix. Such sequences resulting from the interactions in a modulation network will also depend upon prior or subsequent CAM interactions, and thus the coordinate control of cell states by *both* molecular families becomes an important issue.

Some of the functions of the ECM are regulated by a balance between synthesis and degradation of its components, thus altering its combinatorial interactions. Tissues during development show close correlation, for example, between cell movement, cell proliferation, and hyaluronic acid degradation by hyaluronidase, as is seen in the developing chick cornea. We noted in table 7.2 that hyaluronate is associated with certain proteoglycans. In addition, as is also shown in that table, there is a remarkable tissue specificity in the distribution of various proteoglycans, and it therefore seems likely that a sequence of emergence of particular proteoglycans will accompany histogenetic sequences; this is seen locally, for example, in limb buds. Such sequences will in all likelihood reflect changes in the cellular sources of different ECM components as development continues. An example of this is seen during development in the early production of glycosaminoglycans and collagen by epithelial cells, followed later by a much larger production by neighboring mesenchyme.

Unfortunately, unlike that of the known CAMs, the detailed developmental sequence of expression of SAMs and SAM receptors at different embryogenetic sites has not been determined in detail. It is therefore not yet possible to develop a coordinate description of CAM expression along with SAM complex expression. Nonetheless, certain general observations lend some support to the idea of a modulation network of SAM interactions with cells that would influence and be influenced by previous CAM and SAM interactions. In general, at least some CAMs appear very early in development: in the frog, N-CAM and L-CAM are specified (probably by maternal messages) in the blastula; in the mouse, L-CAM can be detected at the two-cell stage. The SAMs, laminin and fibronectin, appear by blastula and gastrula stages, and cytotactin appears at later gastrulation stages. It is pertinent to a possible assignment of function in cell surface modulation that fibronectin receptors appear in a widespread fashion and that antifibronectin antibodies will block gastrulation, presumably by inhibiting cell movement. Fibronectin has also been implicated by Thiery as a molecule that facilitates the movement of neural crest cells. The data on expression sequences of SAMs are at present still scant, however, and obviously much remains to be done to link these sequences to CAM sequences and to the notion of a modulation network.

The idea that both a particular sequence of synthesis of matrix proteins and their interactions can be important in such a network is supported by recent observations on the ECM protein cytotactin. During gastrulation, this protein appears in a sharp wave proceeding cephalocaudally. After fibronectin and laminin have appeared in a variety of sites, including somites, cytotactin appears in the basement membrane of these structures, again in a cephalocaudal sequence. It appears subsequently in the neural crest pathways and, even later in development, is not as widely distributed in the embryo as laminin and fibronectin. Cytotactin also appears at definite local embryonic sites in a patterned order: in the CNS it is synthesized by glia at early stages of cell migration, and in limb bud development it appears at some growth zones but not at others. A striking example of its correlation with periodic pattern formation is seen in somites. Cytotactin appears at the anterior half of each somite at just the time when neural crest cells invade only this part of the somite structure (the sclerotome) as it becomes mesenchymal; this is followed by a rearrangement of the appearance of the proteoglycan to which cytotactin binds into the posterior half of each somite (figure 7.9). The result is an alternating segmented pattern of the two molecules, both of which are synthesized by the somites autonomously. Moreover, cytotactin reduces the motility of neural crest cells, and this effect is mitigated by fibronectin, a molecule bound by cytotactin and found across the whole somite. This example of patterning related to movement and synthesis of proteins that may form a modulation network nicely illustrates the conjugate coordinate role SAMs may play in conjunction with CAMs to yield pattern.

In addition to appearing at different times and places, different ECM proteins have different effects upon various primary processes. The example just mentioned centers upon the effects on

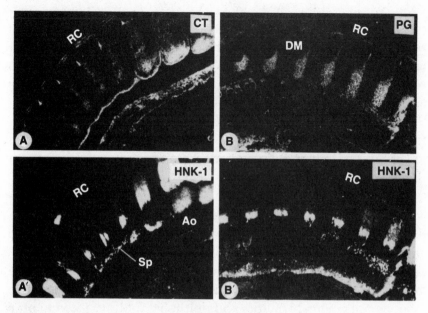

Figure 7.9

Pattern formation correlated with different molecular distributions in SAM networks, as seen in neural crest cell invasion of the sclerotome, the mesenchymal portion of the somites of the chick embryo (see figure 3.2, D). Double-labeled immunofluorescence with HNK-1 (A'-B') and anticytotactin (A) or antiproteoglycan (B) antibodies. HNK-1 antibodies stain migrating neural crest cells. Rostral is to the left. A and A': Parasagittal section through a 34-somite-stage embryo. Cytotactin is expressed in the rostral halves of the sclerotomes (A) and in uniform distribution along the dorsal, ventral, and intersomitic borders of the mature somites. Cytotactin is also seen surrounding the aorta. Within the sclerotome, crest cells have condensed into a compact mass in the rostral half from which the dorsal root ganglion subsequently arises (A'). In contrast, more ventrally located crest cells are evenly distributed along the wall of the aorta, where they will later form the sympathetic plexus. B and B': Parasagittal section of a 42-somite-stage embryo. Cytotactin-binding proteoglycan is found in a wide variety of sites, except within the dermamyotome or epithelial portion of the somites. Within the sclerotome, proteoglycan expression is polarized in the caudal half of each segment (B). Neural crest cells are localized in the rostral halves of the sclerotome (B') but are evenly distributed near the aorta. Fibronectin, which interacts with cytotactin, is found in both rostral and caudal portions of somites (not shown). R, rostral; C, caudal; Ao, aorta; Sp, presumptive sympathetic plexus; DM, dermamyotome; CT, cytotactin staining; PG, proteoglycan staining. (Bar = 200 μm.) (From G. M. Edelman, 1988, Morphoregulatory molecules, Biochemistry 27: 3534–43.)

movement of neural crest cells by fibronectin, which, as Thiery has shown, acts as a positive substrate for migration, and by cytotactin, which is strongly avoided by such cells. It has been found that, in forming certain other structures, CAM and SAM action can also be coordinate. As seen in the central nervous system, for example, an ECM protein such as cytotactin (synthe-

sized by glia) and a CAM such as Ng-CAM (synthesized by neurons) can have *sequential* effects on movement. This has been
revealed by perturbation experiments: in the development of
layers in the cerebellum, univalent fragments of antibodies to
Ng-CAM block granule cell entry from the external granular
layer into the molecular layers, as such cells migrate on radial glia
through the molecular layer to form the internal granular layers.
In contrast, fragments of antibodies to cytotactin have no such
effect but do slow granule cell exit from the molecular layer into
the internal granular layer.

A later but important activity of matrices in modulation networks may be to stabilize the phenotype of particular cells in
tissues by affecting their steady state control of protein synthesis
and expression through global cell surface modulation. For example, mechanochemical properties of the basement membrane
may affect interactions with epithelial cell surfaces. Under the
influence of cortical tractors and epithelial foldings (see chapter
6), of cell division, or of other changes in cell number, the basement membrane may undergo tension. This could modify the
nature of its interaction with cell surface receptors and modulate
cell responses differently at different loci. That such mechanical
interactions involving global modulation may matter is suggested
by observations of Bissell and her coworkers that mammary epithelium steps up casein synthesis and changes cell shape on collag-
enous ECM if it is *floating* on culture cells but not if it is *attached*
to the side walls of the tissue culture vessel. Cells certainly exert
tension on such substrates. Thus, in addition to its *chemical* specificity, the microscopic *physical* structure and the mechanochemical nature of the matrix array may both affect responses to small
molecular signals. *As with differential prevalence modulation of
the CAMs, SAM action therefore can depend not only upon synthetic rates and expression but also upon the higher-order cellular
structures already built up in the neighborhood.* This reciprocal
contextual influence of previous cellular events upon function at
the molecular level bears upon the determination of the state of
the matrix itself and also upon the relation between its mechanochemical functions and its capacity to alter cellular states.

Although the state of our knowledge of the complex functional
aspects of ECM (particularly the interactions of its components

with the cell surface) is still quite incomplete, we may summarize our account by enumerating the major ECM variables affected by and affecting cellular response. The present discussion and that in chapter 6 indicate that ECM can affect cell movement, mitosis, shape, and gene expression. Epithelial-mesenchymal transformations depend at least in part upon matrix interaction. Different cells synthesize different matrix components at different stages of their development. Given the multiplicity of matrix interactions, the various molecular and cell-binding specificities of matrix molecules, the sequences of their expression, the opportunity for combinatorial interactions of these molecules with one another and with cell surface receptors, as well as the markedly different mechanochemical properties of ECM organized in different states, it is not surprising that ECM components are major morphoregulatory elements. As important as they are, however, such components do not always act to determine *initial* structure at all morphogenetic sites. It is clear from our discussions of the feather, for example, that prior CAM interactions are necessary for matrix action; indeed, at certain morphogenetic sites such as barb ridges, such CAM interactions may be sufficient.

Taken together, the CAMs and SAMs provide a very powerful and varied cooperative and complementary means of relating cell place and the interactions of cell collectives to gene expression. The regulatory mechanochemical loops set up by CAM expression sequences and SAM modulatory networks provide a rich basis for the epigenetic determination of form. In addition to CAMs and SAMs, however, there is a third set of morphoregulatory molecules—cell junctional molecules—that plays a role in place-dependent cell surface interaction during development. We turn briefly to these molecules and to the related ultramicroscopic structures built up by their interactions.

SPECIALIZED JUNCTIONS AND CELL JUNCTIONAL MOLECULES (CJMS)

In epithelial cells, there are a number of specialized junctional complexes formed by molecules that differ from CAMs and

SAMs. These include gap junctions, tight junctions, adherens junctions, and desmosomes; gap junctions can also form between cell aggregates in condensing mesenchyme. All of these are well-formed and sometimes elaborate supramolecular structures carrying out various functions, ranging from electrical and chemical cell-cell communication (gap junctions) to sealing apical surfaces of epithelia (tight junctions) or linking defined regions of cell-cell contact with cytoskeletal elements (adherens junctions, desmosomes). We will consider these structures in order, paying most attention to their potential functions in embryogenesis and morphogenesis.

Gap Junctions

These are constituted from oligomeric membrane protein subunits that unite in defined structures (connexons). Connexons interact across the space between apposed cells and allow direct pathways (channels) for communication from cell to cell via ions and small molecules but not macromolecules. They mediate such pathways in almost all animal tissues and open the possibility of coupling cells in collectives. In effect, they constitute molecular channels with alternative conformations and may have gating properties (figure 7.10). The major gap junction protein from liver has a molecular weight of 27 kD. In contrast, the protein from heart has a molecular weight of 45 kD, but only after cleavage of a cytoplasmic tail of 17 kD. Amino terminal sequences of the two proteins from liver and heart share about 43 percent identical and 25 percent homologous residues. In contrast, the gap junction protein of lens fibers has a completely different amino acid sequence. Thus, it is likely that these proteins form a diverse family, the tissue specificity in each case reflecting various modifications of function.

Gap junctions show electrical coupling between cells, but they do not pass molecules greater than 1,000 D. Cells linked by such junctions thus maintain their differentiated identity while allowing ions, cyclic nucleotides, or other small molecules to pass. Gap junctional channels form rapidly between apposed cells (in minutes or seconds) and can form between heterologous cell types provided that they produce homologous channel-forming molecules.

During development, gap junctions form at a variety of sites. In the rat preovulatory follicle, for example, cumulus granulosa cells communicate with the oocyte via gap junctions. At the final stage of oocyte maturation, just before ovulation, this communication is broken. Following fertilization, there is no junctional communication until the eight-cell stage; in the mouse, there is electrical coupling from this stage to the blastocyst stage, but enhanced coupling is compartmentalized and the trophectoderm cells are coupled separately from the inner cell mass cells. Thereafter, gap junctions form variably but, in general, become more and more locally restricted as ECM elaboration and spatial separation of cells both occur. The pattern in complex differentiated tissue reflects this increasing local compartmentalization. For example, in the skin, cells in the dermal layer are coupled widely in collectives of hundreds of cells. In the overlying epidermis, however, coupling is among collectives of only four to six cells, and there is as a rule no coupling between the two layers. So far, it has not been shown whether these extents of coupling reflect domains of growth control or of differentiation events.

One attempt to demonstrate a role for gap junctions in development was made by Gilula and coworkers who injected antibodies to the 27 kD protein into a specific cell in the gray crescent region of the eight-cell *Xenopus* embryo. This operation disrupted dye transfer and electrical coupling, and, at later stages, injected embryos showed loss of the eye, of the trigeminal ganglion, and of anterior somites on the injected side. These results are preliminary; it is not clear yet whether gap junctions play a key signaling role in embryonic induction or in pattern formation. Nonetheless, the finding that they mediate connectivity and compartmentalization in such diverse structures as the skin, the apical ectodermal ridge of the limb bud, and the developing otic placode is consistent with such a role. Moreover, Gilula and colleagues have found that the transfer of signals in the regeneration of *Hydra* to regain its original form after cutting an organism to separate head structures from other structures appears to depend upon the integrity of gap junctions. Of course, the mechanisms of development in later, more complex animal forms do not necessarily have to preserve all of those seen in earlier forms.

Tight Junctions (Zonula Occludens) and Adherens Junctions (Zonula Adherens)

In contrast to gap junctions, tight junctions provide a transepithelial permeability barrier that regulates flow into the extracellular space, and accordingly these junctions are in general positioned in the apical region of epithelial cells (figure 7.10). This actual position may be established via a second junction—the zonula adherens or so-called belt desmosome.

Tight junctions are of particular interest in terms of morphoregulatory interactions because it has been proposed (see the article by Gumbiner and Simons in the review by Stoker) that L-CAM participates in their formation in certain areas and that

Figure 7.10

Diagrams of some specialized junctions. (See text for further descriptions and compare with figure 6.3; see Stoker for more details.) A: The gap junction can pass molecules of sizes up to 1 kD and can electrically couple cells. The diagram shows junctions between two cells, a connexon, and a subunit. (Diagram according to P. N. T. Unwin, 1987, Gap junction structure and the control of cell-to-cell communication, in Junctional complexes of epithelial cells, Ciba Foundation Symposium 125, 78–89, Chichester: Wiley.) B: The tight junction can form a seal in the apical region of an epithelium. (Diagram of Gumbiner and K. Simons, 1987, The role of uvomorulin in the formation of epithelial occluding junctions, ibid., 168–86.) C: Adherens junctions. The domain substructure of adherens junctions (both intercellular and cell-substrate contacts). (According to B. Geiger, Z. Avnur, T. Volberg, and T. Volk, 1985, Molecular domains of adherens junctions, in The cell in contact: Adhesions and junctions as morphogenetic determinants, ed. G. M. Edelman and J.-P. Thiery, 461–89, New York: Wiley.) a: The extracellular domain consisting of the exogenous surfaces to which the cell binds (in an intercellular junction, this domain may consist of membrane components of the neighboring cell). b: The integral membrane domain containing "contact receptor(s)" and mediating the transmembrane linkage to the plaque. c: The membrane-associated plaque domain to which microfilaments attach. d: The cytoskeletal domain attached to the plaque, consisting of actin making up microfilaments and actin-associated proteins. The proportional dimensions of the different domains in the scheme do not represent actual proportions in adherens junctions. D: A desmosome and some of its components. (After D. R. Garrod, M. Steinberg, and W. W. Franke, 1987, Localization of desmosomal proteins, in Junctional complexes of epithelial cells, Ciba Foundation Symposium 125, 67, Chichester: Wiley.) DP I and DP II, desmoplakins; PL, plaque; PM, plasma membrane; IS, intercellular space (about 30 nm); S, sugar. Adherens junctions and desmosomes can interact with different cytoskeletal components (see figure 6.1 and text).

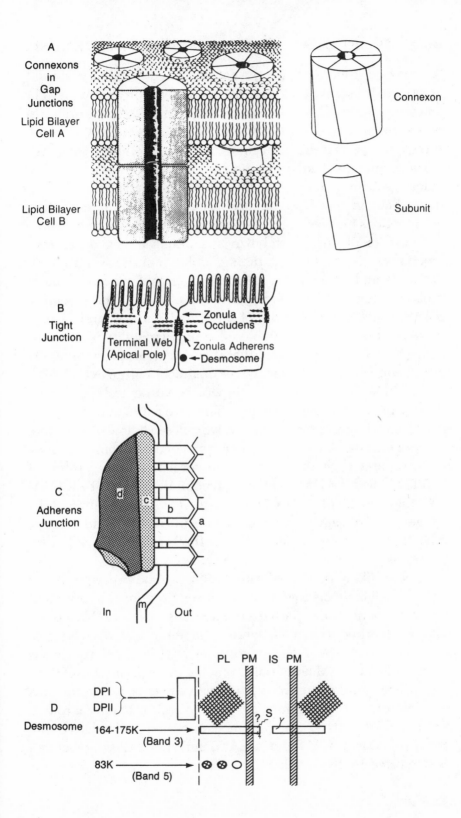

A
Connexons
in
Gap
Junctions

Lipid Bilayer
Cell A

Lipid Bilayer
Cell B

Connexon

Subunit

B
Tight
Junction

Zonula
Occludens
Zonula Adherens
Desmosome
Terminal Web
(Apical Pole)

C
Adherens
Junction

d c
b
a

In m Out

D
Desmosome

DPI
DPII

164-175K
(Band 3)

83K
(Band 5)

PL PM IS PM

? S

this may be responsible for the calcium ion dependence of tight junctional integrity. L-CAM is not always coexpressed with tight junctions, however: in myelin sheaths of the CNS and brain tissues after early neurulation, for example, L-CAM is not present. It thus may be that different tight junctions assemble differently.

The formation of adherens junctions (or belt desmosomes) provides a subapical mechanically integrated contractile network throughout an epithelium (figure 7.10). As we mentioned, adherens junctions may serve to position tight junctions, and certainly they can mechanically stabilize an epithelial sheet. Adherens junctions have contacts at their endofacial surfaces with actin filaments, and intercellular adherens junctions form a continuous subapical belt with an intercellular gap of 200 Å. This is seen in polar epithelia such as those of intestine, pancreas, and kidney; there is, however, considerable structural variability in different tissues. It has been proposed that these structures form a family of cell contacts with similar modes of attachment to cytoskeletal microfilaments by means of interactions with cytoskeletal actin and a vinculin-containing plaque. They are laminated structures consisting of four domains, and, as we will see below, the protein components making up the various types of desmosomes are now being separated. Most recently, an integral membrane protein of 135 kD called A-CAM (which is structurally related to L-CAM and may be identical to N-cadherin) has been identified by Geiger and colleagues (see their article in Edelman and Thiery), who found it to be associated with the formation of adherens junctions.

It seems likely that CAM interactions will be prerequisite for the cell-cell contacts that are in turn required for the formation of tight junctions and perhaps of adherens junctions. Moreover, recent experiments in my laboratory on fibroblast-like cells transfected with L-CAM cDNA suggest that gap junction formation is enhanced as L-CAM homophilic binding occurs. The role of tight and adherens junctions in early inductive events, if any, remains to be determined. Certainly, they would appear to have a role in epithelial integrity during folding events, and a correlative role for two CAMs, L-CAM and A-CAM, in forming these structures is suggested by the evidence.

Desmosomes

The discussion above leads naturally into the last of the families of specialized junctions to be considered here. As we mentioned, the zonula adherens, or the adherens junction that interacts with cytoskeleton, has been called a belt desmosome. Another type of junction that also interacts with the cytoskeleton is the macula adherens, or desmosome proper. This is a rigid plaque, 1.0 to 1.5 nm in diameter, with which intermediate filaments of the cytoskeleton are associated. (For details, the interested reader may consult the combined views of Franke, Garrod, and Steinberg in the book edited by Stoker.) The desmosomal membrane domain and plaque are distinctive: unlike the zonula adherens, they do not show vinculin, α-actinin, L-CAM, or A-CAM. Instead, they have two major polypeptides of 250 kD (desmoplakin I) and 215 kD (desmoplakin II), which are related in amino acid sequence. The desmoplakins bind calcium and appear to require this ion for their formation. Since desmosomes are symmetrical about the line between the cells they join, the desmosomal proteins must recognize one another in their extracellular regions. Indeed, desmosomes can be formed between cells of different tissue origins.

The desmosomal plaque also contains the cytoplasmic portion of a protein of 150 kD to 175 kD (band 3 glycoprotein), and it contains an acidic protein of 83 kD (band 5 protein), which is also present in adherens junctions. Just as adherens junctions interact with actin and vinculin of the cytoskeleton, so desmosomal plaques interact in a definite manner with intermediate filaments: cytokeratin intermediate filaments in epithelial cells, desmin intermediate filaments in cardiac myocytes, and vimentin intermediate filaments in meninges. There is, therefore, specificity in the interactions of different cytoskeletal elements with each of the kinds of junctions. This suggests a specific stabilizing role for each in the forming of epithelia; at present, one cannot exclude the possibility that such junctions with their cytoskeletal interactions could also change the modulation states of cells.

Very little is known about desmosome formation in embryogenesis, but these structures do appear early, just when cytokeratin filaments appear in the morula-blastocyst transformation. Desmosomes can also be seen in trophectoderm cells. Later, desmosomes are found on ectodermal and endodermal cells in the mouse but disappear before ectodermal cells convert to primary mesenchyme. As with the other specialized junctions, what is most needed is knowledge of a detailed sequence of events correlating cell interactions via CAMs and SAMs with those for these more complex structures. Such detailed expression sequences should help establish the successive or mutually dependent nature of CAM, SAM, and CJM functions. It is likely that prior CAM interactions are necessary for the formation of junctions; obviously, however, they are not sufficient for defining complete epithelia.

CONCLUDING SUMMARY

In this chapter, we have considered morphoregulatory molecules that fall into definite functional families: CAMs, SAMs, and CJMs. We lack a complete description of the sequential expression of each of these molecular families as a function of place; however, because the very earliest development (as early as the four-cell stage) begins with epithelia that lack junctions but have CAMs, it seems likely that CAM interactions are the very earliest, SAMs follow closely, and CJMs then appear. Although this *precedence hypothesis* has not been proven, the timing of appearances of L-CAM and the fact that this molecule is needed to form tight junctions, the absence of junctions from the two- to four-cell-stage embryo in the definite presence of CAMs, and the elaborate structure of desmosomes are all in line with this proposed sequence. The main point is that a cascade of interactions of morphoregulatory molecules is required for establishing morphology.

We have seen that CAM interactions involve a series of complex local modulations that can be essential to the formation of inducing collectives and their proper signaling. We have also seen that epithelial-mesenchymal transformations and a series of global modulations affecting cell division and protein expression can depend upon SAM interactions—particularly on interactions with the ECM in a complex modulation network offering many combinatorial possibilities of cell and protein binding. We have seen that cells in linked collectives can communicate through gap junctions while maintaining their differentiated state, possibly signaling the formation of groups of coupled cells responding similarly to inductive signals. Such cells may also be labeled as similar in their collectives by the activity of the cytoplasmic domains of the particular CAMs that link them. Finally, we have seen that the epithelial sheets that fold and form complex structures are linked and sealed at their apices by tight, adherens, and desmosomal structures interactive with the cytoskeleton, at the same time that these sheets interact at their basal surfaces with ECM components of the basement membrane (see figures 6.3 and 7.6). While the picture is incomplete, the evidence supports the view that all of these molecules play mechanochemical as well as regulatory roles in development.

In this, the longest and most technical chapter of the book, it has been my hope to show that the detailed consideration of morphoregulatory proteins is one of the essential tasks of molecular embryology. With the knowledge of these extraordinary morphoregulatory gene products (none of which is necessary to the survival of a cell proper), and the knowledge of the sequence of primary processes in development that they help regulate, we are in a position to ask how we can account for *genetically* determined animal and tissue form. Given the survey presented in the last two chapters and our preceding analysis, *we are forced to consider regulatory models that relate the gene expression of morphoregulatory molecules at particular times and places to the mechanics of formation of cell collectives releasing signals at these places.* The resulting topobiological models, to be discussed in part three, are much more complex than those we reviewed earlier in the book, but they have the twofold advantage of accounting for more of the facts and of linking mechanochemistry to developmental genetics in an explicit fashion. As I have already indicated, I take this to be the central task of molecular embryology.

SELECTED REFERENCES

Edelman, G. M. 1986. Cell adhesion molecules in the regulation of animal form and tissue pattern. *Annu. Rev. Cell Biol.* 2:81–116.

Cunningham, B. A., J. J. Hemperly, B. A. Murray, E. A. Prediger, R. Brackenbury, and G. M. Edelman. 1987. Neural cell adhesion molecule: Structure, immunoglobulin-like domains, cell surface modulation, and alternative RNA splicing. *Science* 236:799–806.

Gallin, W. J., B. A. Sorkin, G. M. Edelman, and B. A. Cunningham. 1987. Sequence analysis of a cDNA clone encoding the liver cell adhesion molecule, L-CAM. *Proc. Natl. Acad. Sci. USA* 84:2808–12.

Takeichi, M., C. Yoshida-Noro, Y. Shirayoshi, and K. Hatta. 1985. Calcium-dependent cell-cell adhesion system: Its molecular nature, celltype specificity and morphogenetic role. In *The cell in contact: Adhesions and junctions as morphogenetic determinants,* ed. G. M. Edelman and J.-P. Thiery, 219–32. New York: Wiley.

Edelman, G. M. 1987. Epigenetic rules for expression of cell adhesion molecules during morphogenesis. In *Junctional complexes of epithelial cells,* Ciba Foundation Symposium 125, ed. M. Stoker, 192–211. Chichester: Wiley.

———. 1988. Morphoregulatory molecules. *Biochemistry* 27:3534–43.

Gallin, W. J., C.-M. Chuong, L. H. Finkel, and G. M. Edelman. 1986. Antibodies to L-CAM perturb inductive interactions and alter feather pattern and structure. *Proc. Natl. Acad. Sci. USA* 83:8235–39.

Chuong, C.-M., and G. M. Edelman. 1985. Expression of cell adhesion molecules in embryonic induction. I. Morphogenesis of nestling feathers. *J. Cell Biol.* 101:1009–26.

———. 1985. Expression of cell adhesion molecules in embryonic induction. II. Morphogenesis of adult feathers. *J. Cell Biol.* 101:1027–43.

Edelman, G. M., and J.-P. Thiery, eds. 1985. *The cell in contact: Adhesions and junctions as morphogenetic determinants.* New York: Wiley.

Edelman, G. M., B. A. Murray, R. M. Mege, B. A. Cunningham, and W. J. Gallin. 1987. Cellular expression of liver and neural cell adhesion molecules after transfection with their cDNAs results in specific cell-cell binding. *Proc. Natl. Acad. Sci. USA* 84:8502–6.

Nagafuchi, A., Y. Shirayoshi, K. Okazaki, K. Yasuda, and M. Takeichi. 1987. Transformation of cell adhesion properties by exogenously introduced E-cadherin cDNA. *Nature* 329:341–43.

Dickson, G., H. J. Gower, C. H. Barton, H. M. Prentice, V. L. Elsom, S. E. Moore, R. D. Cox, C. Quinn, W. Putt, and F. S. Walsh. 1987. Human muscle neural cell adhesion molecule (N-CAM): Identification of a muscle-specific sequence in the extracellular domain. *Cell* 50:1119–30.

Hay, E. D., ed. 1981. *Cell biology of extracellular matrix.* New York: Plenum.

Hynes, R. O. 1987. Integrins: A family of cell surface receptors. *Cell* 48:549–54.

Ruoslahti, E., and M. D. Pierschbacher. 1987. New perspectives in cell adhesion: RGD and integrins. *Science* 238:491–97.

Lee, E. Y.-H. P., W.-H. Lee, C. S. Kaetzel, G. Parry, and M. J. Bissell. 1985. Interaction of mouse mammary epithelial cells with collagen substrata: Regulation of casein gene expression and secretion. *Proc. Natl. Acad. Sci. USA* 82:1419–23.

Warner, A. E., S. C. Guthrie, and N. B. Gilula. 1984. Antibodies to gap junctional protein selectively disrupt junctional communication in the early amphibian embryo. *Nature* 311:127–31.

Fraser, S. E., C. R. Green, H. R. Bode, and N. B. Gilula. 1987. Selective disruption of gap junctional communication interferes with a patterning process in *Hydra*. *Science* 237:49–55.

Stoker, M., ed. 1987. *Junctional complexes of epithelial cells*, Ciba Foundation Symposium 125. Chichester: Wiley.

Larsen, W. J., and M. A. Risinger. 1985. The dynamic life histories of intercellular membrane junctions. In *Modern cell biology*. Vol. 4, ed. B. H. Satir, 151–216. New York: Alan R. Liss.

Hascall, V. C., ed. 1986. *Functions of the proteoglycans*, Ciba Foundation Symposium 124. Chichester: Wiley.

Sawyer, R. H., and J. F. Fallon. 1983. *Epithelial-mesenchymal interactions in development*. New York: Praeger.

See also the reference to Thiery in chapter 6.

PART THREE

═══════

THE MORPHOREGULATOR
HYPOTHESIS:
MECHANOCHEMISTRY
LINKED TO
DEVELOPMENTAL
GENETICS

═══════

8

The Developmental
Genetic Question

ARMED WITH the data from previous chapters on developmental gene cascades, on primary processes of development, and on morphoregulatory molecules, we can now directly confront the developmental genetic and evolutionary questions. We will consider the two questions separately and in order in this chapter and the next one. First, however, it is useful to summarize some of the main facts and conclusions, derived from a variety of fields, upon which satisfactory answers to these questions critically depend. We can do this economically in twelve statements; some may seem obvious or simplistic, but as a collection they subtly transform our view of development.

1. *Development is under genetic control.* While this is obvious, its details are not: a main point is that there are developmentally significant structural and regulatory genes specially dedicated to key events in development; diverse developmentally crucial regulatory genes interact in complex webs. The various types include examples ranging from pair rule and homeotic genes in *Drosophila* to CAM genes in vertebrates.

2. *Developmental events are nonetheless epigenetic and topobiologically controlled.* They emerge first as a result of polar redistributions in the oocyte and then as a result of cellular interactions at particular locations or places, in sequences whose

temporal regulation is long compared with those of intracellular control events. Information about such locations is *not* stored in genes.

3. *Development is regulative.* Alterations of the locations of groups of cells at particular developmental times can be compensated for, within limits. With certain exceptions, this capacity is diminished as developmental events and time proceed: cellular competence decreases and commitment increases with histodifferentiation. The exceptions are metamorphosis, regeneration, and bone repair, in all of which regulative capacities are retained to some extent.

4. *Pattern, not simply cell differentiation, is the evolutionary basis of morphogenesis.* The combination of patterns leading to form is a result of natural selection acting upon developmental variants, the form and phenotypic function of which increase fitness. Thus the particular combination of regulatory genes leading to form in a given species is a result of the natural selection of those organisms whose epigenetic sequences in development led to that form and its phenotypic behavior.

5. *Within a genus, development can show variations in particular morphologic features and patterns but does not alter the overall body plan.* The body plans of existing animal species have been fixed since the Precambrian. A major means by which evolutionary alterations occur in morphology is heterochrony, a change in the time of appearance during the development of characters possessed by ancestors. Such changes reflect alterations in times of response of developmentally significant genes.

6. *The fundamental issue in developmental genetics is the determination of the regulation of pattern mainly by the action of regulatory genes and only incidentally by structural genes.*

Differences between related species such as chimpanzees and humans appear to be due to regulatory-gene action, not to the existence of great varieties of different structural genes in the two species.

7. *The primary processes of cell division, cell and tissue movement, and cell death provide the driving forces for the development of form. The primary processes of adhesion and place-dependent gene expression or embryonic induction regu-*

late these driving forces. Adhesion leads to the formation of epithelia, and its control allows for epithelial-mesenchymal transformation in both directions. Embryonic induction depends upon a series of appositions of epithelia with epithelia, of mesenchyme with epithelia, and of epithelia with mesenchyme in a sequence of events that affect the genes that regulate adhesion as well as the genes that regulate cytodifferentiation. The responses of cells to inductive signals depends upon their proximity and degree of linkage to neighboring cells.

8. *The cell surface plays a special role in these topobiological interactions* because it mediates signals from other cells and the ECM and links with other surfaces to form tissues. It is dynamic, showing transmembrane-controlled global modulation that alters cytoskeletal interactions and cell shape, thereby influencing movement, division, and gene expression.

9. *Three families of morphoregulatory molecules expressed at the cell surface appear to be specifically concerned with cell adhesion events and modulation of signaling events during induction and later histogenesis: CAMs, SAMs, and CJMs.* The genes that regulate the expression of these morphoregulatory molecules are therefore of particular developmental significance. CAMs mediate cell-cell adhesion and border formation between cell collectives. SAMs mediate cell-substrate interactions, including those with ECM and basement membranes. CJMs mediate intercellular communication (gap junctions), apical sealing of epithelia (tight junctions), stabilization of the sheet, and interaction with cytoskeleton (adherens junctions, desmosomes).

10. *There is a close relation between CAM expression, cell adhesion, and border formation between cell collectives during induction and tissue formation.* CAMs are expressed in early cell collectives, and they appear to act by virtue of a series of local modulation events at the cell surface, providing a means for changing their binding under control of the cell. During embryogenesis, CAM expression and modulation follow definite sequences characteristic of each CAM as a function of place. A mapping of CAM borders shows a correlation but not an identity with tissue borders; CAM expression follows cycles that are independent of cytodifferentiation. These cycles are nonetheless

temporally correlated with cytodifferentiation. This is consistent with the early use of CAMs to form a variety of structures, leading to tissues that then vary greatly in later histogenetic development. Alteration of CAM binding alters morphology, and, at least in some cases, alteration of morphology alters CAM expression. In one example (the feather), alteration of *ectodermal* L-CAM function during induction (and therefore of linkage of cells in an epithelium) shows changes in morphology in underlying condensing *mesodermal* mesenchyme, which becomes linked by N-CAM, with consequent changes in pattern. This is accompanied by alterations in the mitotic behavior of cells. In other cases, CAM perturbation leads to alterations in cell migration or in the interaction of cell processes.

11. *The evidence suggests that SAMs can cause global modulation of the cell surface, supporting changes from epithelia to mesenchyme.*   SAMs provide migratory substrates for mesenchymal cells and, in the form of basement membranes, stabilize formed epithelia in tissues. Distributions of SAMs in various places are more general and less spatially ordered on a fine scale than are those of CAMs. By virtue of their multivalent attachment sites and various specificities for one another and for cell ligands, SAMs can provide a combinatorial multimolecular environment for cells that governs particular aspects of differentiation, migration, and mechanical properties by means of a modulation network.

12. *Of the CJMs, gap junction proteins appear to be the most evident candidates for the role of forming structures that allow direct communication among cells in collectives.*   It has not yet been established whether such junctions are essential in regulating embryonic induction. Other junctions formed by CJMs provide a basis for the mechanical integrity of epithelial sheets during folding events and possibly for the effect of tension on primary processes.

It is clear from this summary review that no strictly genetic account alone, not even one involving the detailed analysis of sequences of developmentally important genes, can provide a satisfactory answer to the developmental genetic question. It is equally clear that a purely mechanical or mechanochemical analysis that ignores this genetic control of developmental events is also inadequate: the one-dimensional genetic code *does* specify a three-dimensional animal in time, albeit by epigenetic means. These means assure that, at the macroscopic scale, animal shape is determined by linked chemical and mechanical events occurring in cells and tissues that alter gene expression. Gene expression in turn alters such events through morphoregulatory molecules.

How can the different genetic and epigenetic events be reconciled in detail? *What seems to be required is a place-dependent dynamic regulatory loop that ranges from the gene to the gene product, cells, tissues, and organs, and then back from these structures of higher scale (see table 2.1) to control the expression of the same gene or a different gene.* Such a loop would include those regulatory genes and structural genes affecting the driving force primary processes in such a way as to yield genetic control of pattern. It would also, however, require signals that *go back directly to the gene level* from the level of those morphogenetically significant cell collectives that were formed epigenetically under the influence of the primary processes.

This anticipatory summary sets our goal, which is to answer in detail two questions subsidiary to the developmental question. How can epigenetic alterations of the mechanochemical properties of cells linked in inducing collectives be related to the action of the regulatory genes, thus guaranteeing both morphology and the next inductive event? Above all, how can this occur under overall genetic control, so that it yields the tissue pattern and animal form characteristic of a species?

THE MORPHOREGULATOR HYPOTHESIS

We can now sketch a hypothesis framed to answer these questions. As originally proposed, it was called the regulator hypothesis and was formulated mainly around CAMs. It will be extended here to cover all morphoregulatory molecules and in recognition of this, will be called the morphoregulator hypothesis. I will first give an overview of its major tenets, taking heed of the summary just presented, and then describe the salient details.

We may conclude from our summary that there are four main tasks in formulating an adequate hypothesis. The first is to account for the *epigenetic component* of morphogenesis in terms of cellular processes. The second is to identify those regulatory and structural genes that are chiefly responsible for the *genetic component* of pattern formation and morphogenesis. The third is *to link the epigenetic and genetic* components in order to provide a signal path both to these regulatory genes and to the regulatory genes governing histodifferentiation. These three tasks are the concern of this chapter. The fourth task is to explain how particular combinations and responses of two kinds of regulatory genes in a phenotype *can give rise during evolution* to a particular animal form in a species. This will be considered in the next chapter, which discusses the evolutionary question.

According to the morphoregulator hypothesis, the epigenetic component of morphogenesis comes from the three driving force processes that assure the presence of cells in a sufficient number—cells that are capable of movement in certain states and that are subject to selective removal by death. All of these processes—cell division, movement, and death—depend upon the action or removal of mechanochemical factors, and, in addition to their particular detailed consequences at a particular place and time, their exercise has mechanical consequences that alter form at the scale of both cells and tissues.

Regulation of these driving force processes comes from the processes of adhesion and induction. According to the hypothesis, the major genetic aspects of morphogenesis result from the interaction of these two regulatory processes, as mediated by gene products we have called morphoregulatory molecules. Under cell control, morphoregulatory molecules are capable of promoting cell-cell adhesion, causing epithelial-mesenchymal transformation, and providing substrate pathways for cell movement.

The morphoregulator hypothesis (see table 8.1 for a brief summary of its assumptions and proposals in a slightly different form) states the following. (1) *The essential genetic component of early*

*pattern formation in morphogenesis comes from the existence
and temporal response to inductive signals of those regulatory
genes and structural genes that determine the appearance and
function of morphoregulatory molecules.* The epigenetic component comes from the topobiological response of cells to these
molecules. Tissue differentiation, by contrast, results from the
action of historegulatory genes, the sequences of which are under
the control of selector genes (table 8.1). *In general, morphoregulatory genes act independently of historegulatory and selector
genes. (2) The link between the epigenetic and the genetic components of development is in the inductive signal paths arising from*

TABLE 8.1

The Morphoregulator Hypothesis

Assumptions and Conditions:
1. The cell is the unit of control, but the collective (a group of neighboring cells linked by MR molecules) is the unit of signaling. Collectives are determined by cytoplasmic domains of CAMs linking them and acting through different second messengers (and also possibly by gap junctions).
2. Three kinds of regulatory genes are involved:
   a) Morphoregulatory (MR) genes control structural genes for morphoregulatory molecules. These genes are not necessary for life of a cell but are necessary for pattern.
   b) Historegulatory (HR) genes control structural genes involving all other cytodif-ferentiation events. Such structural genes, specifying general "housekeeping" functions common to most cells and also necessary for the emergence of histodif-ferentiated cells, are required for the life and specific characteristics of any cell and constitute by far the largest of the three classes.
   c) Selector (S) genes, by affecting certain HR genes, restrict expression of sequences of cytodifferentiation at certain places and developmental times.

The MR Hypothesis:
1. The context of epigenetic responses of cells in a collective to inductive signals is set by CAMs forming borders and response characteristics in a cell collective and by a network of SAMs acting by means of global modulation resulting in a *choice* of primary processes (division, movement, death) in a given signaling situation.
2. The essential genetic components linking epigenetic mechanochemical events to gene expression are MR genes. Their action is under independent control from that of HR and S genes.
3. The link is via inductive signal paths arising via adhesion-dominated collectives giving rise to signals between such collectives. Such signals proceed back from the collec-tives to the MR, HR, and S genes to change expression of morphoregulatory mole-cules and cytodifferentiation products.
4. The sequential historical interactions of MR and HR genes via epigenetic paths provide the basis of pattern by controlling temporal sequences of mitosis, movement, death, and further signaling.

---

adhesion-dominated collectives, giving rise to signals that go directly back from these collectives to genes governing morphoregulatory molecules. Embryonic induction proceeds by signaling from *groups* (or collectives) of cells to other groups of cells, not via single cells. The key suggestion is that the signals do not arise until at least one such collective out of a pair of mutually inducing collectives is actually formed under the action of morphoregulatory molecules and their genes. Histogenesis occurs within this framework as a result of similarly conditioned signals to historegulatory genes—those controlling the structural genes responsible for individual cell metabolism and for the structure, shape, and movement of particular cells. Historegulatory genes are essential to the life of the organism and govern all primary processes except adhesion but do not directly govern any products yielding cell-cell or cell-substrate binding. Nonetheless, the control of these genes by a set of selector genes akin to homeotic genes determines pathways of histogenetic expression. We will consider these selector genes later. (3) *The place-dependent coordinate activity of these three kinds of genes—morphoregulatory, historegulatory, and selector genes—leads to overall form and pattern.* This activity depends on a sequence of epigenetic events leading to the formation of inducing collectives. Such a dependence therefore results in a temporal sequence of cycles of gene expression for at least some morphoregulatory molecules, as is reflected, for example, in CAM rules and SAM modulatory networks. As we will see in the next chapter, the particular combinations of the types and the response activities of morphoregulatory and historegulatory genes lead to form in a given species because those combinations have led to morphologies that enhance fitness. The *bounds* of morphoregulatory pattern are therefore determined by evolution, not by development.

These statements together constitute the morphoregulator hypothesis but do not give a detailed mechanistic account of linked genetic and epigenetic expression. We may now embody these ideas in several very specific models based on the CAMs; as we will indicate later, similarly appropriate models can be constructed for SAMs and CJMs. Examining such models should help relate the morphoregulator hypothesis more tightly to the detailed facts that form its basis.

First, let us consider some of its assumptions further. According to the hypothesis, CAMs are key regulators of morphogenetic motion, epithelial integrity, and mesenchymal condensation. A major tenet is that genes affecting CAM expression (morphoregulatory genes) act in early development *independently of and generally prior to* those that control tissue-specific differentiation (historegulatory genes). Consistent with this assumption, CAM expression in most induced areas does initially precede the expression of most cytodifferentiation products. This is consistent, in turn, with the observation that the expression of a given primary CAM type overlaps *different* tissue types, as is seen in a classic fate map (see figure 9.1). It should be noted, however, that the precedence is not absolute: in some cases, such as the formation of primary mesenchyme, a few historegulatory genes may act prior to morphoregulatory genes at particular sites, rendering the mesenchymes from these sites different in their competence. Finally, as the CAM rules show (see figure 7.3), primary CAM sequences may appear several times during the histodifferentiation of a single structure such as the feather or the kidney.

A main function of CAMs is to attach cells in collectives, to form borders, and to regulate movement, and thus a major part of their function is mechanochemical. Although CAMs exist in a relatively small number of specificities compared to the number of histodifferentiated cell types, because of cell surface modulation, *they are capable of a very large number of alterations* in their binding properties, which are graded and nonlinear. To relate this mechanochemical CAM function to CAM expression sequences and to the expression of other gene products concerned with cytodifferentiation, one must assume that chemical or mechanochemical signals act *locally* on cells in collectives. Altered pressure, tension, or flow in the vicinity of a collective of cells held together by one kind of CAM in the neighborhood of another collective held together by a CAM of different specificity, together with the chemical factors released by such collectives, could alter the expression or modulation of the CAMs at cell surfaces. A varying temporal sequence of such expressions would alter morphogenetic movements in different ways and thus lead to changes in specific form and pattern.

With these assumptions as background, let us now examine how local signals could affect morphoregulatory genes for CAMs and SAMs as well as historegulatory genes determining tissue formation. At the level of a given kind of cell and its descendants in a collective, CAM expression may be viewed as occurring in a cycle (figure 8.1). Traversals of the outer loop of this cycle affect morphoregulatory genes, which can lead either to the switching on of one or another of the CAM genes or to their switching off. A switching on and off of the same genes is suggested in the case of mesenchymal cells contributing to dermal condensations as well as in the case of neural crest cells (rule I; see chapter 7). A switching to a different CAM gene or combination of CAM genes is suggested in epithelia (rule II). The subsequent action of historegulatory genes (figure 8.1, *inner loop*) is pictured to be the result of inductive signals arising in the new milieus that occur

Figure 8.1

The morphoregulator hypothesis as exemplified in a CAM regulatory cycle. Early induction signals (heavy arrow at left) lead to CAM gene expression. Surface modulation (by prevalence changes, polar redistribution on the cell, or chemical changes such as E-to-A conversion) alters the binding rates of cells. This regulates morphogenetic movements and formation of cell collectives, which in turn affect embryonic induction or milieu-dependent differentiation. The resulting inductive changes can again affect CAM gene expression as well as the expression of other genes for specific tissues. The heavy arrows at left and right refer to candidate signals for the initiation of induction that are still unknown. These signals could result from global surface modulation as a result of CAM or SAM binding (right) or from release of morphogens affecting induction (left) or from both; in any case, a mechanochemical link is provided between gene expression and morphogenesis. (From G. M. Edelman, 1987, CAMs and Igs: Cell adhesion and the evolutionary origins of immunity, Immunol. Rev. 100:9–43.)

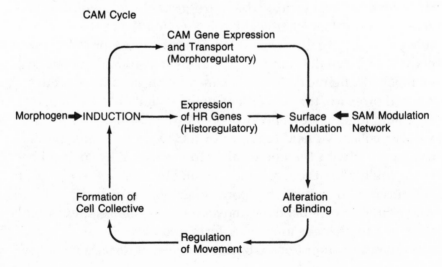

CAM Cycle

historically through CAM-dependent cell aggregation, motion, and tissue folding.

Significant early responses of particular historegulatory genes are determined by particular selector genes, which in this respect resemble the homeotic genes of *Drosophila*. If the expression of certain historegulatory genes led to altered cell motion or shape or altered posttranslational events, this would alter the effects on morphogenesis of subsequent traversals of the outer loop. An example directly affecting the cells containing N-CAM concerns the historegulatory genes that specify the enzyme responsible for polysialic acid synthesis and for E-to-A conversion, events that lead to changes in N-CAM binding rates (see chapter 7). Thus, *within the framework provided by morphoregulatory genes, historegulatory genes can also alter form;* under control of selector genes, they also determine developmental pathways, as discussed below.

Combinations of two CAM cycles with signaling across borders between two collectives linked by different CAMs could lead to a rich set of effects altering the path of morphogenesis. In considering how two such cycles (each related to at least one different CAM) might interact, we are compelled to consider the nature of the signals that activate morphoregulatory and historegulatory genes during induction. It remains unknown whether these signals are morphogens released by cells linked by a particular CAM (figure 8.1, *left large arrow*) or whether they are derived from mechanical alterations of the cell surface or cytoskeleton through global cell surface modulation (figure 8.1, *right large arrow*). Of course, both types of signals might be required in some cases and, as I mention later, growth factor signals are just beginning to be identified. Almost certainly, the signals affecting global cell surface modulation would come from interactions with SAM modulation networks.

We may use the development of the feather to illustrate in a detailed model how modulation of signaling interactions between two different inducing collectives linked by different CAMs—L-CAM in the epidermis and N-CAM in the dermis—can yield pattern. As we discussed in chapter 7, the earliest induction events lead to the expression of N-CAM in more or less circular dermal condensations that form a hexagonal pattern. Perturbation of L-CAM in the *epidermis* altered the *dermal* pattern to stripes and changed the mitotic pattern in the dermis, leading ultimately to distorted feather germs or scalelike structures. Such changes must have been mediated by independent signals affecting each CAM-linked collective. A minimal model based on the exchange of signals between these tissues, one of which (epidermis) has already undergone a CAM cycle and one of which (dermis) is undergoing such a cycle, has been shown to generate these patterns in a computer simulation.

This computer model (figure 8.2) of feather germ induction generates both the normal and the antibody-perturbed patterns. The model simulates individual cells, each capable of signaling mitosis, movement, and differentiation, and it explicitly specifies a causal role for CAMs in the response of cell collectives to inductive signals. In the model, the lateral advance of the dense dermis (in this instance, a result of mitotic activity) is a major constraint on the order of formation of actual condensations. Experimental evidence suggests a minimum of two inductive signals (figure 8.2, A): E_s, produced by L-CAM-linked epidermal cells, and D_s, produced by N-CAM-linked dermal cells. The signals are considered to be diffusible morphogens, but the model is also consistent with direct cell-cell signaling. E_s acts on mesenchymal cells within dense dermis to increase their mitotic rate, turn on N-CAM production, and form condensations. Dermal cells in condensations then produce D_s, which acts upon epidermal cells to induce placode formation and to down-regulate production of E_s over an area slightly larger than that of each condensation. This eventually halts the growth of the underlying dermal condensate.

In normal epidermis, down-regulation of E_s occurs in a cooperative manner, reflecting cell-cell interactions in a collective mediated by L-CAM (*solid curve*, figure 8.2, A). Anti-L-CAM antibodies act exclusively on epidermis, changing the linkage and modulation state of epidermal cells, and by this means could alter production of E_s in three ways: (1) by changing the effect of D_s in down-regulating E_s production, (2) by changing the baseline rate of production of E_s itself, or (3) by changing the time constants of epidermal cellular response to D_s. In the computer simulations, increasing the net production of E_s by combinations

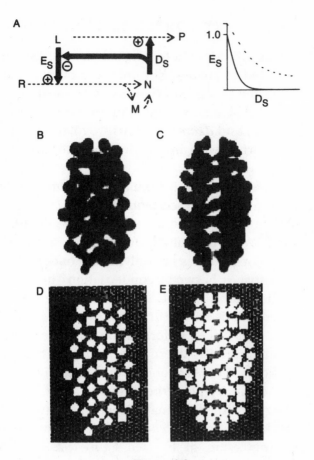

Figure 8.2

Computer model of feather pattern formation (see figure 4.1), illustrating the signal linkage between two CAM cycles. A: Epidermal cells (L) linked by L-CAM produce a signal (E_s). Dermal cells in mesenchyme (R) respond to E_s by increased mitosis (M), by production of N-CAM (N), and by production of another signal (D_s). D_s induces placode formation (P) and down-regulates epidermal production of E_s. Cellular responses to the inductive signals are stochastic. The graph (right) shows plots of the production of E_s as a function of the level of D_s. In the normal case, the interaction is highly cooperative (solid curve); in the antibody-perturbed case, the curve shows a higher baseline and less down-regulation of E_s (dashed curve) because of decreased cooperativity between epidermal cells. The simulations generating the model involved 9,600 epidermal and 3,850 dermal cells, each of which underwent iterated cycles of signaling and response according to the scheme in A. Patterns in B (epidermal E_s level) and D (dermal condensations) correspond to normal development after 350 cycles; those in C and E correspond accordingly to perturbed development in which there was decreased epidermal cooperativity. In B and C, darker regions represent areas of greater down-regulation of E_s because of higher levels of D_s. In D and E, black areas contain no cells, gray areas are mesenchymal cells, and white areas are cell condensations, expressing N-CAM and D_s. Compare these panels with those in figure 7.4, which show the actual experimental findings. (From W. J. Gallin, C.-M. Chuong, L. H. Finkel, and G. M. Edelman, 1986, Antibodies to L-CAM can perturb inductive interactions and alter feature pattern and structure, Proc. Natl. Acad. Sci. USA 83:8235–39.)

of the first two possibilities led to stripes in a robust manner; the third possibility led to stripes, but only in a narrow parameter range. In further modeling experiments, it was assumed that the disrupting of L-CAM linkages of epidermal cells leads to *increased* production and *decreased* down-regulation of E_s in epidermis by interfering with intercellular cooperativity (*dashed curve*, figure 8.2, *A*).

Unperturbed development is simulated in figure 8.2, *B* and *D*. The first condensations form sequentially in the simulation, from the center outward in the midline row, and the final hexagonal pattern depends upon the initial formation of this row. As the front of dense dermis moves laterally, new condensations form laterally to the spaces between condensations in the adjacent medial row. The reason is that, as the dense dermis migrates laterally, these locations are the first ones encountered that have sufficiently high values of E_s to form a condensation. The topobiological determination of pattern depends upon the linkage of response thresholds via CAMs and upon linked signal paths.

Simulation of antibody-perturbed development (figure 8.2, *C* and *E*) also began with a normally developed midline row of condensations. Decreasing the cooperativity of the function reflecting down-regulation of E_s (see figure 8.2, *A*) produced striped patterns resembling the experimental patterns described in chapter 7 (figure 7.3). In the simulation, anti-L-CAM acted on the epidermis to prevent E_s from being sufficiently down-regulated, and, as a result, dermal cell condensation continued laterally, forming stripes of cell condensations. Between condensations, however, E_s was still sufficiently down-regulated to prevent condensation, thus ensuring stripe formation.

The results of the experiments on feather induction and the consistent patterns in the simulations of feather induction fulfill one of the main predictions of the morphoregulator hypothesis, relating the mechanochemical functions of CAMs to inductive signaling. Another of the predictions of the hypothesis is that dynamic changes in bordering cell collectives mediated by CAM expression also affect the subsequent or late expression of specific historegulatory genes at various induction sites. In the case of feather induction, studies of the coordinate spatiotemporal expression of CAM genes and keratin genes may provide a critical test of this prediction. Preliminary results already suggest that the patterns of keratin expression in the perturbed and the unperturbed cases are different.

Further tests and elaborations of the computer model await experimental perturbation analysis using anti-N-CAM as well as anti-L-CAM. One point is sufficiently clear, even at this early stage: in such a dynamic model, CAMs themselves, though necessary, are clearly insufficient to generate a rich diversity of form; the regulatory cycle involving signals and the dynamics of the primary processes of development are the fundamental generators. This view of the operation of CAM cycles also indicates how important it is to identify the signaling system and the chemical nature of the signals to cells that govern the expression of morphoregulatory and historegulatory genes. Repeated patterns of N-CAM and L-CAM expression have been observed in varying environments of cytodifferentiation in the feather (see chapter 7), raising the issue of whether such repetitive CAM patterns arise at different stages and places in response to the *same* signals regardless of the varied action of historegulatory genes.

The analysis of CAM expression and distribution in the feather (see chapter 7) serves in addition to illustrate how a series of CAM cycles applied successively to differentiating tissues can result in borders of morphologically significant structures. In the histodifferentiation of the feather, control of CAM expression is tied first to movement in the induction stage; then to cell division in the stages of induction and barb ridge formation; and finally to cell death in the terminal expression of keratin. In this last stage, *borders* delineating L-CAM-linked collectives become *edges* of barbs and barbules in the final structure (see figure 7.5).

One of the outstanding problems related to the idea of the prior expression of CAM genes and subsequent actions of historegulatory genes is to understand the connection of CAMs to a signal path for the latter genes. We may ask, for example, whether CAMs of different specificity involved in the CAM couples at inductive sites are not merely ligators of their respective adjacent cell collectives. While they obviously carry out this ligating function, it is conceivable that they are not "signal neutral," that is, their *particular* binding properties may be necessary for transmitting particular CAM-related inductive signals. In other words, ligating the cells together nonspecifically in a collective may not be sufficient; *particular* CAMs may be required at particular places. This does not, of course, imply that CAMs *carry* the necessary signals. Nonetheless, *the different cytoplasmic domains of different CAMs may affect cells in different fashions, possibly by linkage to different second-messenger systems, to the cytoskeleton, or to both.*

Given these particular examples, it is useful to discriminate among the various levels of control of the embryonic events leading to form. The morphoregulator hypothesis assumes (table 8.1) that the cell is the unit of control, that the cell surface is the nexus of control events, that cell adhesion and differentiation order the driving forces of the processes of cell movement and cell division, and that adhesion acts by generating local place-dependent signals affecting collectives in CAM-linked couples during epigenesis. These signals are assumed to consist both of morphogens and of mechanochemical factors, involving, for example, the cross-linkage of CAMs and also SAM interactions affecting global cell surface modulation. While the cell is considered to be the unit of control, the unit of induction is considered to be a cell collective of sufficient size linked by a particular primary CAM or combination of CAMs. According to the hypothesis, only such a CAM-linked collective releases signals in the proper order or responds in a defined fashion sufficient to give form.

Among the morphoregulatory molecules that provide the linkage between the genes and the mechanochemical requirements of epigenetic sequences CAMs are thus hypothesized to be particularly important. Linked CAM cycles occurring in various contexts offer a potential solution to the problem of mechanochemical control of pattern, ranging over the various levels from gene through organ and back to gene, during regulative development. According to these topobiological views, "place" in the embryo is established as a historical (i.e., spatiotemporally defined) consequence of modulation and control rather than by prespecified cell addresses or markers.

THE ROLE OF SAMs AND CJMs IN THE HYPOTHESIS

The expression of CAMs as gene products that act as regulators of cellular mechanochemical events in signaling collectives links the one-dimensional genetic code to the higher-order assemblages of cells and tissues. The control of CAM binding makes the necessary rapprochement between developmental genetics and mechanochemistry at cell and tissue levels. In other words, CAMs are proposed as a bridge between *Entwicklungsmechanik* and developmental genetics (see chapter 5).

This statement is not exclusive, however; in previous chapters, we emphasized that while the CAMs are initially necessary as key regulators of pattern, other molecules such as SAMs (e.g., cytotactin), CJMs (e.g., gap junction proteins), and various tissue-specific gene products must also be present to ensure cellular migration, global modulation, and specialization in histogenesis. Although the body of evidence is not as coherent as for the CAMs alone, there are good reasons to expect that a coordination between the expression and function of CAMs, SAMs, and CJMs is essential in development. This is indicated for CAMs and SAMs by the fact that neural crest cells down-regulate N-CAM during their migration as ectomesenchyme in fibronectin-rich and cytotactin-rich regions. It also is indicated by the coordination between Ng-CAM and cytotactin in governing the migration of cerebellar granule cells and radial glia. Furthermore, as we have seen, antifibronectin antibodies have been shown by Thiery to block gastrulation events in the newt, presumably by hindering cell migration events.

Thus, although the facts on expression sequences are not yet as compelling for SAMs as for CAMs, SAMs nonetheless fit the requirements of the morphoregulator hypothesis and, in particular, play a key role in global cell surface modulation. Their regulation and topobiological functions differ from those of CAMs especially because they are extracellular and have properties related to their function in supporting cell migration and forming basement membranes. Being extracellular, they tend to be more widespread in scale and in location, and they spread beyond the cells that synthesize them. As is shown by cytotactin, however, this does not mean that they cannot be synthesized in a place-dependent fashion. It does mean that they are less likely than CAMs to be *directly* or *immediately* regulated by the cell that synthesized them. Instead, it is the overall pattern of the appearance and regulation of SAM receptors and of the synthesis of *multiple* SAMs that is likely to be a major factor in their action, along with their degradation and subsequent reshaping by enzymes such as proteases. Given their global modulating properties, multiple binding sites, polyfunctionality with respect to binding, and interactions with one another, *the SAMs provide a molecular basis for the connecting of cell state to two main functions deriving from movement as a driving force. These are cell migration after mesenchymal transformation and epithelial folding, to which SAMs contribute by providing a basis for polarity and for the tensile properties* discussed by Jacobson, Odell, and Oster.

We have suggested that SAMs form a modulation network with combinatorial properties that result from the sequential and differential synthesis of polyfunctional ECM proteins interacting at different embryonic sites as a function of time. Such topobiologically significant synthesis certainly occurs with cytotactin; specific variations in different proteoglycans in different tissues (see table 7.2) suggest that they, too, are synthesized in such a manner. With the rich combinatorial possibilities of molecular and cellular binding inherent in such matrix proteins, different degrees and forms of global cell surface modulation could ensue at different embryonic sites. This would be expected to alter mesenchymal transformation, migration, and cell division, reflecting the particular modulation sites (and SAM receptors) present on cells in a given location as well as the kinds of ECM molecule combinations able to interact with such sites. The action of such a network is schematized in figure 8.3.

According to this view, SAMs are important modulatory components in the morphoregulatory scheme. One would not expect them to play as immediate or as early a role as CAMs in border formation or in rapid responses to inductive signals. Nonetheless, one would expect them to play roles that are synergistic with

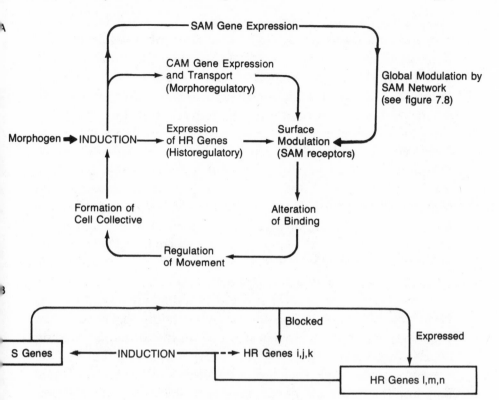

Figure 8.3
Effects of induction on a CAM cycle and SAM modulation network (A) and on selector gene action (B). Compare with figure 8.1. The notion of selector genes was first suggested by A. Garcia-Bellido; see reference in chapter 4.

CAMs at certain sites of induction. Because of their freedom from control by the cells that synthesized them, however, it seems unlikely that they will in general show a *cycle* of control (except possibly through their cell receptors or integrins, for which such a cycle has not yet been shown). Instead, they are more suited to interactions that can be controlled by later events of enzymatic alteration and by resynthesis. They are also more suited to the stabilization of structures and, through global cell surface modulation, they will govern which of the primary processes (division, movement, death) can proceed *under adequate signaling conditions.* In other words, they set the context of response.

With CAM cycles and SAM modulatory networks, we have been able to give reasonably specific examples and models of morphoregulatory systems. Our present state of knowledge, however, allows us to say little about the third family of morphoregulatory molecules, the CJMs. Certainly, gap junctions are a prime candidate for the role of synchronizing and linking certain signals between and among cells in an inducing collective. Collectives necessary for induction, such as the apical ectodermal ridge of the developing limb bud, are all linked by junctions. Moreover, as we already mentioned, there is suggestive evidence that the blocking of gap junctions with antibodies leads to failure of normal morphogenesis. It is an intriguing finding that gap junctions form readily as a result of CAM linkage of cells in a collective and that, as in tight junctions, prior CAM linkages of cells may be required for gap junction formation. If this were generally so, one would perhaps begin to understand the basis of interaction that makes a group of cells into such a collective. The data on the role of L-CAM in tight junction formation and A-CAM in adherens junction formation certainly leave open the possibility that CAM linkage also precedes the formation of some of the more specialized cell junctions, and together these observations support the precedence hypothesis. With CJMs, CAMs may simultaneously affect cellular morphology and vectorial protein processing while also forming cell collectives with inductive potentials. Although the role of cell junctions in signaling is obscure, through their interaction with different components of the cytoskeleton (actin and α-actinin, for adherens junctions; intermediate filaments, for desmosomes), these structures must at least lend mechanical stability to epithelia, modulating how they fold and influencing the polar traffic of molecules along their cell membranes. But they also may affect global modulation events through these linkages.

Despite these unresolved issues, the major outlines of the morphoregulator hypothesis are reasonably clear. The overall scheme consists of CAM cycles interacting with SAM modulation networks (and possibly gap junction formation) in a series of mechanochemical linkages. These linkages alter signaling events, affecting morphoregulatory genes specifying CAMs, SAMs, CJMs, and also various historegulatory genes. The coupling of these cycles and networks involves two parallel (i.e., largely independent) sets of signals to morphoregulatory and histeregulatory genes. The sequential expression of these genes is epigenetic and place dependent and, in general, for histeregulatory genes, it is historical or irreversible. It is the dynamics of expression of morphoregulatory molecules interacting with morphogenetic signals over many levels of organization and recursively affecting cellular driving force processes that ultimately leads to form. By such means, structure at higher levels can be linked with local topobiologically conditioned signals, ensuring the sequential action of the next set of genes, whether morphoregulatory or histeregulatory. And while development is irreversible, the same kinds of CAMs may be used in different contexts for regeneration and metamorphosis.

HISTOGENETIC PATHWAYS

The scheme we have elaborated leaves a further very important issue unresolved. How are histeregulatory genes controlled in such a fashion that, even at nearby terminal induction sites (e.g., pancreas and liver), completely different proteins are expressed in a stable manner that is fixed after cellular commitment? At this point, the data on gene cascades from the work on *Drosophila* are of particular significance. *It appears likely that certain sequences of regulatory-gene expression must restrict or inhibit the expression of sequences of other genes.* Thus *the expression of certain of these histeregulatory genes may preclude the expression of others as a result of the influence of selector genes that resemble homeotic genes.* The expression of particular sequences of morphoregulatory genes in cycles and networks may epigenetically first restrict the signals to histeregulatory genes in particular groups. Whether certain of these histeregulatory genes are in addition linked under similar *cis* or *trans* controls remains a subject for investigation.

An enormous body of work is now converging upon the issue of the regulation of tissue-specific genes in animal cells—enhancers, upstream regulators, *cis-* and *trans-*acting factors. Moreover, the characterization of genes for growth factors and oncogenes and the analysis of DNA-binding elements contiguous to homeo-box sequences should, together with this work, yield a much clearer picture of developmental gene regulation. This is not the place to review these important issues; the interested reader may consult some of the reviews mentioned in the reference list. At this point, it is nevertheless worth mentioning that mutations in sequences specifying DNA-binding domains could alter their specificity for regulatory sequences in the genome. Many onco-gene and homeobox products are in fact expressed during mor-phogenesis and often in spatially and temporally restricted patterns. Candidate signals for induction such as TGF-β are be-ginning to be identified. Moreover, cephalocaudal distributions of different homeobox sequences are being identified in verte-brates. It would not be incompatible with the morphoregulator hypothesis if particular growth factors or morphogens were found to appear in specific spatiotemporal patterns during induc-tion and morphogenesis.

Given the assumptions of the morphoregulator hypothesis, it is reasonable to suggest that CAM genes will *not* be under control of tissue-specific enhancer elements. Instead, one would expect that morphoregulatory genes for CAMs will have a characteristic reversible response to specific signals, which can operate inde-pendently of signals to tissue-specific historegulatory genes. It is these latter genes that one would expect to respond more or less irreversibly to their signals.

According to the morphoregulator hypothesis, it is thus likely (in analogy to homeotic genes in *Drosophila*) that selector genes (or S genes) exist that allow this local expression of certain sets of historegulatory genes and at the same time restrict the expres-sion of others (see figure 8.3). S genes need not be numerous but could be activated in different sequences in different locations to yield a large set of different sequences of cytodifferentiation. Activation of S genes by induction may result in the formation of DNA-binding proteins with such a role. Whatever the case, it is clear that such a "modular" organization, limiting historegula-tory responses to certain sequences of gene expression, must be present in addition to CAM cycles and SAM modulation net-works in order to account for the details of histogenesis *at partic-ular locations*. Although, in general, morphoregulatory genes act first, at no time is it precluded that a small number of historegulatory genes are engaged before morphoregulatory genes act. Indeed, in certain mesenchymal cells, such events could account for the restriction of their inductive potential before any extensive morphogenetic shaping takes place.

To the uninitiated reader, it is only fair to say that, in considering historegulation, I have not discussed many subjects that are essential to molecular embryology and particularly to molecular histology. These include the control of mitotic lineages, the activity of various growth factors, and the details of differentiation itself. One wishes to know where and when differentiation occurs, how it is related to various cell lineages, and how its timing is controlled in detail. These are all very important, as their extensive coverage by many authors indicates. But I do not believe that, necessary as they are, they can alone explain how morphology is related to gene action. I have emphasized the idea that only through linkage by morphoregulatory molecules of cells into collectives can the coordinated release of such factors and the response to them yield form and tissue. In the morphoregulator hypothesis, the details of driving force processes such as cell division and movement and the signals that drive them are treated in black-box fashion. If the overall outline of the hypothesis is confirmed, it will be increasingly important to understand the details of these processes so that we may explain the origin of particular histologies.

In brief summary, and as a suggested answer to the developmental genetic question, we may say that, according to the morphoregulator hypothesis, the regulatory path consists of chemical signals and mechanochemical signals (resulting in global modulation) that together switch morphoregulatory genes for CAMs. CAMs and SAMs then regulate morphogenetic motion and, indirectly, mitosis, and these together affect induction between pairs of collectives. At certain sites, this in turn switches on selector genes and particular historegulatory genes and also switches the CAM morphoregulatory genes on or off in CAM cycles. The changes in cell shape or motility and alteration of CAM chemistry that result from historegulatory gene action can lead to altered form even if expression of a given CAM cycle remains unchanged. SAM modulatory networks play a role in governing

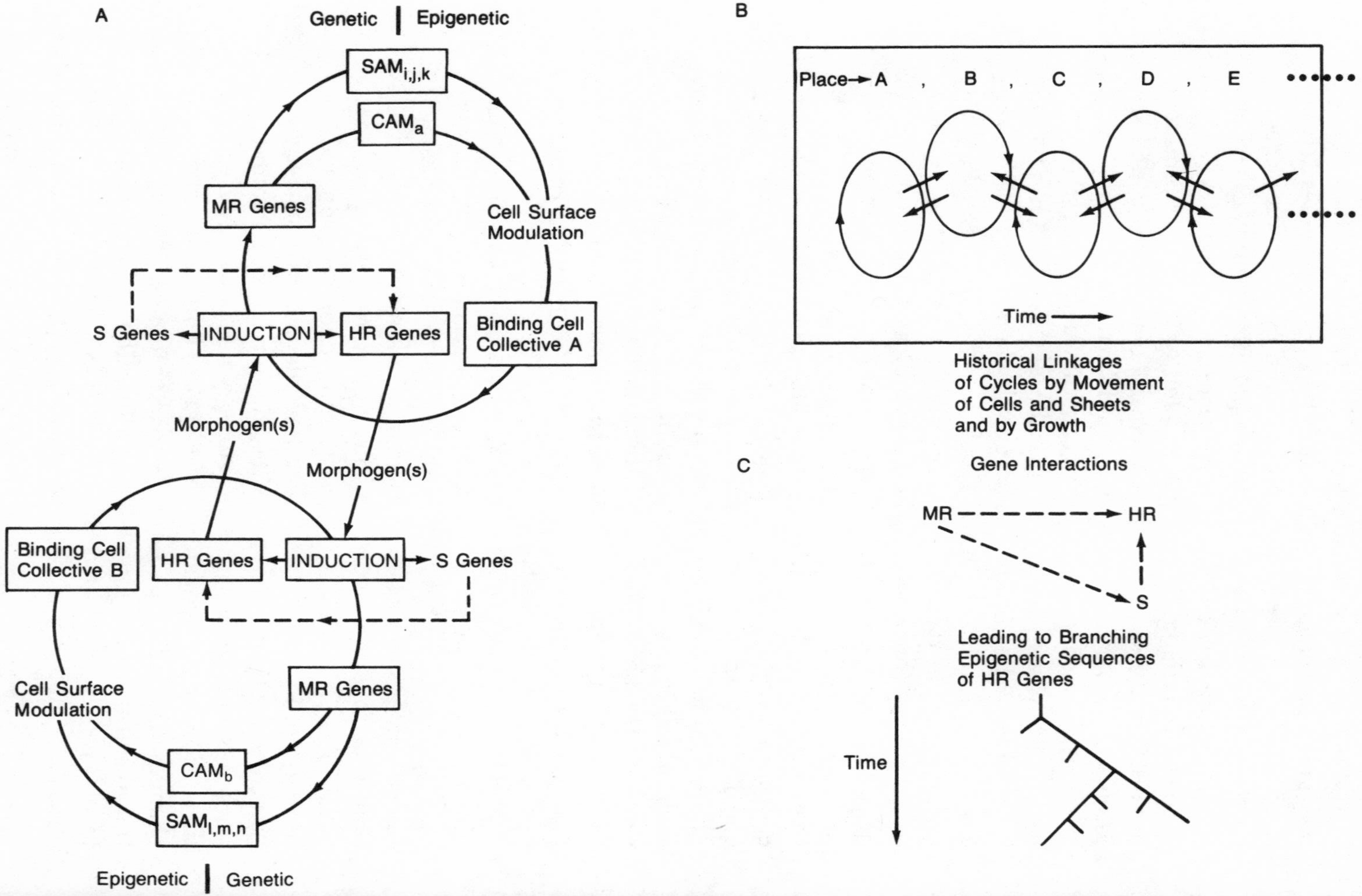

A

Genetic | Epigenetic

$SAM_{i,j,k}$ — CAM_a

Cell Surface Modulation

Binding Cell Collective A

HR Genes

MR Genes

INDUCTION

S Genes

Morphogen(s)

Morphogen(s)

INDUCTION — S Genes

HR Genes

Binding Cell Collective B

MR Genes

CAM_b — $SAM_{l,m,n}$

Cell Surface Modulation

Epigenetic | Genetic

B

Place → A , B , C , D , E

Time →

Historical Linkages of Cycles by Movement of Cells and Sheets and by Growth

C

Gene Interactions

MR ---→ HR ←--- S

Leading to Branching Epigenetic Sequences of HR Genes

Time →

which primary process acts, and they also determine epithelial-mesenchymal transformations and cell migrations. In these various ways, mechanochemical events are linked to gene action in epigenetic sequences.

An outline of the morphoregulator hypothesis and its conditions was already given in table 8.1. A diagram incorporating the mutual effects of MR, HR, and S genes as they are coupled by CAMs and SAMs acting on two cell collectives that are mutually inducing is given in figure 8.4. As the figure indicates, a historical sequence of such interactions linked by movement (and therefore affected by CJMs) leads to form and pattern in a given species. The temporal factors governing the response of MR, H, and S genes must be set by evolutionary alterations of various signal thresholds for *cis* and *trans* regulation. As we will see in the next chapter, the morphoregulator hypothesis provides a means of explaining several aspects of the evolutionary question, ranging from the nature of developmental constraints on evolution to the mechanistic bases for the heterochrony that provides a major developmental means of affecting morphologic evolution.

Figure 8.4

Combined responses of MR and HR genes in interacting cell collectives subject to CAM cycles. MR genes for SAMs and CAMs affect global modulation, which conditions whether cells will change shape, move, or divide; they also affect local modulation, which couples cells in a collective. S genes suppress HR gene expression at particular times and places; HR genes affect cytodifferentiation. The cycle starts when a morphogen (an HR gene product of collective A) triggers induction of a collective of cells linked by CAMs that is globally modulated by SAMs. This collective (B) releases a second morphogen or morphogens, which then alters the original collective. As is suggested in panel B, a succession of such signals across different collectives formed in time at different places and with varying rates of movement and growth could give rise to form. In such interactions, there is control by a cascade of genes (see panel C), but unlike the repeated expression of CAM genes, the epigenetic sequences of structural gene expression will show a branching pattern in time. CAM_a, a given CAM; CAM_b, a different CAM; HR, historegulatory; MR, morphoregulatory; $SAM_{i,j,k}$, $SAM_{l,m,n}$, different SAM modulatory networks; S, selector. In an actual case, cells in a single collective may express more than one CAM. See also table 8.1.

SELECTED REFERENCES

Edelman, G. M. 1984. Cell adhesion and morphogenesis: The regulator hypothesis. *Proc. Natl. Acad. Sci. USA* 81:1460–64.

———. 1985. Expression of cell adhesion molecules during embryogenesis and regeneration. *Exp. Cell Res.* 161:1–16.

———. 1985. Evolution and morphogenesis: The regulator hypothesis. In *Stadler genetics symposium series on genetics, development, and evolution*, ed. T. Gustafson, L. Stebbins, and F. J. Ayala, 1–28. New York: Plenum.

———. 1986. Molecular mechanisms of morphological evolution. In *Molecular evolution of life*, Chemica Scripta, vol. 26B, ed. H. Baltscheffsky, H. Jörnvall, and R. Rigler, 363–75. Cambridge: Cambridge University Press.

Gehring, W. J. 1987. Homeoboxes in the study of development. *Science* 236: 1245–52.

Ruddle, F. H., C. P. Hart, A. Awgulewitsch, A. Fainsod, M. Utset, D. Dalton, N. Kerk, M. Rabin, A. Ferguson-Smith, A. Fienberg, and W. Mcginnis. 1985. Mammalian homeo box genes. *Cold Spring Harbor Symp. Quant. Biol.* 50: 277–84.

Krumlauf, R., P. W. H. Holland, J. H. McVey, and B. L. M. Hogan. 1987. Developmental and spatial patterns of expression of the mouse homeobox gene *HOX 2.1*. *Development* 99:603–17.

Sharpe, C. R., A. Fritz, E. M. DeRobertis, and J. B. Gurdon. 1987. A homeobox-containing marker of posterior neural differentiation shows the importance of predetermination in neural induction. *Cell* 50:749–58.

Adamson, E. D. 1987. Oncogenes in development. *Development* 99:449–71.

Wilkinson, D. G., J. A. Bailes, and A. P. McMaleon. 1987. Expression of the proto-oncogene *int-1* is restricted to specific neural cells in the development of mouse embryos. *Cell* 50:79–88.

Smith, J. C. 1987. A mesoderm-inducing factor is produced by a *Xenopus* cell line. *Development* 99:3–14.

Weeks, D. L., and D. A. Melton. 1987. A maternal mRNA localized to the vegetal hemisphere in *Xenopus* eggs codes for a growth factor related to TGF-β. *Cell* 51:861–67.

Rosa, F., A. B. Roberts, D. Danielpour, L. L. Dart, M. B. Sporn, and I. B. Dawid. 1988. Mesoderm induction in amphibians: The role of TGF-β2–like factors. *Science* 239:783–85.

Serfling E., M. Jasin, and W. Schaffner. 1985. Enhancers and eukaryotic gene transcription. *Trends Genet.* 1:224–30.

See also John and Miklos in chapter 4, Jacobson et al. and Thiery in chapter 6, and Gallin et al. (1986) in chapter 7.

9

The Evolutionary
Question

IN CHAPTER 5, it was pointed out that no mechanistic explanation of development, not even one complete at the molecular
level, is sufficient to account for a particular morphology. Instead,
it was suggested that a mutual interaction was required between
evolutionary processes selecting for form and the developmental
genetic processes leading to its emergence. It was further suggested that phenotypic transformation in evolution occurred as
a result of the natural selection of forms arising mainly from
genetically mediated changes that affect developmental dynamics. This implies not only that there are general biological and
ecological factors affecting the evolutionary emergence of animal form but also that there are developmental constraints on
evolution. We are brought back to the evolutionary question in
a more specific form: *How is the morphoregulator hypothesis,
which was proposed to answer the developmental genetic question, reconciled with extensive changes in animal form in relatively short evolutionary time periods?*

We will reconsider this question here in terms of the developmental and topobiological mechanisms suggested in previous
chapters. The main aim is to explain how the morphoregulator
hypothesis can rationalize the relation between genetic change

and heterochrony, postulated to be a major evolutionary basis for change in form (see chapter 5). A secondary aim is to consider how particular developmental constraints on evolution arise as a result of topobiological interactions among primary processes. In other words, we are concerned first with how evolution affects development and then with how development affects evolution.

NONLINEAR RELATIONS BETWEEN GENETICS, DEVELOPMENT, AND EVOLUTION

Before carrying out this program, we must review a number of facts and conclusions related to the actual means by which various genetic mechanisms can give rise to morphologic novelty. First, it is important to understand that *development of form cannot be straightforwardly related to genetic change, because the relation of function to new morphologic structures is not simple or direct.* This conclusion follows from a variety of factors that are worth listing because they set the evolutionary question in perspective. (1) Development is driven by primary processes that show stochastic and nonlinear local interactions that depend upon local mechanochemical factors, and these are not prefigured in genes. (2) There are topobiological constraints upon the size, movement, and interaction of cell collectives, and, as a result, certain interactions cannot be mechanically realized. (3) Different developmental pathways can in some cases lead to the same morphologic result. We will call this developmental degeneracy. (4) During early periods, in which morphology is isolated from function, development has a self-regulating character. This self-regulation results from threshold dependences upon signaling processes operating at multiple levels and scales, ranging from the gene to organized cell collectives. (5) Certain major genetic controls of continuous morphologic change are polygenic, and the effects of even a single gene on such change can be pleiotropic. In other words, a mutation can lead simultaneously to more than one form of morphologic change. (6) Later *compensatory* functional interactions between large-scale but separate developmental systems such as bones, muscles, and the nervous system can alter the phenotypic effects of genetically induced variation. (7) Similarly, changes in the *behavior* of an animal of a given phenotype (upon which natural selection acts) can compensate for genetically induced changes. Behavior thus is in fact a continuation of certain developmental processes, as we will see in the next chapter. (8) Natural selection of actual morphologic forms is conditioned by ecological variables acting on the adult phenotype. Because these are historical, even a complete answer to the developmental genetic question in terms of proximate causes could not alone account for actual developmental sequences.

All of these factors set limits on the evolution of phenotypes, morphologic novelties, and adaptations. By *morphologic novelty,* I mean macroevolutionary changes such as the transition from reptilian scales to feathers. By *adaptation,* I refer to the process by which organisms change to increase fitness. In the Darwinian sense, this is the expected number of offspring produced by a type. In the Fisherian sense, it means the per capita rate of increase of a type. Although, in some evolutionary contexts, the effects of qualitative changes in a gene product can be related directly to such notions of fitness, we conclude from our list of factors that, in morphologic evolution, this is generally not true. Clearly, neither adaptation alone nor morphologic novelty alone suffices to account for the existence and fitness of phenotypes— both must operate within particular developmental and ecological constraints.

Although we will take the position here that epigenesis can provide the major basis for change in animal form, its dynamics are constrained by the need to match the various primary processes of development. The picture of these dynamics painted in previous chapters indicates that they are context dependent, self-regulating, and nonlinear. Large changes in some of the primary processes can have relatively small effects. On the other hand, relatively small changes in *certain locations that are topobiologically significant* can have huge effects. It is useful to give a few examples of those effects, illustrating some of the listed factors that tend to mask the relation between fitness and genetic change. I will choose for brief mention examples of developmental degeneracy, developmental self-regulation, and some instances of compensatory functional interactions to illustrate these nonlinearities; all three factors can have marked effects on evolution.

A good example of developmental degeneracy is seen in the morphology of the scapula in different species, as was shown by Oxnard. Extensive analysis reveals that the scapulae of a large number of mammalian species fall into three forms. The functions of the shoulder in locomotion apparently sharply constrain the myriad possible shapes of mammalian shoulder girdles. One variate separates different monkeys and apes in relation to the tensile forces the shoulder can withstand. A second separates arboreal and terrestrial forms and is related to the advantage of placing the shoulder joint more laterally yielding the greater mobility required in trees. The third separates man, baboons, and ungulates from all other forms and, in the last of the species, seems to be linked to the need to place the scapula more distally for greater extension in running. These variates were almost certainly achieved by a variety of developmental pathways, and this example of developmental degeneracy shows how indirect and context dependent is the constrained selection for final function of the small number of morphologic structures derived from these pathways.

The self-regulating character of development and the effects of selection on development itself provides another example that must also be carefully analyzed. In his classic work, the great embryologist Roux pointed out that development can be separated into an autonomous period, in which organization can be constructed independently of activity, and a subsequent period, in which the epigenetic sequences and growth depend upon functional activity. In certain species such as *Ambystoma,* there may be a remarkable and relatively fixed sequence of neuromuscular and musculoskeletal activities leading to immediate coordinated behavior after hatching. In other species with elaborate motor skills such as cats or monkeys, however, the patterns of motion in the fetus are neither apparent sequences nor emergent replicas of the later motions of the born behaving animal (see table 9.1). Behavioral embryology thus covers a wide range of evolutionary variates, and their character is a complex function of phenotypic selection.

We will consider some developmental bases of behavior sepa-

TABLE 9.1

Some Examples of Compensation and Nonlinear Functional Interactions of Morphological Elements

---

1. Neuromuscular activity to yield appropriate synaptic connections to muscle. Motor behavior in development unrelated to adult motor patterns (see Hamburger 1963).
2. Sequenced motor patterns in development related to adult behavior (in *Ambystoma*—see Coghill 1929).
3. Adaptability of muscle and bone to altered stresses in adult that are compensatory for early morphology. Evolutionary changes in jawbone of piranha fish entail large rearrangements of structure of head and muscle insertions (see Alexander 1975).
4. Requirement for two stages, one without and the second with neural activity to produce neural mappings (e.g., retinotectal projections—see Schmidt 1985).
5. Adaptive alteration of motor pattern after evolutionary change in muscle insertion with subsequent large alteration in adaptive radiation patterns (cichlid fish—see Liem 1974, 1980).
6. Neuronal group selection in somatic time (see chapter 10).

---

rately in part four. Here we may usefully mention some further related examples illustrating the compensatory interactions of nervous, muscular, and skeletal systems and showing how indirectly and yet how profoundly genetic change may affect final behavioral function (table 9.1). Of these examples, perhaps the most striking are the consequences of changes in the pharyngeal jaws of cichlid fish. During evolution, these fish developed a synarthrosis of the lower jaw, synovial joints in the upper jaws, and an important shift of the insertion of their fourth levator muscles. These structural changes led to an important functional change that separated the grasping, mastication, and deglutition of food. This change freed the premaxillary and mandibular jaws to evolve different specializations for different foods in different species and led to an explosive adaptive radiation and concomitant rich morphologic variation. That the brain and nervous system could adapt to such changes without immediate compensatory mutation is yet another example of the effects of epigenetic compensatory mechanisms in morphogenetic change.

All of these observations on developmental degeneracy, nonlinear functional interactions, and compensatory functional interactions indicate that, although the effects of morphogenetic change can be very indirect, they can nonetheless be enormously significant. Before dwelling further on the issue of how flexible various epigenetic mechanisms are, we may ask how they themselves respond directly to mechanisms of mutation and selection. The examples we have chosen so far must not blind us to the fact that development itself, though not *simply* related to mutational change, is nevertheless greatly susceptible to mutation and selection at early stages. Inductive mechanisms can change in phylogeny, for example, and the same structures can arise evolutionarily by a different series of mechanisms. Examples of the latter include differences both in gastrulation mechanisms (fish, chick, frog) and in formation of the neural tube (see chapters 3 and 6 and the references by Ballard and by Alberch).

The evidence I have reviewed so far makes a convincing case that development bears a nonlinear relation to mutational change. Given the self-organizing and threshold-determined character of development, it is not surprising that *most* genetic change alters developmental processes by alterations not of structural genes but of particular regulatory genes, as is proposed in the morphoregulator hypothesis. *But the evidence also indicates that this conclusion is not sufficient to answer the evolutionary question. We obviously need a combined genetic and epigenetic analysis, interpreted in terms of ecological requirements.* We turn now to that analysis, first taking up a new view of the mechanism and meaning of heterochrony based on the morphoregulator hypothesis and then reconsidering what the existence of developmental constraints on evolution means in terms of the hypothesis.

CAM AND SAM REGULATION AS A BASIS FOR HETEROCHRONY

It may be useful to summarize the morphoregulator hypothesis in a slightly different form in order to show how it provides a molecular framework relating developmental genetics and morphogenesis to evolution. As it applies to developmental genetics, the hypothesis can be succinctly expressed in the following six statements.

(1) Cell adhesion molecules (CAMs) play a central role in morphogenesis by acting through adhesion as steersmen or regulators for other primary processes, particularly morphogenetic movements. CAMs exercise their regulatory role by means of local cell surface modulation. (2) Genes for CAMs—and, to some extent, for SAMs—are expressed under control of morphoregulatory genes in schedules that are prior to and relatively independent of genes for expression of particular networks of cytodifferentiation in different organs. (3) This control of CAM and SAM structural genes by morphoregulatory genes is responsible for the body plan, as is seen in fate maps. In animals such as the chicken, this plan is reflected in a topological order: for example, a simply connected central region of N-CAM surrounded by a contiguous simply connected ring of cells expressing L-CAM. As we might expect from statement 2, CAM boundaries in such maps overlap named tissue boundaries. We will illustrate this later in figure 9.1. (4) Morphogenetic movements are resultants of the inherent motility of cells and of CAM expression as it is coordinated with the presence of substrate adhesion molecules (SAMs) such as fibronectin and cytotactin. Such movements, regulated by CAM and SAM modulation, are responsible for bringing cells of different history together to create various embryonic inductions. (5) CAMs can be expressed in cycles during histogenesis, and their expression in neighboring inducing collectives helps delineate borders between inducing collectives. At certain stages, induction events can also lead to expression of historegulatory genes, some of which are under the control of selector genes; the resultant cytodifferentiation is coordinated with CAM type. (6) Complementing the action of CAMs, SAMs can form modulatory networks that alter the character of cell migration, the folding of epithelia, and mitotic responses that lead to pattern.

According to this summary picture, although the primary processes provide the key morphogenetic driving forces, *the temporally regulated expression* of morphoregulatory genes and particular historegulatory and selector genes provides a large part of the *selectivity* that guides and kinetically constrains the interaction of primary processes during the generation of form.

The morphoregulator hypothesis can now be extended to suggest that CAM and SAM gene regulation provides a *molecular basis for heterochrony*. According to the classic view, heterochrony is a genetically controlled change in the developmental rates of appearance of the *morphologic traits or characters* seen in ancestors. In chapter 5, we mentioned Gould's account of how Haeckel, who invented the term, came to grief by emphasizing recapitulation as the main mode by which ontogeny and phylogeny are related. To account for this relation, Gould proposed instead a series of heterochronic states based on alterations in regulatory genes. These include various kinds of heterochrony such as neoteny, progenesis, paedomorphosis, and hypermorphosis. (For details, the reader should consult Gould's book, referenced in chapter 5.) It might seem that this heterochronic analysis in terms of morphologic structures leaves the field to von Baer, whose laws (see chapter 5) may appear at this level to be correct. But a number of exceptions to his formulation also occur. Von Baer's formulation fails, for example, in comparing early events such as gastrulation, which in some vertebrates differs in detail both temporally and geometrically. The possibility must be raised that *heterochrony applied at the level of formed tissue structures considered to be homologous is an inadequate concept and that a different basis is necessary to explain heterochronic change.* Instead, if the genetic control of morphogenesis is as indirect as I described it in the preceding section, it is perhaps no surprise that establishing homologies of structures does not lead to a secure means of understanding phylogenetic connections of developmental events.

How can the issue be reconciled? I propose that heterochrony may be explained in terms of *molecular* embryology, that is, in terms of morphoregulatory molecules whose regulation is based on topobiological principles. We must therefore see whether the morphoregulator hypothesis can be applied to resolve the evolutionary question. The pivotal point of the hypothesis is that CAMs at the cell surface act either directly or indirectly to influence primary processes. Even in very early events such as gastrulation, CAM expression must, for example, play a direct role in the control of motion that is the result of the play between cellular motility, tension in tissue sheets, and adhesion. Whether a cell moves is determined by a balance between its inherent motility and the alternative opportunities provided by cell-cell adhesion mediated by CAMs and by cell-substrate adhesion mediated by SAMs. Differences in mobility and in epithelial-mesenchymal transformation caused by small changes in the regulation of such molecules could lead to large changes in the geometry of gastrulation, for instance.

The key proposal is that small changes in the response times of morphoregulatory genes for CAMs and SAMs as a result of mutations affecting cis- *or* trans-*acting elements could lead to large nonlinear changes in expression sequences and morphology.* The results of this molecular heterochrony could be far-reaching. According to this picture, it is possible to understand why different vertebrates might share a basic body plan and yet have different gastrulation patterns, morphogenetic movements, and details in their fate maps. Natural selection during evolution would allow only those organisms to survive in which individual particular combinations of variant morphogenetic movements and variant CAM gene expressions led to the appropriate functional inductive sequences. But more than one such covariant combination could occur (another form of developmental degeneracy), and successful combinations of movement patterns and gene expression that are quite variant from species to species (even at early developmental stages) could yield *similar inductive sequences.* In this scheme, natural selection acts to eliminate inappropriate movements by selecting against organisms that express CAM genes in sequences leading to failure of induction. On the other hand, any variant combination of movements and timing of CAM gene expression (resulting from variation in morphoregulatory genes) that leads to appropriate inductive sequences will in general be evolutionarily allowed. Whether that selection takes place or not depends upon the phenotypic expression of the altered form and upon its effects on fitness.

If this key extension of the morphoregulator hypothesis is true, large morphological variations will be possible in short evolutionary times because of the enormous effects upon morphogenesis of even small permitted changes in CAM or SAM regulatory genes. This analysis suggests a plausible way by which the critical early determinants of form can arise from certain embryonic molecular processes: structural genes for a few CAMs of different specificity are expressed according to an evolutionarily stabilized topological plan and under temporal control of morphoregulatory genes that are largely independent of the historegulatory genes involved in later cytodifferentiation. This allows for great variation in the details of fate maps from species to species (see figure 9.1) but at the same time tends to conserve the basic body plan. This does not imply that a new body plan cannot arise by such means. However, because of the rarity of satisfactory major changes and because of the ecological constraints discussed in chapter 5, a major change of this type is very unlikely to occur.

The morphoregulator hypothesis asserts that CAM and SAM regulatory genes are the *minimal* set likely to be instrumental in morphologic evolution, although other genes affecting the primary processes would obviously be equally important at certain developmental stages. For example, independent but *covariant* alterations occur in morphogenetic cell movements, and timing of CAM regulatory gene expression during evolution could lead to similar functioning phenotypes both at the developmental level and in the behaving animal.

A major prediction of the hypothesis, as it bears on this idea of covariance, is that the CAM fate maps (see figure 9.1 for an explanation) of organisms such as chick and the frog will be highly similar despite the large differences in early morphogenetic movements, geometry, and topographic details seen in the two species of embryo. The *topology* is expected to be the same in various species with similar body plans because similar inductive sequences within and between different germ layers in all likelihood require similar borders between different CAMs. This topological requirement would be strongest at the earliest times (for example, in primary induction), and it would also hold for the distribution among particular germ layers of a given kind of CAM. Occasional deviations, if they occur at all, would be expected only at later times of organogenesis, when most inductions have already occurred. Recent experiments have lent strong support to this prediction—chick and frog CAM fate maps (figure 9.1) and expression sequences reflecting CAM rules are similar, but consistent with the idea of molecular heterochrony, the two species show clear-cut differences in the *relative timing* of primary CAM expression during development.

This extension of the morphoregulator hypothesis simplifies certain problems of relating genetic change to evolutionary change. Because of the wide dynamic range and possible temporal permutations of cell surface modulation events, for example, the developmental and evolutionary effects of the variant expression of a rather small number of genes related to cell adhesion could be momentous. The assumptions made in the morphoregulator hypothesis are thus genetically parsimonious: *small changes* in timing or response by alterations of a small number of CAM or SAM regulatory genes could have large nonlinear effects upon form and pattern in relatively short periods of evolutionary time. These changes could occur without the need for large numbers of complementary changes in many different structural genes. The parallel nature of the loops of the CAM cycle and combinatorial aspects of the SAM modulation network would allow florid variations within the same general morphologic scheme. It is not difficult to incorporate into this scheme molecular heterochronic mechanisms leading to various changes in form related to sexual maturation such as progenesis, neoteny, and paedomorphosis (see Gould): small changes in the timing of expression of morphoregulatory genes for CAMs in the cycle (possibly under direct or indirect hormonal influences) could lead to large changes in form that could be effected readily by driving force processes in development. The changed forms could then be selected in evolution because of their adaptive advantages. This implies that the actual response characteristics of CAM and SAM regulatory genes and the kinds of signals leading to these responses in a given species are determined within that species by these ecological variables, not merely by ontogenetic events.

The key idea underlying the proposal of the morphoregulator hypothesis as a basis for heterochrony is that morphologic resemblances in different species will be in terms of timetables and sequences of CAM and SAM expression, and that various large changes in form will occur by small changes in the responses to signals of CAM and SAM regulatory genes. Such changes as are seen in paedomorphosis or neoteny are ascribed in this view to alterations in the extent to which various developmental primary processes are allowed to continue before switching to a new CAM cycle or modulation network. Delay could, for example,

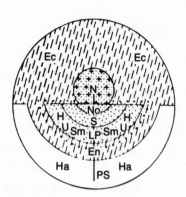

A

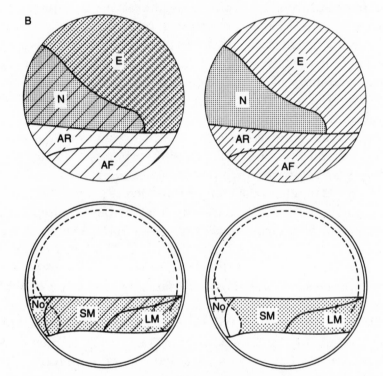

B

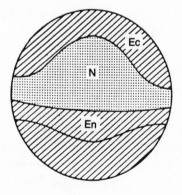

C

lead to size changes involving extensive mitosis and growth. Acceleration could lead to diminution in the size of inducing collectives, with nonlinear consequences for subsequent events.

One of the most intriguing possibilities is that these effects on CAM linkage could take place in endocrine areas during metamorphosis, leading to massive changes in the release of hormones affecting target areas. Conversely, metamorphic target areas may, unlike their neighboring tissues, have indefinitely delayed expression or sequencing of CAM cycles, an expression that

Figure 9.1

Comparison of composite CAM fate maps in chick and frog. Classic fate maps are constructed by labeling cells and following their fates, mapping the origin of these cells or their progeny onto a chosen structure at a given stage (see Slack 1983, in reference list to chapter 3, for further discussion). The structures chosen here for mapping and comparison are the chick blastoderm (A) or the frog gastrula (B, C), and the regions mapped are for a stage after major organ formation. A composite CAM fate map consists of CAM developmental distributions mapped onto a classic fate map. A: Chick. The distribution of N-CAM (stipple), L-CAM (slashes), and Ng-CAM (crosses) on tissues of five- to fourteen-day-old embryos is mapped back onto the tissue precursor cells in the blastoderm. Additional regions of N-CAM staining in the early embryo (five days) are shown by larger dots. In the early embryo, the borders of CAM expression overlap the borders of the germ layers, that is, derivatives of all three germ layers express both CAMs. At later times, overlap is more restricted, as a result of operation of CAM rules (see figure 7.3). N-CAM disappears from somatic ectoderm and from endoderm, except for a population of cells in the lung. L-CAM is expressed on all ectodermal and endodermal epithelia but remains restricted in the mesoderm to epithelial derivatives of the urogenital system. The vertical bar represents the primitive streak (PS); Ec = intraembryonic and extraembryonic ectoderm; En = endoderm; N = nervous system; No = prechordal and chordamesoderm; S = somite; Sm = smooth muscle; Ha = hemangioblastic area; H = heart; LP = lateral plate mesoderm; U = urogenital system. B: CAM fate maps in the frog Xenopus, comparing the areas of the superficial and deep layer of the embryo that will give rise to tissues expressing either N-CAM (dotted) or L-CAM (slashed) at stage 20 of development (top left) or in the adult (top right). Fate maps at top left and middle are seen rotated 90° compared with those of the chick; both superficial and deep layers are shown. Just as in the chicken, after an initial overlapping of the territories of expression of the two CAMs, these molecules became segregated in two contiguous and simply connected regions in the adult. The presence of N-CAM in frog adult muscle and heart was determined biochemically; all other determinations were made by immunocytochemistry. C: The frog adult composite map for the superficial layers (B, top right), rotated 90°; compare with A, the map for the chick. N, prospective neural area; E, prospective epidermal area; AR, prospective archenteron roof; AF, prospective archenteron floor; SM, prospective somite mesoderm; LM, prospective lateral mesoderm. See figure 6.5 for diagrams of gastrulation in frog embryos. (Modified from K. L. Crossin, S. Hoffman, M. Grumet, J.-P. Thiery, and G. M. Edelman, 1986, Site-restricted expression of cytotactin during development of the chicken embryo, J. Cell Biol. 102:1917–30 [A]; and G. Levi, K. L. Crossin, and G. M. Edelman, 1987, Expression sequences and distribution of two primary cell adhesion molecules during embryonic development of Xenopus laevis, J. Cell Biol. 105: 2359–72 [B].)

is invigorated only after the appropriate hormonal stimulus appears at metamorphosis. Very large or structurally radical changes could occur by either or both of these means. One can envision, therefore, that the morphoregulator hypothesis may be directly applicable to metamorphosing or regenerating systems. A particularly important feature of the hypothesis is that *it allows dissociation of developmental effects in different regions, down to the scale of inducing collectives, which in certain instances could decrease in size and number of cells to some minimal level during evolution.* This allows developmental and evolutionary flexibility and also decouples local morphologic changes from general processes of size increase or growth.

During development, thousands of genes must be expressed to provide a functioning phenotype. The genetic parsimony of the morphoregulator hypothesis is applicable to CAM and SAM genes but not necessarily to the historegulatory genes that are an equally important part of a CAM cycle. Against the topobiological background provided by morphoregulatory gene products, evolution of historegulatory genes could be elaborate. This would result in modulation of primary processes, refinement of regional function, and even, in some cases, to alteration of form itself. Such cases might include changes in polysialyl transferase enzymes altering N-CAM binding, changes in cytoskeletal elements modifying cellular motility, and elaboration of novel peptide signaling elements altering rates of CAM or SAM production.

One of the challenging tasks of molecular embryology will be to determine the minimal number of morphoregulatory and historegulatory genes necessary to specify a complex appendage or organ and to identify which of these genes are affected by S genes. One prediction of the morphoregulator hypothesis is that the ratio of morphoregulatory to historegulatory genes is small. Another is that the actual molecules mediating the signaling steps in induction need not constitute a very large or exotic repertoire. Growth factors and various peptides are reasonable candidates for this role; although one would expect to find a variety of such factors of different specificity, place of expression and history of expression are expected to dominate the effects of signaling.

This survey and extension of the morphoregulator hypothesis suggests a resolution to the problem of how small numbers of genetic changes can lead to relatively large changes in form and phenotypic function in relatively short evolutionary times. But, however effective, the powers of such topobiological systems are not unlimited. Indeed, because of their very topobiological character, they place sharp constraints on the forms that can be achieved, even in the absence of stabilizing selection by ecological variables, as was discussed in chapter 5. Let us turn, finally, to this issue, which illustrates that *genetics and epigenetics must act together to yield a balance between the creation of possible morphological novelty and various functionally adaptive developmental constraints. It is this balance that gives rise to phenotypic diversity and that accounts for the scarcity or absence of certain phenotypes.*

DEVELOPMENTAL CONSTRAINTS ARISING FROM TOPOBIOLOGICAL CONSTRAINTS

Developmental events provide a strong basis for the evolution of new forms. However, given the very nonlinear character of CAM cycles and SAM modulation networks and their dependence upon complex mechanochemical events and sequences, it is clear that certain combinations and interactions must fail. This is because successful inductive sequences depend both on molecular dynamics and on the covariance of driving force processes to yield the next set of signals for further epigenetic change. Aside from weakly adapted forms that might survive, there are downright failures and impossibilities inherent in particular topobiological combinations.

A variety of strong limits are placed upon certain innovations. These include (1) the limits of cellular mechanochemical processes (e.g., speed of cellular motion, tension, response times of cytoskeletal elements); (2) the continuity requirements and size limits of collectives involved in induction; (3) the large numbers of topobiological constraints on morphological movements of epithelia and migration of mesenchyme; (4) the spatial requirements for, and response times of, the signal loops from organized inducing collectives to regulatory genes; (5) the limits on the macroscopic properties and structure of materials forming the musculoskeletal system and connective tissue components of organs; and (6) the various limits of behavioral adaptations in organisms with richly endowed central nervous systems. The first four items on this list are concerned with constraints mainly affecting early developmental events, where environmental interactions are minimal. The last two items relate to limits of compensatory features (see table 9.1 and chapter 10) in which epigenetic alterations can occur (as in metamorphosis) during various actual environmental interactions with developing systems.

All of these constraints indicate that, even if the mechanisms proposed in the morphoregulator hypothesis apply, the number of *covariant* alterations in morphoregulatory genes interacting within the limits of control of primary processes to yield *successful* inductive structures must still be a very small fraction of all possible variants that might be produced. This is particularly true of changes early in development. Later alterations involving secondary CAMs and various historegulatory gene activities might have more "exploratory leeway" not only because of the reduced relative scale of cellular motion (see table 2.1 and figure 3.2) but also because cellular activity and function may come to dominate or compensate for the altered morphologic interactions resulting from genetic innovation (table 9.1). These nonlinear effects introduce discontinuities and directionalities into the morphogenetic process that must ultimately constrain the kinds of phenotypes that can be selected to increase fitness. This is just what would be expected if CAMs and SAMs provided a major link between the genetic code and the complex mechanochemical processes that result in three-dimensional form.

A remaining important problem, not considered in this book, is to understand how such a molecular view of heterochrony can be used to relate homologous structures in development. This task, which has been pursued by systematists since Haeckel, is particularly challenging because the dynamic molecular picture of morphogenesis painted here allows both for developmental degeneracy and for an extraordinary diversity of interactions among body parts that could yield the same functional result in a phenotype. Although one would in many cases expect homologies drawn from structure to hold across species lines, in other cases, structures that appear homologous may have arisen by different molecular dynamic paths and have been selected for similar function. Only by having a detailed knowledge of both the controlling genetic cascades (with comparisons of regulatory genes) and the related molecular and mechanochemical sequences of development will we understand the evolutionary connections of developmental and adult structures in related species. We are far from this level of detail. Meanwhile, the extended morphoregulator hypothesis provides a satisfying, albeit provisional, view of the relation between the developmental genetic question and the evolutionary question. The challenge is to subject this hypothesis to more extensive tests in a variety of species focusing on a clear-cut set of predictions. While it is by no means proven, it provides an intellectually satisfying framework within which developmental genetics and evolution may be related.

SELECTED REFERENCES

Ballard, W. W. 1981. Morphogenetic movements and fate maps of vertebrates. *Am. Zool.* 21:391–99.

Alberch, P. 1985. Problems with the interpretation of developmental sequences. *Syst. Zool.* 34:46–58.

———. 1987. The evolution of a developmental process. In *Marine biological laboratories lectures in biology,* vol. 8, ed. R. A. Raff and E. Raff, 23–46. New York: Alan R. Liss.

Ballard, W. W. 1976. Problems of gastrulation: Real and verbal. *Biol. Sci.* 26:36–39.

Løvtrup, S. 1974. *Epigenetics: A treatise on theoretical biology.* New York: Wiley.

Wright, S. 1932. The roles of mutation, inbreeding, cross-breeding, and selection in evolution. *Proc. Sixth Int. Congr. Genet.* 1:356–66. (See also R. N. Brandon and R. M. Bevrian. 1984. *Genes, organisms, populations: Controversies over the units of selection.* Cambridge: MIT Press.)

Edelman, G. M. 1986. Molecular mechanisms of morphological evolution. In *Molecular evolution of life,* Chemica Scripta, vol. 26B, ed. H. Baltscheffsky, H. Jörnvall, and R. Rigler, 363–75. Cambridge: Cambridge University Press.

Coghill, G. E. 1929. *Anatomy and the problem of behaviour.* Cambridge: Cambridge University Press. Reprint. New York: Hafner, 1965.

Hamburger, V. 1963. Some aspects of the embryology of behavior. *Q. Rev. Biol.* 38:342–65.

Alexander, R. M. 1975. Evolution of integrated design. *Am. Zool.* 15:419–25.

Schmidt, J. T. 1985. Factors involved in retinotopic map formation: Complementary roles for membrane recognition and activity-dependent synaptic stabilization. In *Molecular bases of neural development,* ed. G. M. Edelman, W. E. Gall, and W. M. Cowan, 453–80. New York: Wiley.

Bock, W. J. 1965. The role of adaptive mechanisms in the origin of higher levels of organization. *Syst. Zool.* 14:272–87.

Oxnard, C. E. 1968. The architecture of the shoulder in some mammals. *J. Morphol.* 126:249–90.

Roux, W. 1984. The problems, methods, and scope of developmental mechanics. Reprinted in *Defining biology: Lectures from the 1890s,* ed. J. Maienschein, 105–48. Cambridge: Harvard University Press.

Maienschein, J., ed. 1986. *Defining biology: Lectures from the 1890s,* Cambridge: Harvard University Press.

Liem, K. F. 1974. Evolutionary strategies and morphological innervations: Cichlid pharyngeal jaws. *Syst. Zool.* 22:425–41.

———. 1980. Adaptive significance of intra- and interspecific differences in the feeding repertoires of cichlid fishes. *Am. Zool.* 20:295–314.

Lewontin, R. 1968. *Population biology and evolution.* Syracuse: Syracuse University Press.

See also references to Raff and Kaufman in chapter 1 and to Gould, Maynard Smith et al., Bonner, Arthur, and Alberch in chapter 5.

PART FOUR

DEVELOPMENT AND
BEHAVIOR

10

Developmental Variation
and Somatic Selection:
Neural Darwinism

I T MIGHT BE THOUGHT that the proposal of a provisionally satisfactory explanation reconciling morphologic evolution with developmental genetics would be a fitting ending point for an introduction to topobiology. But a special case will be made here for extending the inquiry into neurobiology and the development of the brain, for topobiology has reached its height of refinement in this structure. Moreover, the development and functioning of the brain offers a unique opportunity to inquire into the larger significance of epigenetic variation. In this chapter, we will therefore go beyond the molecular and cellular level, to the basis for the behavior of the whole animal, and attempt to show that topobiological principles are important to that behavior. This means that we will touch upon certain psychological and physiological issues not ordinarily considered to be part of developmental biology.

The most highly developed brains are morphologic marvels in which the principles we have discussed are exploited and extended in a staggeringly complex yet beautifully unified fashion. As we indicated in the preceding chapter, a number of the compensatory aspects of continuing morphogenesis are related to the brain and its connected neuromuscular and skeletal agents, the so-called motor ensemble. Furthermore, the actual behavior that arises from brain activities strongly affects phenotypic selection, and it in turn rests on special developmental principles. From the standpoint of topobiology, two of the most significant are the evolution of extensively connected mapped structures in the brain and the importance of somatic variation and selection in brain function. At the level of such function, we may mention two striking examples in which evolution and development interact: bird song, in which ethologically determined inherited patterns are mixed with learning, and perceptual categorization, in which an animal can generalize its recognition to a large variety of patterns after confronting only a few. These functions depend upon the development of neural maps and upon somatic or synaptic variation.

The functioning of the brain in behavior and the principles by which it develops pose severe challenges to any genetically determinist notion of development. Even the relatively large human genome has hardly a fraction of the DNA that would be required directly to specify the connectivity of the brain (see figure 2.1). If we consider the developmental and behavioral alterations of synapses, the requirements become even steeper. It must be that epigenetic principles underlie brain function, allowing somatic adaptation to novelty to occur. Consistent with this conclusion are the facts that during phylogeny the brain is the most variable of all complex organ systems and that in higher vertebrates the telencephalon (which gives rise to the cerebral cortex) is the most variable of brain regions.

It has been customary to consider the brain as a kind of computer with certain inherited programs that receive and code input information from the world and guide adaptive action accordingly by calculation. This instructionist point of view appears on the surface to have much merit, but upon close scrutiny it is not easily reconciled with a variety of developmental, morphologic, and behavioral observations. I will suggest here instead that variance in developmental cellular populations can be a topobiological factor of major significance, the analysis of which gives rise to a new view of brain function. A number of key observations about this kind of variation have been made over the last decade.

A brief account of these challenging observations and of a particular population theory, the theory of neuronal group selection (especially its developmental aspects), will be presented here to show how morphogenetic events affect actual and potential brain function. This account, when taken together with the morphoregulator hypothesis, will indicate that the obligate variation in neural structure that arises as a result of topobiological mechanisms is not just "noise" (see page 183). Instead, the theory of neuronal group selection holds that variation in connectivity and signal patterns in individual brains is both adaptive and essential to the performance of subtle behaviors. To reveal this, we will provide just a sketch of the theory; the interested reader may consult original sources for greater detail. I will assume a minimal knowledge of neuroanatomy and discuss neural function in somewhat simplified terms.

The brain in complex animals, such as human beings, consists of sheets, or laminae, and of more or less rounded structures called nuclei. Each of these structures has evolved to carry out functions in a complex network of connections, and each consists of very large numbers of neurons. The connection to the outside world is by means of specialized neurons called sensory transducers, which make up sense organs and provide the input to the brain. The brain's output is by means of neurons to muscles and glands. In addition, parts of the brain (indeed, the major portion of its tissue) receive input only from other parts, and they give outputs to other parts without intervention from the outside.

How do neurons connect with each other, and how are they arranged within nuclei and laminae? The major means of connection is the synapse, a specialized structure in which electrical activity passed down the axon of the presynaptic neuron (figure 10.1) leads to release of a chemical (neurotransmitter) that in turn induces electrical activity in the postsynaptic neuron. As is shown diagrammatically in the figure, synapses can change their efficacy—presynaptically by changes in the amount and delivery of transmitter and postsynaptically by altering the chemical state of

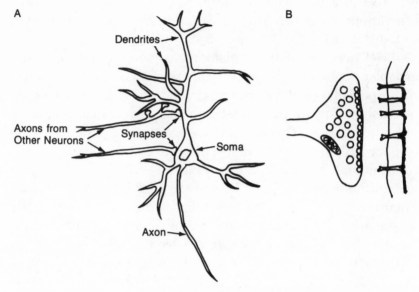

Figure 10.1

Simplified diagrams of neurons in circuits and of synapses. A: Axons from near or distant neurons make contact with a particular neuron either on its body (soma) or on its branching processes, called dendrites. Axons carry electrical activity that can release a neurotransmitter when it reaches a synapse; developing axons are called neurites. After interacting with appropriate receptors, the neurotransmitter in turn can trigger the recipient neuron (or postsynaptic neuron) to fire electrically. B: A synapse. The circles in the structure on the left represent vesicles containing neurotransmitter in the presynaptic neuron. The postsynaptic neuron projects receptors (the Y-shaped structures) into the cleft between the pre- and postsynaptic membranes. These receptors bind transmitter released from the presynaptic vesicles and trigger the responses of the postsynaptic neuron. (From G. M. Edelman, 1985, Neural Darwinism: Population thinking and higher brain function, in How we know, *ed. M. Shafto, 1–30, San Francisco: Harper & Row.)*

receptors and ion channels. Neurons themselves can be arranged anatomically in a variety of complex ways but are sometimes disposed into maps, a very important principle in complex brains. An example is the correspondence of portions of the cerebral cortex responsive to light touch on the skin to the order of the skin on different body parts (see figure 10.7 for a representative case). This type of mapping is called somatotopy.

These kinds of arrangements are brought about by a series of developmental events, beginning with the formation of the neural plate and passing through neurulation (formation of a neural tube), migration of neural crest cells, cell migration, neurite (fiber) formation, connection and synapse formation, and cell death. Some of these processes are shown in the cartoon summarizing the main events in figure 10.2. Although the connectivity of the complex neuronal systems in areas of the central nervous system (particularly those that are mapped) is similar from individual to individual, it is not identical. Indeed, as the second panel of figure 10.2 shows, there is considerable variation both in the shapes of individual neurons in a class and in their connection patterns. This is perhaps not surprising, given the stochastic nature of the driving forces provided by primary processes such as division, movement, and death—in some regions of the developing nervous system up to 70 percent of the neurons die before the structure in that region is complete.

The topobiological dependencies of the developing nervous system are particularly striking. Nowhere is this seen as clearly as in the formation of maps, such as the map of visual space formed by the so-called retinotectal projection. In this instance, neurites from the ganglion cells of the retina form the optic nerve, the fibers of which then map in a definite fashion to a region that in animals like the frog is called the optic tectum (figure 10.3). Stimulation by a point of light of a particular point on the retina will lead to stimulation of neurons in a particular region of the tectum, and the responding cells are arranged in a definite map.

The arrangement of this map is achieved during development in at least two steps. The first, which involves extension of neurites by optic fibers in overlapping arbors, forms a coarse map and does not require neural activity. The second step, in which the map is refined and becomes much more precise in some species, requires neural activity in the ganglion cell fibers and tectum. Such map formation in animals like the goldfish or the frog is dynamic, and connections shift and reassemble as differential growth occurs in the retina and the tectum.

Although it is not known whether all of these mechanisms apply to the formation of every mapped area in the brain, it is likely that many of the steps are the same. *From a topobiological point of view, what makes such maps particularly interesting is that epigenetic events creating form from place during embryogenesis must to some extent anticipate various interactions of the*

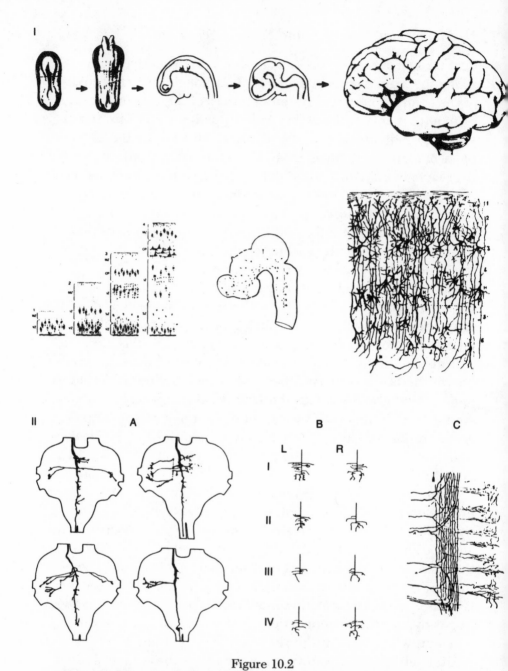

Figure 10.2

I. *Cartoons of some neuroembryological events, showing development from neural groove to cerebral cortex (top row) and production of layers or areas by cell movements (bottom row). The various processes are outlined in the text; it is noteworthy that, at one stage of their careers or another, all neurons are gypsies, migrating for short or long distances.*
II. *Anatomical variability of various neural patterns.* A: *Four examples of variability in the branching of the descending contralateral movement detector (DCMD) in the meta-thoracic ganglion of* Locusta migratoria. *(From K. G. Pearson and C. S. Goodman, 1979, Correlation of variability in structure with variability in synaptic connections of an identified interneuron in locusts,* J. Comp. Neurol. *184:141–65.)* B: *A schematic represen-*

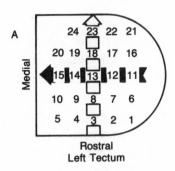

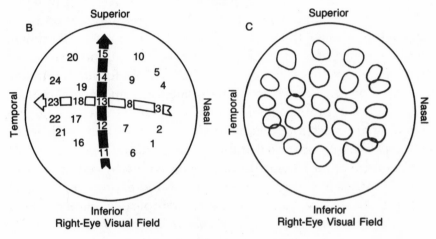

Figure 10.3

Retinotectal map in Xenopus. *An electrode was inserted in the tectal neuropil at each of the numbered electrode positions* (A), *and the region of visual field that elicits activity at each electrode position number was determined* (B). *The entire visual field region (shown in* C) *that elicits activity at the electrode tip, which is the sum of signals from many optic nerve fiber terminals, is termed a multiunit receptive field. (From S. E. Fraser, 1985, Cell interactions involved in neuronal patterning: An experimental and theoretical approach, in* Molecular bases of neural development, *ed. G. M. Edelman, W. E. Gall, and W. M. Cowan, 481–507, New York: Wiley.)*

tation of the branching sequence of a fiber from an ommatidial receptor neuron of Daphnia magna. *Neurons on the left (L) and right (R) of four genetically identical specimens (I,II,III, and IV) are shown. (From E. R. Macagno, V. Lopresti, and C. Levinthal, 1973, Structure and development of neuronal connections in isogenic organisms: Variations and similarities in the optic system of* Daphnia magna. *Proc. Natl. Acad. Sci. USA 70:57–61.) C: A longitudinal section of the posterior and lateral columns of the spinal cord to show the arrangement of the posterior roots and the origin of the collaterals. (S. Ramón y Cajal, 1889–1904,* Textura del sistema nervioso del hombre y de los vertebrados, *3 vols., Madrid: Moya.) Note the variability even in repeated structures.*

two-dimensional surfaces of sensory receptor sheets (e.g., retina or skin) with the three-dimensional world in which the animal moves and receives stimuli. Obviously, this puts constraints on the evolutionary and developmental realization of mapped neural regions.

So far, what I have described in a brief and coarse fashion sounds very much like the organization of a vast telephone exchange and perhaps even like that of a digital computer. In many ways, the brain does indeed behave like these systems. But when we look at certain detailed structural features and certain functional behaviors of the nervous system, the analogy breaks down, and we confront a series of problems the mutual implications of which amount to a series of interpretive crises for neuroscience.

The *structural crises* are those of anatomy and development. Although the brain looks like a vast electrical network at one scale, at its most microscopic scale, it is not connected or arranged like any other natural or man-made network. The network of the brain is made during development by cellular movement, extensions, and connections of increasing numbers of neurons, as we have just seen. It is an example of a self-organizing system. *An examination of this system during its development and at its most microscopic ramifications after development indicates that precise point-to-point wiring cannot occur.* In general, therefore, uniquely specific connections cannot exist. If one numbered the branches of a neuron and correspondingly numbered the neurons it touched, the numbers would not correspond in any two individuals of a species—not even in identical twins or in genetically identical animals (see figure 10.2).

To make matters worse, neurons generally send branches of their axons out in diverging arbors overlapping with those of other neurons, and the same is true of certain processes (called dendrites; see figure 10.1) on recipient neurons. We saw an example in discussing the arborization of optic nerve fibers on the tectum. The point is that, if we asked a particular neuron which input came from which other neuron in the overlapping set of dendritic connections, it could not "know."

The existence of principles of development that lead to variance in connections, and of overlapping arbors with unidentifiable (and not necessarily repeatable) patterns of synapses, creates a crisis for those who believe that the nervous system is precise and "hardwired" (like a computer). We may ask, How is this crisis met by conventional explanations, if it is recognized at all by those who believe the idea of the brain as a computer?

First, in such explanations, variations below a certain microscopic level are considered to be "noise," a necessary consequence of the developmental dilemma. Second, the absence of uniquely specific connections is treated by arguing that higher levels of organization, such as maps, either do not need such connections or compensate for their absence in some fashion. And the absence of anatomically identified synaptic inputs can be dealt with by assuming that neurons use a code much in the way that codes can be exploited to identify phone credit card users or computer users. Of course, in neurons, the presumed codes would relate to the frequency, spacing, or type of their electrical activity or to the particular chemical transmitters with which they are associated (figure 10.1). Notice that all these explanations assume that individual neurons carry information just as certain electronic devices carry information. I will argue later that this is not a defensible assumption and that these explanations are inadequate.

Before I do so, however, let me turn to a related series of difficulties, which I will label *functional crises,* pertaining more to physiology and to psychology. The first of these is that, if one explores the microscopic network of synapses with electrodes, the majority of them are not expressed, that is, they show no detectable activity. They are what have been called silent synapses. But why are they silent, and how does their silence relate to the signals, codes, or messages that are supposed to be expressed?

A more striking dilemma, which I will later discuss extensively, concerns the function and interactions of maps of the kind we have considered for the retinotectal system. Despite the conventional wisdom of anatomy books, there are major temporal fluctuations in the borders of maps in some brain laminae. Moreover, maps in each different individual appear to be unique. Most strikingly, the variability of maps in adult animals depends upon the available input. This does not seem a dilemma at first; after all, computers can change their "maps" upon alteration of software. But the functioning maps of the nervous system are based on *anatomical* maps—at this level, they are changed in the adult brain only by death of neurons. If the functioning maps are changing as a result of "software" changes, what is the code that can give two different individuals with variant maps the same output or result? One conventional explanation is to say that there are alternative systems in the brain that can handle changing input, each alternative fixed and hardwired but switched differently by changing input. As we will see, however, the facts show that the variance of maps is not discrete or two-valued but continuous, fine-grained, and, at the same time, extensive.

The next two functional crises bring us closer to psychological dilemmas of the most profound kind. The first casts doubt on the idea that complex behavior of animals with complex brains can be explained solely by learning. Indeed, I believe that *this crisis highlights the most fundamental problem of neuroscience: How can an animal initially confront a small number of "events" or "objects" and, after such exposure, adaptively categorize or recognize an indefinite number of novel objects even in a variety of contexts as being similar or identical to the set that it first encountered?* Put briefly, how can an animal recognize an object at all? How can it then generalize and "construct a universal" in the absence of that object, or even in its presence? The fact is that this kind of generalization can occur in pigeons, without language, as I will discuss later. Usually, explanations of this profoundly challenging problem rely upon the existence of hidden cues, not obvious to the experimenter, or treat the world of the responding organism as if its "objects" or "events" came with labels on them. But, in reality, the world with its "objects" is an unlabeled place—the number of ways in which macroscopic boundaries can be partitioned by an animal in an econiche is very large, if not infinite. Furthermore, the assignment an animal may make is relative, not absolute, and it depends on its adaptive needs.

Lest it seem that we are drifting from topobiology to philosophy, let me sharpen the issue and point out that such adaptive partitions of "objects" depend upon maps, and map formation in development is a topobiological example par excellence. Nowhere in the developing embryo does the definition of place have more significance for development, for behavior, or for the evolution of a species.

But how do such maps interact to give defined resolution of objects and clear-cut action or behavior? In humans, a consideration of this question leads to what I will call *the homunculus crisis: the unitary appearance to a perceiver of perceptual processes that are nevertheless known to be based upon multiple and complex parallel subprocesses and upon many maps.* (In the visual system, there may be as many as twenty interconnected brain centers.) Who or what organizes such a unitary picture— "computations," "algorithms," "invariants," or the homunculus, a little man who has in his head yet another homunculus and so on ad infinitum? Who is at home? If it is a homunculus, how could he have been constructed during the developmental wiring of the brain by his cousin, whom we may call the electrician? We have already seen that if he exists, such an electrician has constructed some very odd wiring during development.

Clearly, *any satisfactory developmental theory of higher brain function must remove the need for homunculi and electricians at any level and at the same time must account for object definition and generalization from a world whose events and "objects" are not prelabeled by any a priori scheme or top-down order.* This sounds less and less like the tasks to which computers are put. How can we meet the issue? I have proposed that the problem is of precisely the same order as that faced by Darwin when he considered the origins of taxonomic order and the origin of species without assuming divine intervention or a superhomunculus. To support this contention, I must take up a few of the main ideas of population thinking, discuss some examples, and then propose how an extension of this analysis to the development and function of the nervous system in somatic time can dispose of the dilemmas and crises I have been discussing. We will see that topobiological principles play a major role in a satisfactory brain theory.

POPULATION THINKING

Before Darwin, thinking about the origin of biological order was under the sway of an idea that has been variously called the great chain of being, the *scala naturae,* typological thinking, or, for short, essentialism. Since Plato, nature had been assumed to consist of classes, or taxa, defined by properties from the top down, fixed and in plenitude. In this view, individual variation was a noisy inconvenience to be ignored, or it was considered a symptom of the fallibility of our earthly life. In any case, the origin of species was assumed by definition.

In creating population thinking, Darwin made it clear that individuality was of the essence, that variance in a population was real and not just noise. Indeed, such variance was the basis for change. Upon this basis, natural selection acted through the environment to select those individuals whose adaptations were on the average "better," that is, eventually leading to their higher rate of reproduction.

Briefly put, these are the basic notions of population thinking. As we already saw in chapters 5 and 9, they provide the main underpinnings for the central theory in biology. Practically all of Darwin's presuppositions, except for his genetics, were correct. Variation within the population is not informed as to outcome; it occurs by chance. Overall, the environment is remorselessly independent, and on the average the best adapted will have the largest number of descendants. It is not a pleasant thought for certain wealthy benefactors of modern science whose generosity may be motivated by ideas of immortality that the less fit must eventually die. Nonetheless, these are the basic premises of the theory of natural selection.

Although the evolutionary system works over aeons of time, research in the last two decades indicates that other selective systems such as the immune system can operate in somatic time, that is, within an organism during its lifetime. Let us turn to this very specific example of somatic selection to see what it reveals for our present considerations of how the brain might operate. Its consideration will also provide a beautiful example of evolutionary opportunism, for its key molecules appear to have been derived from CAM precursors. The immune system is represented by molecules and cells in the blood capable of telling the difference between self and not-self at the molecular level. It is clearly a noncognitive system, despite the attempt of certain Russian biologists (and now Americans) to prove that it is *directly* influenced by the brain. Nevertheless, it is a system of exquisite specificity: in confronting two huge, otherwise identical protein molecules, for example, the immune system can recognize the difference of one carbon chain tilted differently in each by just a few degrees. Moreover, it can tell these molecules apart from all other molecules and retain the ability to do so once it has initially developed it.

Given all the different compounds that organic chemists can construct that certainly never existed before in the evolution of the human species, how is it that one's body can positively distinguish them and thus distinguish self from not-self in this refined fashion? The theory that prevailed before our most recent modern knowledge is the so-called theory of instruction. It assumed that, in the immune system, a foreign molecule transferred information about its structure to the combining site of the antibody molecule and then removed itself, much as a cookie is impressed in dough by a cookie cutter. That folded site or crevice would represent an informed recognizing site, which could then recognize all further instances of the particular foreign molecule. It is obvious why this was called the theory of instruction: information about three-dimensional structure was transferred from the molecule to be recognized to the molecule (the antibody or immunoglobulin) that would recognize it.

This simple and elegant theory turned out to be false and has been replaced by another notion, embodied in the so-called theory of clonal selection. At first, the idea behind this newer theory seems quite at odds with common sense. The theory proposes that, prior to confrontation with any foreign molecule, one's body already has the capability of making a huge repertoire of *different* antibody molecules, each with a different shape at its binding site. When a foreign molecule is introduced into the body, it polls a group of cells (lymphocytes), each with a different kind of antibody on its surface, and binds to those cells in the repertoire having antibodies that are more or less complementary to it.

An analysis of the complete chemical structure of antibodies was carried out in the author's laboratory several decades ago. It showed that the polypeptide chains of these molecules contain constant and variable regions and that the variable regions are the basis of the repertoire (figure 10.4). When an antigen binds to an antibody with a variable region of sufficiently close complementary shape, it stimulates that cell to divide and make progeny cells bearing more of that kind of antibody with that same complementary shape. This group of daughter cells is a clone, the asexual progeny of a single cell, and this is a case of differential reproduction by clonal selection. It is a particularly intriguing recent finding that N-CAM is related to immunoglobulin molecules and to their evolutionary cousins on lymphocytes that together form the so-called immunoglobulin superfamily (figure 10.4). It would not be surprising if it were found that the precursor of present-day CAMs and immunoglobulins was concerned with cell adhesion, for regulation of the response of immune cells depends upon cell-cell interaction. This idea (reviewed in a re-

Figure 10.4

Homology of N-CAM with members of the immunoglobulin superfamily (see also figure 7.1 and compare the various domain arrangements). It is an attractive hypothesis that self-nonself recognition characteristic of immune responses arose from self-self recognition by adhesion mechanisms involving an N-CAM precursor. A: Alignment of the five internally homologous segments (I to V) common to the ld, sd, and ssd chains, showing their similarity with each other and with a member (see B) of the Ig superfamily (one-letter amino acid code). Residues are numbered consecutively from the amino terminus of the mature N-CAM polypeptides. Residues identical in all five N-CAM regions and highly conserved among Ig-like proteins are marked with triangles; *the cysteines proposed to be involved in intradomain disulfide bonds are indicated by* closed triangles. *Residues identical in two or more sequences are* boxed. *B: Amino sequences from the variable (V_L) and constant (C_L) regions of the light chain of an Ig. (Conventions as in A.) C: Model of N-CAM showing homologous loops (I to V) in the region common to all three polypeptides* (open bar). *The base of each loop corresponds to the proposed intradomain disulfide bond. The cell membrane is indicated by* stippling, *and the extracellular and intracellular regions are to the left and right, respectively. The membrane-spanning region and carboxyl terminal segment common to the ld and sd chain are indicated by the* solid bar, *while the cytoplasmic domain unique to the ld chain is indicated by the* hatched bar. *The unique segment of the ssd chain is indicated by the* open bar *and* dashed line *below. Numbers 1 to 19 correspond to exons in the chicken N-CAM gene, and their relative boundaries in the protein are noted by* transverse lines. *D: Some diagrams of Ig superfamily members including N-CAM. (See G. M. Edelman, 1987, CAMs and Igs: Cell adhesion and the evolutionary origins of immunity, Immunol. Rev. 100:9–43.)*

A

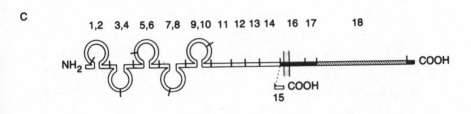

B

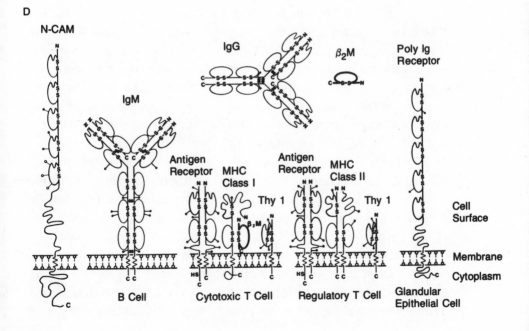

cent issue of *Immunological Reviews;* see references) has received further support from recent findings by T. Kaufman and M. Seeger of Indiana University. N-CAM–like sequences were discovered by these workers in the genome of *Drosophila,* a species that does not possess an adaptive immune system or immunoglobulins (personal communication).

With a little thought, one can detect some very interesting properties of the immune selective system. First, there is more than one way of recognizing a particular shape above any given threshold criterion for matching shape. Second, the system has the potential for memory. Consider, for example, that after presentation of the foreign molecule to a particular group of cells, some cells stop dividing but the rest go on to the end producing antibodies of the kind that would recognize the original foreign molecule. Because some have divided, but not all the way to the end, they constitute a larger number of identical individuals than was originally present, each waiting to respond to another presentation of the foreign molecule. This is a form of cellular memory that can last for an entire lifetime.

Our discussion of population thinking, the immune system, and somatic selection converges upon two key statements. (1) In evolution, essentialism and typological thinking are incorrect; instead, taxa are formed from the bottom up by natural selection upon variant individuals in populations. (2) In the immune system, instructionism is wrong; instead, recognition of nonself occurs by clonal selection acting upon variant antibodies produced in somatic time. In both cases, a form of classification upon novelty occurs, an adaptation so refined that the initial idea used to explain it was instructionist—whether it assumed creation by design for species and structures, or the instructive transfer of information on foreign molecules to antibodies as they are built.

Now we can come back to a key question about the brain: *In its order, does the brain provide the basis for the recognition of novelty and for generalization upon a few presented instances by instruction and information processing, or is it, at its most fundamental level of operation, a somatic selective system based upon variance in populations of neurons, variance that arises first during development because of topobiological constraints?*

Can we make a case for neural Darwinism? To answer this question, we must first discuss a population theory of brain function based on selection and consider the evidence in its favor. This theory should be able to resolve the crises I have described and, in doing so, reconcile these crises at various levels of anatomical, physiological, and psychological function into a unified developmental picture. Otherwise, it would be no improvement over current views.

THE THEORY OF NEURONAL GROUP SELECTION

Because some of its premises touch upon rather detailed and specialized facts concerning nervous systems and their function, this theory can be described here only in a somewhat skeletal form. For a more complete account, the interested reader may consult the book *Neural Darwinism*. The theory has three major premises, two of which can be stated in a reasonably simple fashion. The third is more difficult and will be considered separately in a later section.

The first premise of the theory is that, because of the epigenetic influence of morphoregulatory mechanisms, large numbers of variant connections are formed during development in a particular brain area, *connections that, at their finest ramifications, differ from individual to individual.* These variant connections arise because of the dynamics of primary processes under local constraint of the morphoregulatory molecules and because various processes of developmental selection take place. This selection occurs by means of synaptic reinforcement, neurite extension and retraction, cell migration, and cell death (see figure 10.2). Moreover, *because these processes are more or less local in scale and because neurites in general have restricted lengths, it is assumed that groups of more strongly connected neurons are formed in nuclei or laminae of the brain.* In any such region, a group comprising from hundreds to thousands of cells represents neurons that are more closely connected to each other than to neurons in other groups. The ensemble of all such groups in a region constitutes a repertoire of structural variants—a *popula-*

tion that is called the *primary repertoire*. After anatomical formation of such groups during development by means of dynamic processes of cell adhesion that control cell motion and process extension, certain connections are selected over others, and the others disappear. The existence of variance is not contrary to the fact that overall tracts and particular neurons can follow definite pathways. These can be established by expression through modulation of particular CAMs and SAMs. (For more details, the reader may consult chapter 5 of my book *Neural Darwinism.*)

The next major premise of the theory states that, *once such a variant primary repertoire is built, a second process of selection occurs during the animal's sojourn in its environment after a certain stage of development. The network no longer changes in its geometry to any great extent. Instead, at any time, those groups that respond best to a given input are selected by increasing the efficacy of their synaptic connections.* This results in differential amplification of the strengths of certain connections and in suppression of others, and leads to the formation of a *secondary repertoire. Certain individuals (i.e., groups) in that repertoire will be more likely to respond to further presentation of similar or identical input signals (or stimuli) than will those that were not selected.* Nonetheless, although the unit of selection is a group, different groups may compete for neurons, and some neurons in a group may be used to form other groups after competition occurs. Selected groups are functional entities.

The result of this selection from an already selected anatomical repertoire is the establishment of more than one way of adequately responding to a particular input. This idea that there exists a large number of structurally different groups that may respond in a functionally similar way to a given input or stimulus is called degeneracy. We have already considered a related idea in chapter 9. Degeneracy is a fundamental property of selective systems, and it is the means by which such systems can respond to novel stimuli that are similar but not identical to an original stimulus. It is, in fact, the necessary basis upon which generalization can be performed by a nervous system. We mean by generalization the ability to respond to large numbers of novel members of a class after presentation of just a few numbers of that class.

Degeneracy is not in itself sufficient, however, to support generalization. To understand this point, *we must consider the third premise of the theory of neuronal group selection, which is called reentry, and also take up the issue of categorization of a stimulus world that is not named or ordered a priori.* This is the most difficult aspect of the theory, and we must digress a bit to consider how the world of "objects" or "events" that constitutes the environment for an animal with a brain might be categorized. After that, we can consider the significance of the third premise, reentrant signaling in the brain, and its relation to this process of categorization and generalization. This digression may appear to take us far from the molecular, anatomical, and developmental aspects of topobiology. But it will in fact help establish an important topobiological point related to the evolutionary question: the nature of the maps set up in development to allow individual animals to categorize their environment adaptively. Moreover, according to the theory, development never stops: *the alteration of synapses as a result of experience, leading to a patterned distribution of their changes in strength, is a topobiological one.* These patterns depend as much upon cellular responses to place (this time on receptor sheets and connecting neural networks) as do earlier developmental events. What differs from early topobiological descriptions is the mechanism and the nature of the signaling. Let us turn, therefore, to signaling and stimuli as they impinge on the nervous system.

STIMULI, OBJECTS, AND SETS

What is the nature of the stimulus? Is it an essential class—does the world come packaged with labels, as some of the essentialists felt the jungle did for tigers? In other words, is a stimulus a list in which singly necessary and jointly sufficient features will define an object—a chair, a table, a leaf, a particular niche, a vein on a leaf, what have you? Or is it, rather, an arbitrary class, something that the animal simply names for convenience, with no necessary relation to its other members? These questions have a kinship with certain fundamental philosophical questions of realism and nominalism.

Studies on people and on pigeons that we will take up later suggest that neither of these modes reigns. Instead, it appears that a variety of disjunctive features or exemplary properties are used by animals to categorize and generalize. Before we describe some of these results, it may be useful to note that real-world stimuli can be grouped into so-called polymorphous sets. These are sets in which disjunctive sampling of features constitutes a class and in which neither necessary nor sufficient conditions are required. If a group of things can be characterized by n attributes (where n is not a small number) and any disjunctive combination of m of these features is chosen (where m is less than n), then an ensemble of these combinations constitutes a polymorphous set. In contrast, if to define a set we insisted upon n features out of n, it would be an essentially defined set, and if we insisted upon only one out of n, it would be a nominally defined set. The example shown in figure 10.5 may serve to make these

Figure 10.5
Polymorphous sets. Set I contains "at least two of round, doubly outlined, or centrally dark." Set II does not. (From G. M. Edelman, 1985, Neural Darwinism: Population thinking and higher brain function, in How we know, *ed. M. Shafto, 1–30, San Francisco: Harper & Row. After I. Dennis, J. A. Hampton, and S. E. G. Lea, 1973, New problems in concept formation,* Nature *243:101–2.)*

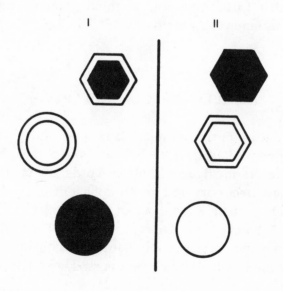

ideas clearer. The difference between the two groups of patterns is difficult to discern. But when we are told that members in set I can be characterized by "at least two of round, doubly outlined, or centrally dark," the distinction between the two sets is clear.

According to the theory of neuronal group selection, characterization of the world of real stimuli is, in general, polymorphous. But if, to the animal, the world of stimuli is a world of polymorphous sets, the disjunctive properties of which can change depending on the context, the circumstance, or the adaptive needs of the animal, how can that animal use its brain to categorize and generalize in an adaptive manner? Before attempting to answer this question in terms of the third premise of the theory of neuronal group selection, let us take up some evidence that animals *can* indeed categorize and generalize without the advantage of language.

Consider two examples of categorization—one by pigeons, of visual images and scenes, and one by babies, of objects and their boundaries prior to the acquisition of speech. The pigeon experiments were done by Herrnstein and Cerella. Cerella presented pigeons with images of oak leaves in an operant conditioning mode. After several rewarded presentations, the pigeons positively discriminated oak leaf images from images of all other kinds of leaves. One might surmise that the pigeon's capacity to discriminate these forms was based upon some innate capacity that evolved by natural selection; after all, pigeons and their precursors might have lived among trees, and certain adaptive advantages might have operated on a "hidden cue." But Herrnstein's experiments definitely refute this. He presented pigeons with randomly chosen pictures made by a scuba diver of fish in a variety of contexts. After seeing a small number of these with operant rewards, the pigeons positively discriminated among novel pictures, preferentially picking images of fish from among a wide variety of such images differing in local features and contextual cues.

Pigeons do not live among fish. Moreover, pictures of a particular woman could be used to train a pigeon, after which new images of that particular woman would be positively discriminated in a variety of contexts. One must not assume that the pigeons (which certainly lack language as we know it) are recognizing fish as "fish" or women as "women." Indeed, Cerella has shown that after recognizing cartoon images of Charlie Brown (of *Peanuts* fame) and discriminating these from those of Lucy, the pigeons would still recognize Charlie Brown if his head was delineated under his feet. The recognition appears to be largely upon disjunctive collections of local features.

On the basis of these findings, it seems safe to say that the pigeons can generalize without language. In view of the novelty of the images presented in different contexts, it appears likely that they are recognizing polymorphous sets by particular local features, although this conclusion is less certain. Above all, we can conclude that this behavior cannot be explained by any account of conventional learning. There must exist some additional structural features of pigeon brains that *already* permit such behavior even though reward learning is involved in the original training sets of pictures. No digital computer based on instruction or information processing that we know of can carry out such a general mode of visual pattern recognition without a language and very extensive object descriptions.

Now, consider how babies recognize objects. The experiments of Spelke suggest that four-month-old babies visually determine object boundaries in two dimensions or in depth by means of the systematic motion of those boundaries relative to occluding objects and a background. A stationary rod occluded by a horizontal one is seen as two separate rods. If this rod is moved horizontally while still occluded, it is seen as a single rod. For our purposes, the most interesting finding is that two separate shapes are perceived as one object if they are apposed and made to move together. It seems that a baby (before major language acquisition and the ability to grasp objects definitely) does not "parse" an object by singly necessary and jointly sufficient lists of attributes such as color, shape, and texture, although it may seize upon these to discern the object's motion. For the infant, an "object" is constituted by systematic relative motion and occlusion of perceived boundaries. This trait does not appear to be learned in any conventional sense but seems, rather, to reflect properties of the infant's visuomotor system. Furthermore, it seems to be general, that is, it is applied to any moving collection.

After this brief account of these two examples of generalization, we may turn to the question of how a nervous system could be equipped to carry out such tasks. This requires a return to the theory of neuronal group selection—specifically, to its third premise, which is called reentrant signaling, a form of signaling that occurs mainly between maps.

REENTRY IN MAPS AND CLASSIFICATION COUPLES

Animals receive a rather small sample of all possible stimuli. If the world of stimuli consists of potential polymorphous sets to be sampled by an animal according to its adaptive needs, how can an animal generalize from a small sample? This must reflect an inherent capacity of neural networks. According to the theory of neuronal group selection, that property emerges from three features of the brain: (1) reentrant circuits, (2) the degeneracy of repertoires of neuronal groups, and (3) the arrangement of some of these repertoires in maps.

If an object is not predefined or labeled, the nervous system must be able to sample certain different features of that object independently and in parallel, for example, through different sensory modalities. In other words, it must be able to sample disjunctively or partition a collection of object features in a variety of independent ways. It must also be able to correlate certain collections of features to constitute entities such as moving boundaries. In this procedure, it must not, however, completely lose cues about the spatiotemporal continuity and place of an object. Above all, in going from one level of organization of neuronal groups to another in a different part of the brain in short times, it must be able to correlate *previous* samplings of the same object with *current* ones, even though the objects, which do not come labeled, may move and may be occluded.

The requirement for independent sampling is a requirement for a parallel process, and it is well known that the brain is a highly parallel processor. *But how, if objects are not labeled, can such a parallel system keep track of them? According to the theory, this is accomplished by reentrant connections mapping*

one set of degenerate groups forming a repertoire to another
independently mapped repertoire (figure 10.6). To be concrete,
suppose that feature detection (observation of corners, crossings,
line stops) could be performed by the visual system. (In fact, we
know that, as a result of evolution, such capacities exist inborn
and are tuned by experience.) Suppose that, at the same time, the
somatosensory system gets light touch signals from the hand
moving on the object boundary, correlating the continuity of that
boundary and its various attributes: sharp, broken, smooth. This
correlation may not be as refined as feature detection, but, as a
result of motion, it *connects* attributes. Imagine that the neural
signals pass independently from each of these sensory systems to
separate maps, constituting ordered representations of the visual
field or of the body representation for light touch. Now if, as a
result of development, there *already* exists a reciprocal set of
cross-connections between these two maps that can potentially
alter their connection strengths as a function of time, we have
the basis for a reentrant network.

Figure 10.6

A classification couple using reentry. Neurons (those in the visual system, for example)
act as feature detectors, inheriting that capacity as a result of evolution. They map on
the left to some higher-order lamina in the brain (map 1). Other neurons (e.g., those
related to light touch on a moving finger) act as feature correlators, tracing an object by
motion, as is shown on the right. These neurons map to another lamina (map 2). The two
maps map onto each other by reentrant connections, so that groups in one map may excite
groups in the other. This allows the parallel simultaneous sampling of disjunctive charac-
teristics constituting a polymorphous set in the stimulus (figure 10.5); because of the
reentrant connections, these characteristics can be connected in the responses of higher-
order networks. In this way, certain more general characteristics of an object representa-
tion can be connected with other particular characteristics. (Modified from G. M.
Edelman, 1985, Neural Darwinism: Population thinking and higher brain function, in
How we know, *ed. M. Shafto, 1–30, San Francisco: Harper & Row.)*

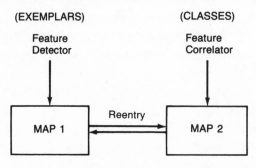

Groups chosen in one map connected by these reentrant connections to groups independently chosen in the other can have their connection strengths increased as a result of simultaneous experience and stimuli. Thus the *parallel independent sampling* of features on one side and of correlations of features on the other, each chosen disjunctively, can now be *related* to each other. Such an arrangement constitutes the minimal structure capable of independently sampling object attributes for the purpose of classification. This is equivalent to saying that at least two different disjunctive modes of sampling must be correlated. In this case, these modes were local visual features and continuity to touch. The smallest unit capable of carrying out such correlations (illustrated in figure 10.6) is called a classification couple. Obviously, in real nervous systems, more than two channels of sampling within or between modalities can be and usually are employed, and we should therefore talk of classification n-tuples, for the brain has an extraordinarily large number of coupled channels and maps even in one system. For example, there is evidence in the visual system of primates for as many as twenty such areas linked by neuroanatomy, much of which is reentrant. These properties are seen in other sensory and higher order systems. Indeed, *perhaps the most striking property of advanced brains is that, to a degree not seen in any other known material object, they are reentrantly mapped.*

Notice that the independent sampling meets the requirement for disjunction in dealing with polymorphous sets—there is no necessary "prelabeled" coupling. Notice also that the arrangement into maps in the nervous system increases the chances of maintaining spatiotemporal continuity (and place) in signals that arise from sampling an object. Finally, notice that the function of reentrant connections between the maps is to help maintain that continuity while selectively linking collections of particular features to other independent correlations of object properties. This is just what is required to characterize polymorphous sets, particularly of objects that are changing place and therefore changing the stimuli to receptor sheets.

To show that such reentrant mapped networks based on a selectionist principle can really carry out certain kinds of classification and generalization, a new kind of automaton, called Darwin II, has been built. The machine is simulated in very large digital computers as a selective system with 10,000 groups and 10^6 connections, and it is constructed as a classification couple. The world of Darwin II is the stationary collection of all two-dimensional figures in black and white and of a given scale. One side of the couple, called Darwin, consists of an analog of visual feature detection. It is responsible for individual representations: it selects simulated neuronal groups giving unique responses to each different stimulus. If a particular collection of features in a stimulus is repeated often, it strengthens the "synapses" or connections of the groups selected, so that they are more likely to respond upon subsequent presentations.

The other side of the couple, called Wallace, is responsible for tracing outlines of objects. It yields similar responses or selections of groups when the correlated traces are similar, even for objects that are locally very different—for example, a short, fat letter A with a low bar, and a rotated, thin long letter A with a high bar.

Reentry between the higher-order networks of Darwin and Wallace gives an interaction between individual and class representations, tying together their independently selected neural groups by strengthening the synapses of the reentrant connections. At this point, presentation of an old individual stimulus can call up groups corresponding to other old stimuli by reentrant linkage (associative memory). Moreover, presentation of novel stimuli of the same class as those previously experienced can do the same (generalization).

The performance of Darwin II, which is solipsistic (free of forced learning or programming by its builders), is far from error free. Indeed, as one might expect, it makes errors about 20 percent of the time. Notice, however, that within the limits of its construction it deals with novelty and that its successful performance does show the self-consistency of the theory of neuronal group selection. A more recent automaton, Darwin III, has a motor system, an eye, and an arm with sensors for light touch. This selective automation simulates a small animal that deals with moving objects and has real motor responses in its classificatory behavior, bringing even greater force to the argument for the consistency of neural Darwinism.

These constructions, however, have no bearing upon whether the theory is *true* for real nervous systems. Let us therefore turn to that subject and ask what kind of evidence is required to substantiate neural Darwinism. Besides reentrant circuits and maps, both of which have been amply demonstrated in the brain, the theory of neuronal group selection has two empirical requirements. First, there must be a generator of diversity during the development of neural circuits, capable of constructing definite patterns of groups but also of generating great individual variation. Variation must be introduced during development by a molecular process at the level of cell-to-cell interaction. Second, there must be evidence for neuronal group selection and competition in brain maps and reentrant circuits. This must occur at the level of changes, not in the pattern of the circuitry, but in the efficacy of preformed connections or synapses. Evidence for these two requirements would fulfill respectively the requirements of the theory's first and second premises.

TOPOBIOLOGICAL EVIDENCE FOR THE THEORY

At this point, it will come as no surprise to the reader that the evidence on the action of CAMs during brain development supports the first premise of the theory and provides an origin of anatomical diversity. This is so because the primary processes are dynamic and stochastic and because, by its very nature, the morphoregulator hypothesis *must* introduce local variation at the scale of individual cells as it establishes general patterns in form and tissue structure. The necessary somatic variation required by the theory of neuronal group selection is supplied by the dynamics of cell surface modulation of CAMs. Neuronal patterns are not assured by preassigned molecular addressing on each cell to construct a "jigsaw puzzle" pattern by which networks are hardwired. Instead, a relatively small number of CAMs and SAMs on the surfaces of cells switch on and off in sequences defined by their local environment. This dynamic switching, in a refined version of the morphoregulator hypothesis, changes the patterns of cell motion, of process attachment, and, ultimately, of the connections formed. (For a model of neuronal pathfinding based on these ideas see chapter 5 in *Neural Darwinism.*)

If these mechanisms apply, one should be able to demonstrate that perturbations of CAM binding alter neural morphology (and function) and that perturbation of neural function leads to changes in CAM expression and distribution. Both of these are required by the dynamic signal loops of the morphoregulator hypothesis.

Perturbation of binding has been seen in a number of systems using univalent fragments of specific antibodies. Anti-N-CAM perturbs orderly connections of the developing neural retina in organ culture. Anti-Ng-CAM perturbs fasciculation (side-to-side binding) of neurites of dorsal root ganglia in culture. Indeed, in this case, it may be that an authentic signal for a CAM has been found: in certain cells in which N-CAM and Ng-CAM are present at constitutive levels, nerve growth factor (a protein growth factor) strongly enhances synthesis of Ng-CAM but not of N-CAM. Anti-N-CAM placed in the tectum of living frogs disrupts formation of the retinotectal map by causing alterations in the pattern of extending neurites and leads to distortions and alterations in the precision of the map. As a final example, we may mention again the differential effect of a CAM and a SAM on the migration of cells in the cerebellum. During development, external granule cells migrate on radial glia of the cerebellum to form a molecular layer and finally rest in a more internal layer, the internal granular layer. Anti-Ng-CAM blocks migration into the molecular layer and slightly alters movement of external granule cells already arrived in that layer. In contrast, anticytotactin does not block migration into the molecular layer but slows cells in the molecular layer or prevents their exit to the internal granule layer. Thus, correlated dynamic control of a neuronal CAM (Ng-CAM) and a glial SAM (cytotactin) has different but complementary effects on a primary process leading dynamically to neural structure (layer formation) and to local variance.

The other requirement of any theory proposing that neural structure is created dynamically by selective means is that the modulation or maintenance of certain CAMs at certain levels of expression depend on signals that result from the actual morphology of the interactive structures. Disruption of the morphology should lead to altered CAM (or SAM) expression. As we have already mentioned, this has been shown in the peripheral nervous system following the section or crushing of a nerve. A complex series of alterations ensues in the expression of N-CAM, Ng-CAM, and cytotactin. The alteration differs at different levels of a connected circuit, ranging from the muscle supplied by the nerve (where, after injury, N-CAM synthesis is enhanced and this CAM is distributed over the entire muscle cell surface) to the Schwann cells that help repair the injury (where N-CAM and Ng-CAM expression is enhanced) and the segment of the spinal cord on the affected side (where N-CAM and Ng-CAM expression is altered in ventral regions). These changes are gradually reversed after regeneration.

Several genetic disorders affecting neural connectivity also show changes in CAM modulation, expression level, or distribution, providing less direct proof of change of modulation. Notable are cerebellar connection disorders in the mouse (*staggerer*) in which E-to-A conversion of N-CAM is strongly delayed, and dysmyelinating diseases in which N-CAM, Ng-CAM, and cytotactin are altered in the interaction between peripheral glia (Schwann cells) and neurons at the so-called nodes of Ranvier.

All of these examples support the idea of dynamic morphoregulation. Because cell surface modulation of CAMs on neurons depends epigenetically upon the results of an orderly sequence of environments and places in which signals are exchanged, it gives a relatively orderly set of circuit patterns. But locally there is no preassigned exact attachment of a particular neuronal cellular process to another. We have here a principle not only of common structure and regulation in the formation of every nervous system but also of necessary somatic variation. The consequence is that no two nervous systems, even those of twins, can be alike at the level of their fine structure. Notice, however, that the fulfillment of the requirement for a source of diversity of anatomical pattern is a necessary but not a sufficient condition for the theory to be supported. We must still show that the second premise, selection among synapses to change their strengths in an already connected nervous system, can occur topobiologically and in a competitive or Darwinian manner.

Synaptic Competition Induced by Topobiological Signals

Evidence fulfilling the second premise of the theory comes from some extraordinary topobiological experiments on adult monkeys carried out by Merzenich and his coworkers. These experimenters prepared detailed maps of the portion of the cerebral cortex (the major lamina of the brain) that is concerned with the early signals for light touch (figure 10.7). They did this by measuring the electrical response of neurons in two areas (the so-called area 1 and area 3b) as they touched various parts of the monkey's fingers and hand in a systematic fashion. By such a procedure, they could locate the receptive field of a neuron—the part of the skin surface that made the neuron fire. Working systematically, they found continuous regions of cortex corresponding to adjacent receptive fields. These constituted a map representing the skin surface of the hand, smooth on the palm and hairy on the back. They then subjected the monkeys to a variety of procedures to see how the maps responded. These procedures consisted of severing one of the three main nerves to the hand, removing one or more digits, and repeatedly stimulating one area, such as the finger pad, by training the monkey to tap its finger for a reward.

The key results of these experiments may be summarized briefly. First, every monkey had a unique map, unlike that of any other monkey. After the median nerve that supplies the smooth skin of the first, second, and half of the third digits was severed, a remarkable change occurred immediately in the map of the owl monkey (figure 10.7). A blank (unresponsive) area appeared, but more of the dorsal region of the hand (hairy skin) was represented in areas where it was not previously apparent. Map boundaries changed even for map regions related to the remaining two nerves (radial and ulnar). Then, over a period of months,

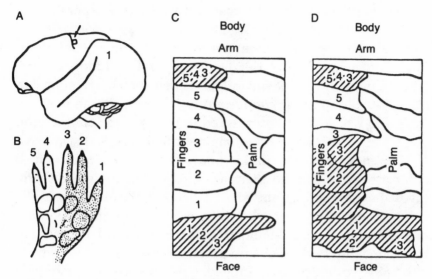

Figure 10.7

Diagrams illustrating the dynamism and variability of maps serving the sensory modality of light touch in the central cortex of the adult owl monkey. A: A diagram of the brain; the arrow *points to the mapped area shown enlarged in C and D. B: A diagram of the palm and digits of the monkey's hand. The* shaded portion *of the palm is served by the median nerve, the cutting of which causes immediate changes in the normal map (C), leading to map D. In C is shown a map of a normal monkey's cortical area representing the palm and fingers. It is made by stimulating small areas of skin and electrically recording from minute areas around single neurons in the cortex to determine their receptive fields. After the median nerve is severed, the map changes, as is shown in D. The main changes include an increase in the amount of representation of the dorsal skin (shown as* diagonally hatched areas *in C and D) and a shift in map boundaries for digits, even those represented by the cortical projections of the two uncut nerves (the radial and ulnar) that also serve the hand. These changes are not due to nerve regrowth. Up to six months later in the adult monkey, the map boundaries continue to shift if the median nerve is not repaired. (From G. M. Edelman, 1985, Neural Darwinism: Population thinking and higher brain function, in* How we know, *ed. M. Shafto, 1–30, San Francisco: Harper & Row. Modified from M. M. Merzenich, J. H. Kaas, J. T. Wall, R. J. Nelson, M. Sur, and D. J. Fellerman, 1983, Topographic reorganization of somatosensory cortical areas 3b and 1 in adult monkeys following restricted deafferentation,* Neuroscience *8:33–55, and from M. M. Merzenich, J. H. Kaas, J. T. Wall, R. J. Nelson, M. Sur, and D. J. Fellerman, 1983, Progression of change following median nerve section in the cortical representation of the hand in areas 3b and 1 in adult owl and squirrel monkeys,* Neuroscience *10:639–65.)*

if the cut median nerve was not allowed to regenerate, the map areas were rearranged in the cortex to correspond to maps assigning territory to either radial or ulnar nerves. There was no evidence that this was because neurons in the mapped regions underwent major regrowth and rewiring. Finally, without any surgery at all, it was found that a monkey tapping one finger showed enlargement of the mapped region corresponding to that finger—a topobiological example that is very compelling.

The changes seen by these investigators involved continuous movement of map boundaries over considerable distances of cortex. The bulk of the evidence suggests that such movements are attributable to *synaptic changes* resulting from alteration in the input. They have been interpreted in terms of the competition for particular cortical cells among neuronal groups that receive overlapping arbors of incoming neurons corresponding to much wider areas of the hand than are apparent in the maps themselves. In other words, the anatomical arrangement consists of widespread overlapping arborizations, and, from these overlapping structures, map boundaries are constructed (depending upon the input) by selecting neuronal groups through alterations of their synaptic strengths. Indeed, a detailed computer simulation based on the notions of neuronal group selection and synaptic populations yields results very similar to the experimental results.

The experimental and theoretical work on the somatosensory system provides just the picture of somatic competition and selection or neural Darwinism proposed in the theory of neuronal group selection. Maps are dynamic; they are based on a degenerate repertoire of neuronal groups with variant connections formed during development; and it is synaptic selection that decides the outcomes—in this case, the borders of map boundaries. It is extremely difficult to explain these results in terms of fixed, hardwired neural systems. The results and their analysis indicate that selection is always going on, even in adult brains.

TOPOBIOLOGY AND SOMATIC SELECTION

We could discuss a number of other areas in which the theory of neuronal group selection has received support—for instance, in studies of the development of bird song—but the two examples I have given will, I hope, serve to indicate that the theory can explain a number of different and otherwise paradoxical findings.

Indeed, each of the issues discussed as crises at the beginning of this chapter actually provides support for the idea of neuronal group selection. Let me briefly show how this can be true.

Under this population view of the nervous system, in which form is dynamically created from place at a large number of different levels, the structural crises precipitated by the absence of precise point-to-point wiring, by the absence of uniquely specific connectivity at the finest ramifications, and by the divergent overlap of dendritic and axonal arbors all dissolve. It is, in fact, just these features of variance one would require to create rich degenerate repertoires for selection. These diverse features are not "noise"; they are necessary variance in neural populations. We have already seen how the regulation of cell interactions by CAMs in embryonic development necessarily leads to both pattern and diversity.

As for the functional crises, silent synapses are not the sign of failure in message transmission. Instead, they are metastable indicators of selection events occurring over the entire population of synapses in a region. As I just mentioned, the fluctuations in map borders are signs of neuronal group selection and of successful group competition. The problem of generalization is resolved by reentrant maps connecting different degenerate repertoires of neuronal groups. Finally, multiple parallel processes of reentry between maps are required in order to construct a perceptual response. The apparent coherence and the unitary properties of that response relate to the final process of generalization and memory through reentry that emerges from such systems. Just as Darwin's view eliminated the need for creation by design, showing how taxa can be evolved (bottom-up) from populations through natural selection, so this selectionist view of the brain eliminates the need to create perceptual categories from the top down. *Synaptic changes in linked neural maps leading to such categories are perhaps the most exquisite result of epigenetic processes creating form from place.* Topobiology at a minute scale reaches its highest point of evolutionary sophistication in complex brains containing many such maps, and its principles provide a central basis for the workings of such brains.

Neural Darwinism has not yet been accepted or disproved.

But if its premises are correct, we may conclude that the brain is not simply a logic machine; it is not constructed like a digital computer, and if it is a selectional system, an effective procedure (one defined by an algorithm) cannot be given or constructed for all its activities a priori. (For a discussion of this point see the papers by Reeke and myself in the references.) The fundamental construction of the brain is bottom-up through evolution and ontogeny by means of natural and somatic selection. As a developmental system, it is constructed through a succession of topobiological principles to deal with open-ended situations related to adaptation by generalization in a world that is not locally labeled or named; it is not, in general, rigidly programmed and is not reversible. Sense and survival are its rulers; in humans, logic is only its housekeeper. No one will deny that in such social animals as human beings, information processing occurs through social transmission and language. But that evolutionary fact, which has created Larmarckian social transmission rules, does not invalidate the essentially Darwinian nature both of the evolution of the brain and of its somatic selectional processes that together govern our fundamental cognitive behavior.

In this chapter, I have reached beyond the molecular level to aspects of function related to phenotypic behavior, including physiology and psychology. I have done so to show that topobiological principles range from CAM cycles to the large loops in brains connecting sensory and motor systems back to developing synaptic populations. In one case, cellular motion is an important driving force and, in the other, motion of the entire animal or its parts. In both cases, the extraordinary and compelling concept is how form and function are tied together by evolutionary and somatic selection, yielding pattern and variation both of which have selective value. The proposed topobiological answers to the developmental genetic question and the evolutionary question are thus connected not only by new notions of heterochrony but also by new applications of population thinking to the question of development and somatic variation. By this means, the genetic code is shown to be tied to the molecular, cellular, organismic, and behavioral scales.

SELECTED REFERENCES

Edelman, G. M. 1987. *Neural Darwinism: The theory of neuronal group selection.* New York: Basic Books.

Edelman, G. M., and L. H. Finkel. 1984. Neuronal group selection in the cerebral cortex. In *Dynamic aspects of neocortical function,* ed. G. M. Edelman, W. E. Gall, and W. M. Cowan, 653–95. New York: Wiley.

———. 1987. Population rules for synapses in networks. In *Synaptic function,* ed. G. M. Edelman, W. E. Gall, and W. M. Cowan, 711–57. New York: Wiley.

Cowan, W. M. 1978. Aspects of neural development. *Int. Rev. Physiol.* 17:150–91.

Edelman, G. M. 1973. Antibody structure and molecular immunology. *Science* 180:830–40.

———. 1974. The problem of molecular recognition by a selective system. In *Studies in the philosophy of biology,* ed. F. J. Ayala and T. Dobzhansky, 45–56. London: Macmillan.

———. 1987. CAMs and Igs: Cell adhesion and the evolutionary origins of immunity. *Immunol. Rev.* 100:9–43.

Dennis, I., J. A. Hampton, and S. E. G. Lea. 1973. New problem in concept formation. *Nature* 243:101–2.

Herrnstein, R. J. 1982. Stimuli and the texture of experience. *Neurosci. Biobehav. Rev.* 6:105–17.

———. 1985. Riddles of natural categorization. *Philos. Trans. R. Soc. Lond. (Biol.)* 308:129–44.

Cerella, J. 1979. Visual classes and natural categories in the pigeon. *J. Exp. Psychol. (Hum. Percept.)* 5:68–77.

———. 1980. The pigeon's analysis of pictures. *Pattern Recogn.* 12:1–6.

Kellman, P. J., and E. S. Spelke. 1983. Perception of partly occluded objects in infancy. *Cognit. Psychol.* 15:483–524.

Kaas, J. H., M. M. Merzenich, and H. P. Killackey. 1983. The reorganization of somatosensory cortex following peripheral-nerve damage in adult and developing mammals. *Annu. Rev. Neurosci.* 6:325–56.

Edelman, G. M., and G. N. Reeke, Jr. 1982. Selective networks capable of representative transformation, limited generalization, and associative memory. *Proc. Natl. Acad. Sci. USA* 79:2091–95.

Reeke, G. N., Jr., and G. M. Edelman. 1984. Selective networks and recognition automata. *Ann. N.Y. Acad. Sci.* 426:181–201.

———. 1987. Real brains and artificial intelligence. *Daedalus* 117:143–73.

Pearson, J. C., L. H. Finkel, and G. M. Edelman. 1987. Plasticity in the organization of adult cortical maps: A computer model based on neuronal group selection. *J. Neurosci.* 7:4209–23.

See also references to Cowan and Le Douarin in chapter 6, and to Coghill, Hamburger, and Schmidt in chapter 9.

11

Coda: The Other Side
of Biology

THIS BOOK has been unabashedly theoretical in its stance. My main purpose in taking that stance is to call to the attention of even expert specialists in biology the fact that the framework in which we have undertaken the task of understanding biology is radically incomplete. DNA and the findings of molecular biology are not alone "the answer to life"—there is another side to biology, that of epigenesis. Epigenesis operates by means of place-dependent molecular signaling over many scales of biological organization finally to reach back to DNA. The cell responding to place-dependent mechanochemical schemes and the organism obeying rules of both natural and somatic selection are the controlling units in topobiology. And while we have restricted ourselves to pursuing the implications of the subject to metazoan development, it is obvious that certain of its aspects extend down even to prokaryotes.

Many of the ideas I have proposed here will have to suffer revision; indeed, some will have to be rejected as more evidence connecting molecular genetics to development and evolution accumulates. The coordinate functioning of thousands of genes is required for the development of complex animals, and we are now probably not too much closer to a *detailed* solution to the problems of epigenesis than biologists were in 1945 when

Schrödinger wrote *What Is Life?* But we may take heart in the fact that, following the appearance of that book, the attempts to transform the problems of heredity and to produce a molecular transformation of the ancient problem of preformation succeeded in a remarkably short time—no more than a decade and a half. The problems we have considered here are in one sense more challenging because they require not only a molecular approach to epigenesis but also the merger of several very large and complex fields, including evolution and ecology. Moreover, genetics itself was very well formulated by Schrödinger's time— although not molecular, it had a quite robust theory of the gene as a linear entity, providing a basis for continued analysis at the molecular level.

We cannot say that this is yet so for development. While the theories advanced here are an attempt to move in the direction of unification, they have hardly been tested over a long enough period of time and with a sufficiently great variety of examples to afford any degree of confidence. Nonetheless, as some of the evidence I have quoted shows, they *can* be tested and modified and they do serve to focus attention upon the linkage of the developmental genetic and the evolutionary questions at a molecular level. They all share the idea that epigenesis leading to form depends upon a type of place-dependent signaling through many levels of organization. The places that govern the signaling are created in time by the previous signaling events. They are genetically constrained because the morphoregulatory molecules that are essential to their creation are under the influence of special sets of regulatory and structural genes. They are somatically variant, at least at a fine scale, because they have been generated by dynamic cellular processes. Both natural and somatic selection operate on organisms to effect this variance and constrain it. It appears that somatic variance is important in brain function; whether it has a physiological role in other organ systems remains to be seen.

We may conclude in the broad mode by stating that evolution leads to phenotypic changes in morphologic pattern mainly by genetic perturbations of topobiologically constrained developmental processes. These processes, while complex, follow definite rules, as we have seen for CAM expression. And while they lead dynamically to an extraordinary number of morphologic states, the number of these processes and their attendant morphoregulatory molecules is not huge. Instead, these processes are applied repeatedly and create new contexts that lead to nonlinear changes in which the same rules can be interpreted in different fashions. Differences in time and place are at the heart of such topobiological transformations. Topobiological processes show degeneracy in their pathways—several different genetic and epigenetic changes can lead to morphologically and functionally similar results or transformations. As a result of such properties, development is self-regulating and nonlinear; as a further consequence, even though it is stochastic, it can yield regularities. Development is nonetheless directional and historical, and as such it is, in general, irreversible.

My attempt in this book has been to suggest that a molecular analysis of this complex historical process is feasible, particularly given the powerful research tools provided by molecular biology and immunology. Such a molecular approach is sensible, however, only if pursued against the larger background provided by an analysis of morphologic evolution. This in turn requires a developmental analysis of the origins and limits of morphologic novelty and phenotypic transformation and a genetic analysis of the regulatory loops and special gene products governing primary processes. Both of these efforts must be reconciled with evolutionary ecology—the selection of morphs in habitats in terms of their function and fitness. The complexity of this challenge is enormous—indeed, in the case of the evolution of higher brain functions, it is staggering. Nevertheless, in the dialogue across many disciplines that has been facilitated by the growth of molecular approaches to embryology, some common themes can be discerned. When they are finally linked into a fully coherent theory of morphologic evolution, we will have a biologically satisfactory answer to Schrödinger's question, and the other side of biology—epigenesis—will finally be in the light.

ABBREVIATIONS

CAM	Cell adhesion molecule
CJM	Cell junctional molecule
DGR model	Digital gene regulator model
ECM	Extracellular matrix
HR gene	Historegulatory gene
ld polypeptide	Large domain polypeptide of N-CAM
MR gene	Morphoregulatory gene
PI model	Positional information model
RD model	Reaction-diffusion model
S gene	Selector gene
SAM	Substrate adhesion molecule
sd polypeptide	Small domain polypeptide of N-CAM
SMPP model	Strict mechanical pattern propagation model
ssd polypeptide	Small surface domain polypeptide of N-CAM

GLOSSARY

Allometric growth A basic alteration of patterned proportions changing nonisometrically with scale. If y is the variable of interest, x is body size, b is the slope of a logarithmic plot, and a is the intercept at unity, allometric growth is represented as $y = ax^b$.

Amnion The innermost membranes surrounding embryos of reptiles, birds, and mammals; thus, amniotes are vertebrates that develop in an amnion. Contrariwise, anamniotes are vertebrates that develop without an amniotic membrane (cyclostomes, fishes, and amphibians).

Animal pole The pole of the egg characterized by abundant cytoplasm and little yolk, and which gives rise to the nervous system; considered by eighteenth-century embryologists to be an "animal" region.

Anlage A German term used to signify the embryonic primordium of an organ or of an embryonic part.

Antibody Immunoglobulin molecules possessing binding sites for antigen (see *Immunoglobulin*).

Antigen A molecule containing structures or determinants that can elicit an immune response. Cellular reactions or a synthesis of circulating antibody may result from recognition of an antigen (see *Antibody, Clonal selection*).

Axon The neuronal process that carries the action potential to another neuron or muscle.

Barbs, Barbules Barbs are strands of keratinized cells that make up the vane of a feather. Barbules are branches of the barbs, and hold the barbs together by hooklets on their ends.

Behavioral embryology The study of the motions and response patterns of embryos in relation to later elements of behavior.

Biogenetic law Haeckel's dictum that "Ontogeny is a recapitulation of phylogeny," which is an idea that has not stood the test of time or the brunt of facts either from the genetics or the developmental dynamics of various species.

Blastomere   One of the early cells of a dividing egg, sometimes distinguished as either large cells (macromeres) or small cells (micromeres).

Blastula   A ball-like, hollow structure following cell division, itself consequent upon fertilization of an egg. Its central cavity is known as a blastocoel. A related structure is the blastoderm found in avian embryos, a disk-shaped structure arising in the same way. Both structures precede the gastrula (see *Gastrulation*). The formation of a blastopore (leading to a blastocoel) leaves a lip of tissue (the dorsal lip) capable of primary induction. This is the organizer of Spemann (q.v.).

Body plan (Bauplan)   The main organization of animal forms dependent on axis, symmetry (axial, radial, etc.), appendage type, and number that is characteristic of species within a genus. *Baupläne* in animals have not altered since the Precambrian period.

Cell address   The notion that the position of a single cell within an organism is specifically determined by a marker or by molecular recognition.

Cell adhesion molecules (CAMs)   Glycoproteins, intrinsic to and mobile in the plane of the cell membrane, that link the cells bearing them to other cells in cell-cell adhesion. Primary CAMs appear early in embryogenesis on derivatives of all three germ layers. Secondary CAMs appear somewhat later on a more restricted set of tissues. Most CAMs bind homophilically. So far, three CAMs have been extensively described that are calcium independent in their binding, and three different CAMs that are all related to each other have been shown to be calcium dependent. Different CAMs have different binding specificities, and a cell can express more than one kind at any given time.

CAM cycle   The expression of particular CAMs after inductive signaling, followed by cell surface modulation, the control of movements, and collective formation, all leading in turn to further influences on inductive signaling. Such cyclic and recursive controls can lead to morphogenetic change while influencing signals to historegulatory genes as well. CAM cycles have been seen in structures as diverse as kidneys and feathers. Two CAM cycles can be coupled via interactions of two inducing collectives.

Cell collective   A term used to designate a set of cells that are more or less closely linked by morphoregulatory molecules. Such sets can range in number from hundreds to thousands of cells. Alternatively, a group of adjacent cells with a similar phenotype acting as a source or target for signals.

Cell cortex   The most peripheral shell of cytoplasm underlying the plasmalemma of a cell and containing many membrane-associated proteins and cytoskeletal structures.

Cell junctional molecules (CJMs)   These comprise a variety of proteins that interact to form cell junctions. Different proteins contribute to: gap junctions, which allow passage of molecular signals of up to 1 kD from cell to cell; tight junctions, which form apical seals in epithelia; adherens junctions, which link cells and connect to actin in the cytoskeleton; and desmosomes, which link cells and connect to intermediate filaments in the cell.

Chemoaffinity model   The idea proposed by Sperry to account for order and pattern in the nervous system stating that cells have markers (down almost to the level of the individual neuron) governing their ordered relation to each other.

Chordates   Members of the phylum Chordata possessing a notochord, pharyngeal gill slits, and a dorsal nerve chord (including tunicates, lancelets, and vertebrates).

Classification couples (and n-tuples)   Terms used in the theory of neuronal group selection to refer to two independent sampling systems (e.g., vision and active touch) whose central nervous system maps are reentrantly connected. The smallest unit of perceptual categorization.

Clonal selection   The idea proposed by Burnet that specific antibody production occurs by selection from a population of lymphocytes, each of which carries an antibody of a single kind and which would replicate following stimulation by binding to an appropriate antigen (see *Somatic selection*).

Clone   The asexual progeny of a single cell.

Compensatory functional interactions   Nonlinear cooperative interactions among systems such as muscles, bones, and nervous systems that can buffer, damp, or alter the effects of genetically induced variation. This is also true of behavior itself.

Competence   The ability of cells at a given stage to be induced. This is of more or less restricted duration.

Complexity   The general increase in cell numbers, types, arrangements, and forms leading to increasing diversity in phenotypes during evolution.

Convergent extension   A term used to describe the convergence of cells of the marginal zone of the frog egg while they extend and intercalate themselves during involution of this zone to bring about a narrower array. Convergent extension is the key to gastrulation movements in spherical eggs of the frog.

Cortical tractor model   A hypothetical set of mechanisms proposed by Oster and colleagues to explain the folding of epithelial sheets. These mechanisms are based on cortical flow in epithelial cells of plasmalemma and actin-myosin complexes; inequities in such flow can lead to exchange of cells in an epithelium and to forces that cause curvature of sheets, as in neurulation.

Cytokinesis   Division or segmentation of the cytoplasmic part of a cell, with segregation of daughter nuclei to separate cells so that it becomes two or more cells. Cytokinesis usually occurs in parallel with nuclear division; when cytokinesis is omitted, multinucleated cells or syncytia may result.

Cytoskeleton   A complex multiprotein assembly that influences interactions throughout the cell, leading to changes in cell shape and movement. It consists of tubule proteins (tubulins with associated proteins, dyneins, and kinesin), of microfilaments consisting of actin interacting with a variety of other proteins including those contributing to motion, and of intermediate filament proteins such as vimentin, desmin, and cytokeratin. The cytoskeleton is a highly dynamic structure, and some of its components are required for cell surface modulation.

Degeneracy   The existence of developmental paths or morphologies with different structure but equivalent function. Developmental degeneracy is the term applied to the fact that different developmental pathways can lead to the same morphologic result.

Dendrites   Branching neuronal processes receiving synaptic input.

Determination   The attainment of a more or less final state of differentiation of a tissue after induction of its competent precursors.

Developmental constraints   Usually used to refer to the fact that the dynamics of development and of developmental genetics do not permit all envisionable phenotypes but only a small subset. Thus the term is used in reference to evolution, specifically morphologic evolution. Constraints include the limits of cellular mechanochemistry, the various size limits and continuity limits of inducing collectives, limits on migrations and epithelial-mesenchymal transformation, various spatial requirements of signal loops, structural requirements on neural and skeletal systems, and limits on behavioral adaptations.

Developmental genetics   The use of genetics (mutant genes) to analyze one or another aspect of a developmental (e.g., embryological) event.

The developmental genetic question   How does a one-dimensional genetic code specify a three-dimensional animal? One of the two major questions addressed in this book (see *The evolutionary question*).

Developmental view of evolution   The idea that evolution is a process of phenotypic transformation resulting largely from genetically mediated change in developmental dynamics which is itself altered throughout phylogeny. In this view, evolution leads to changes in morphology via genetic perturbations of topobiologically constrained developmental processes.

Differentiation   Progressive specialization of developing cells; the result of differential gene expression.

Digital gene regulator (DGR) model   A hypothetical developmental model based on gene cascades for *Drosophila* development. It is based on a series of *discrete* subdivisions of cell populations by local gene interactions. Control of pattern is achieved by local discrete expression of a number of regulatory gene products in a sequential cascade that is combinationally degenerate (i.e., more than one combination of inducing regulators can give the same inductive result). Redistribution of the regulators by epigenetic means in each segment allows further subdivision events.

Econiche   Roughly, the habitat (including food sources) occupied by individuals of the same and different competing species.

Ectoderm   The most superficial of the three germ layers; gives rise to the nervous system and epidermis.

Egg asymmetry or polarity   Maternally determined distribution of factors in the egg endoplasm and surface governing the formation of poles with different inductive capabilities and competence. An example is the formation of animal and vegetal poles in the frog egg.

Egg cleavage   Postfertilization mitotic cell divisions characterized by an absence of net cell growth. Holoblastic cleavage is that in which the entire egg participates (characteristic of mammalian eggs). Meroblastic cleavage is restricted to one superficial region of the egg (the nonyolky part) and is found in some fishes, reptiles, and birds.

Embryo   Refers to a developing organism prior to birth or hatching.

Embryonic induction   A form of milieu-dependent differentiation occurring during embryogenesis. In this process, cells of different histories are brought together by morphogenetic movements, exchange signals as collectives, and undergo differential gene expression. Induction generally takes place between a pair of such collectives. Most of the time, but not always, induction is asymmetric; the timing of induction in this case depends on the induced tissue, but its location depends on that of inducing tissues (one or a series) called inducers or inductors. When the inducer is specifically required, induction is instructive; when many tissues can serve as inducers, it is permissive. The relative positions of cells at particular times are critical for induction. Induction is a paradigmatic topobiological event.

Endoderm   The innermost of the three germ layers; gives rise to the gut and related structures.

Endoplasm   A term used to refer to the cytoplasmic portion of a frog's egg below the cortical layer.

Entwicklungsmechanik   The term used by Roux in 1894 to plead for a new science of *developmental mechanics* whose task was to reduce the formative processes of development to the natural laws that underlie them. Unfortunately, this important program, which preceded molecular embryology, bypassed the study of evolution.

Epidermis   The outer ectodermal tissue of skin; in the early embryo it consists of periderm and ectoderm.

Epigenesis   The changes over time of cellular states as a result of previous cellular states and cooperative interactions occurring at particular places during growth and development. Epigenetic changes are often irreversible, and, to this extent, epigenesis is a historical process.

Epigenetic sequences   The developmental expression of genes followed by the expression of apparently unrelated genes in time scales that are long compared to those during which control of intracellular events occurs. According to the morphoregulator hypothesis (q.v.), this is the result of the signaling interactions of cell collectives under the influence of morphoregulatory molecules governing primary processes of development.

Epithelial-mesenchymal transformation The conversion in state from tightly linked polar cells with a basement membrane to loosely associated cells (migratory or stationary) surrounded by an extracellular matrix. Such a conversion can occur in either direction. When it occurs from mesenchyme to epithelium, it is sometimes called condensation.

Epithelium Sheets or masses of cells more or less tightly linked by CAMs and various junctions, showing definite cellular polarity with apical seals, junctional coupling of various extents, and a basal structure resting on a basement membrane.

Essentialism and typological thinking The notion of a priori categories, the great chain of being, or Platonic categories. The opposite of population thinking.

Eukaryote An organism with cells whose nuclei have nuclear envelopes, chromosomes, and nuclear divisions leading to mitosis or meiosis.

The evolutionary question How is an answer to the developmental genetic question (q.v.) reconciled with relatively rapid changes in form occurring in relatively short evolutionary times? The major question underlying the analysis of morphologic evolution, and one of the two major concerns of this book (see *The developmental genetic question*).

Expression rules and sequences The appearance or removal of particular CAMs in a defined fashion at particular sites or tissue derivatives in development. Such sequences have not been as clearly worked out for substrate adhesion molecules and their receptors or for CJMs.

Extracellular matrix (ECM) components Substrate adhesion molecules (SAMs), including collagens, glycoproteins such as laminin, fibronectin, cytotactin, proteoglycans, and the nonprotein hyaluronic acid, all of which contribute to the extracellular matrix.

Fate The end of the process of cell determination resulting in a particular histodifferentiated state of a cell at a given location.

Fate map Classic fate maps are constructed by labeling cells and following their fates for a defined period of time, and then mapping the origin of these cells or their progeny onto a chosen structure (e.g., the blastoderm) at a given stage. A composite CAM fate map consists of CAM developmental distributions mapped onto a classic tissue fate map.

Fitness The result of adaptation. In a Darwinian sense, the expected number of offspring produced by a type. In the Fisherian sense, the per capita rate of increase of a type (a supervenient property).

Gamete   Refers to a mature reproductive cell, either egg or sperm.

Gap gene   Genes in *Drosophila* that in mutant form result in deletions of groups of segments.

Gastrulation   Formation of primary germ layers—ectoderm, mesoderm, and endoderm—by a set of morphogenetic movements prior to or coincident with the folding of the embryo into a structure topologically equivalent to a tube within a tube. The resulting structure is called a gastrula. The geometry of gastrulation differs in different species, as does the relative contribution of movement, division, and cell death. In all cases, gastrulation results from migration, sheet movement, epithelial-mesenchymal transformation, and embryonic induction.

Gene network or cascade   Refers to the fact that a group of different developmentally important genes interact in various fashions to regulate development at particular topobiologically significant sites.

Genus   A taxonomic division comprising various closely related species within a family.

Global cell surface modulation   Alteration in the mobility of a majority of cell surface proteins, of cytoskeletal states, of cell shapes, and of mitogenic signal processing after cross-linkage of certain glycoproteins of the cell surface. First seen after interaction of the cell surface with concanavalin A; forms of global modulation are seen with matrix proteins such as cytotactin and fibronectin.

Gray crescent   A cytoplasmic region in some amphibian eggs that is grayish in color and that correlates with the future dorsal side of the embryo.

Hensen's node   Cell collectives in the ectoderm of the avian gastrula at the anterior end of the primitive streak. It is analogous to the organizer or dorsal lip of the blastopore in the gastrula of amphibians.

Heterochrony   Alterations of tissues and form in development by mutations that lead to changes in the relative rates of development of different body parts or traits. Such temporal shifts result in dissociation between rates of development of somatic traits and those of gonads. Also used specially in this book as molecular heterochrony (q.v.)—different alterations in rates of responses of morphoregulatory genes (see also *Progenesis, Neoteny, Recapitulation, Paedomorphosis, Hypermorphosis*).

Historegulatory (HR) genes   One of the three kinds of regulatory genes that are important to morphogenesis according to the morphoregulator hypothesis. HR genes regulate structural genes other than those for CAMs, SAMs, and CJMs, and the products of these genes are essential for the life and histodifferentiation of a cell. *Within the framework provided by morphoregulatory gene action,* alterations in HR genes can also lead to changes in shape.

Homeobox sequence   A highly conserved 180–base-pair sequence encoding a protein structure with homology to certain bacterial DNA-binding proteins. Homeobox sequences are associated with particular genes in *Drosophila* such as homeotic genes but have also been found in other species including vertebrates.

Homeotic mutations   Mutations (typically in *Drosophila*) that result in the formation of structures in one part of the embryo that are normally appropriate to another part of it. Homeotic mutations appear to be concerned with developmental pathways altering the *fate* of particular groups of cells.

Homophilic and heterophilic binding   Homophilic binding of a CAM on a cell refers to binding to the same kind of CAM on an apposing cell. Heterophilic binding is to another kind of molecule or receptor.

Hypermorphosis   Prolongation of development so that an adult trait appears in a preadult shape. Leads to a form of recapitulation, as Gould puts it, "by prolongation." A category of heterochrony (q.v.).

Immunoglobulin (Ig)   Any antibody produced by B cells. The basic Ig is a tetramer consisting of two identical large (H = heavy) and two identical small (L = light) polypeptides, held together by disulfide bonds. Other classes differ in heavy chain structure and number of units.

Inner cell mass   Cells in the inner compartment of the blastula of a mammalian embryo that are destined to form the embryo proper as well as some of its membranes.

Instructive   Any developmental factor specifically necessary to determine cell fate (see *Permissive*).

Integral protein   Protein possessing a transmembrane spanning region, a cytoplasmic tail or domain, and an extracellular domain.

Junctions (gap, tight, adherens, desmosomal)   Specialized areas of cell-cell contacts mediated by different characteristic morphoregulatory proteins. Close apposition of plasma membranes and nearby cytoplasmic specializations are characteristic of each type.

Keratin   A family of intermediate filament proteins with high sulfur content found in differentiated epidermal, hair, feather, and scale cells.

Larva   The early form of an animal (as seen, for example, in frog tadpoles) that at birth or hatching is morphologically unlike its parent and must metamorphose before assuming the adult characteristics.

Limb bud(s)   The anlage or rudiment of the limbs in vertebrate embryos.

Local cell surface modulation   Alterations in the prevalence (or surface density), posttranslational chemical structure, polarity, or cytoplasmic domain of a particular cell surface receptor. Applied specifically to the large number of changes that alter CAM binding, it applies as well to receptors such as integrins.

Macroevolution   Evolution of taxa above the species level occurring, in general, at slower rates than species evolution. Macroevolution can give rise to morphologic novelties such as the change from scales to feathers.

Mechanochemical events   Changes in cell shape, cell number, cell movement, and cell contact. Such events are mediated via molecules of the cytoskeleton, molecules governing cell motion and division, and morphoregulatory molecules. Such events lead to changes in the shape of cells and of cell collectives, and thus they eventuate in changes in form. At a higher scale, they are responsible for the mechanics of the formed animal.

Mesenchyme   A loosely associated group of cells (either stationary or migratory), each of which is usually surrounded by an extracellular matrix. Often used to refer to cells in this state from mesoderm, but the term is not exclusive to cells from this layer.

Mesoderm   The middle germ layer that gives rise to muscle, connective tissue, skeleton, and various other structures.

Metamerism   A term applied to the presence of a pattern of periodically repeated body units, segments, or metameres.

Metamorphosis   Transformation of a larva into an adult form.

Metazoa   Sexual organisms that are multicellular, arising from protozoan ancestors and radiating extensively during the late Precambrian era (0.7×10^9 years ago). There are two great branches of their phylogenetic tree, protostomes and deuterostomes (q.v.), the embryology of which differs in detail.

Microevolution   Evolutionary processes acting on species, showing short generation times and genetic recombination.

Molecular embryology   The study of molecules regulating the development of an embryo from the formation of gametes to the adult animal. This field includes the study of cell differentiation, but it also must seek to explain morphogenesis and some aspects of morphologic evolution. It aims to link molecular genetics to the mechanochemistry of cells by analyzing defined signal paths.

Molecular heterochrony   The idea that mutations leading to changes in CAM cycles or SAM regulatory networks can cause changes in the timing, coordination, and covariance of key morphologic events, thus leading to a basis for an answer to the evolutionary question (q.v.). Consequently, small changes in the response times of morphoregulatory genes for SAMs and CAMs could lead to large nonlinear changes in expression sequences and morphology. The addition of the notion of molecular heterochrony to the morphoregulator hypothesis leads to the extended morphoregulator hypothesis.

Morph   Any of the genetic forms or individual variants that account for genetic polymorphism.

Morphogen   A term applied to any molecule presumed to influence morphogenesis but specifically applied to inducing signals. May include growth factors, hormones, etc.

Morphogenesis   The process by which animal form is generated.

Morphologic evolution The study of the developmental and ecological origins of animal form and tissue pattern. Includes the study of how genes can define animal shape and phenotypic function in developmental and evolutionary time.

The morphoregulator (MR) hypothesis A hypothesis linking control of epigenetic primary processes to a set of genetic elements (morphoregulatory, historegulatory, and selector genes) in order to account for morphogenesis. The linkage occurs via morphoregulatory proteins acting in CAM cycles and SAM modulatory networks. If confirmed, this hypothesis would provide the basis for an answer to the developmental genetic question (q.v.).

Morphoregulatory (MR) genes One of the three major kinds of developmentally important regulatory genes postulated to control morphogenesis according to the morphoregulator hypothesis. MR genes control the expression of structural genes for CAMs, SAMs, and CJMs.

Morphoregulatory molecules Molecules (usually proteins) at cell surfaces or in substrates such as extracellular matrices. Expression and interactions of such molecules lead to changes in cell shape and movement, to linkage among cells, and to new forms of regulation of gene expression. The term includes CAMs, SAMs (and their receptors), and CJMs.

Mosaic development A pattern of cell differentiation and fate, fixed or determined early by a defined set of cell locations, sometimes even of a single blastomere. In some species, such a cell can give rise fixedly to a definite set of later structures. There are different degrees of mosaicism and regulation in different species.

Neoteny Retardation of somatic development with respect to the normal course of reproductive maturation (see *Progenesis* for the other heterochronic process leading to *Paedomorphosis*). A category of heterochrony (q.v.).

Neural crest A special collection of cells located early at the top of the neural tube but migrating to various locations during embryogenesis. By this process, they give rise to the entire peripheral nervous system, ganglia, melanocytes, and various craniofacial structures.

Neural Darwinism A general term referring to the collected statements of the theory of neuronal group selection (q.v.).

Neural plate A thickened region of the dorsal ectoderm of a neurula giving rise to the neural tube, which in turn gives rise to the brain and spinal cord.

Neuronal group selection A process by which sensorimotor activity leads to selective strengthening or weakening of populations of synapses. Also applied to the ideas of neural Darwinism (q.v.).

Neurula The structure or stage of morphogenesis following gastrulation and neutral induction in which a neural plate curves into a neural groove and finally closes into a neural tube. The entire process is called neurulation.

Notochord   An axial structure of mesodermal origin underlying the neural tube.

Oncogene   A gene responsible for neoplastic growth of a host cell, which may be introduced by a tumor virus, and which can be stably inherited.

Organizer of Spemann   The dorsal lip of the blastopore, capable of forming a whole embryo after transplantation to another part of the embryo (see *Blastula, Gastrulation*).

Optic tectum   A central station in the visual pathway of many vertebrates receiving retinal fibers; located in the midbrain.

Paedomorphosis   The retention of traits characteristic of a juvenile ancestral form by a sexually mature descendant form (see *Neoteny, Progenesis*). A category of heterochrony (q.v.).

Pair rule genes   Genes in *Drosophila* that in mutant form result in deletion of alternate sequential units.

Pattern formation   The processes by which ordered arrangements of cells or their products are attained. A term used generally and specifically in relation to morphogenesis. Any spatiotemporal ordering of molecules, cells, or tissues may form a pattern, which can then occur at different scales. Morphogenesis depends on pattern formation which, at its finest scale, depends on spatial distribution of both positive ("excitatory") or negative ("inhibitory") signals. Some theories of morphogenesis postulate "prepatterns," steady-state distributions of molecules providing cues to cells.

Perceptual categorization   The discrimination of objects or events from other objects or events or from background by means of the functioning of anatomical and physiological arrangements in the peripheral and central nervous system.

Permissive   Any developmental factor that permits differentiation to occur but does not specifically instruct cell fate (see *Instructive*).

Place-dependent mechanisms of gene expression   Mechanisms by which the dynamics and temporal sequences of driving force primary processes are regulated by morphoregulatory molecules to create form. This notion defines a place—a relative position of adjoining cell collectives at a given time that will then release (and respond to) new signals for morphoregulatory gene expression.

Placodes   Distinctly patterned local ectodermal structures giving rise to various regional specializations. Examples include precursors of ganglia (e.g., optic or nasal placodes) and early precursors of skin appendages such as feathers. Local rearrangements of cell shapes, movements, and differentiation in placodes give rise to particular structures.

Pleiotropic action of a gene   Alteration in a single gene that can affect many unrelated sites and lead to more than one form of morphologic change.

Polarity   A graded organization along one of the major embryonic axes.

Polygenic control   Control of morphological variation by multiple genes. Applicable to continuous genetic variation related to alterations in size.

Polymorphous sets   Sets that do not require either necessary or sufficient conditions for distinguishing their members. Applied to stimuli in nature received by the nervous system in the context of the earliest categorization events.

Population thinking   The idea that individuality and variance in a population is real and that it provides a source for selection events. First enunciated by Charles Darwin.

Positional information (PI) models   The idea of cell patterning proposed by Wolpert that a cell can read signals already present in a spatial prepattern and alter or confirm its address (see *Cell address*).

Precedence hypothesis   The notion that the CAMs appear first in development to link cells, followed later by appearances of SAMs and CJMs, respectively. This entails the idea that CAM interactions are required prior to the formation of various junctions. In some cases, it has been shown that specific CAMs actually take part in junction formation.

Preformation   The ancient idea that animal form was already present in one or the other of the gametes. Contrasted with epigenesis and now supplanted by the notion that form is specified by particular genes working through the genetic code.

Primary induction   The early induction occurring just before or at gastrulation. A classic example is that occurring through interaction with the dorsal lip of the blastopore (Spemann's organizer), a region capable of inducing formation of an entire embryo when transplanted to a different region of the early gastrula. Primary induction is also called neural induction because one of its first steps is induction of the neural plate. All other embryonic inductions (e.g., for heart, liver, feathers, etc.) are called secondary.

Primary processes of development   The major processes of cells that affect embryogenesis and morphogenesis. Driving force processes include cell division, cell and tissue motion, and cell death. Regulatory processes include cell-cell and cell-substrate adhesion, and milieu-dependent differentiation or embryonic induction.

Primitive streak   The axial thickening in the ectoderm of the gastrulas of reptiles, birds, and mammals that is the site of ingression of cells to form a layer called the mesoblast, which finally becomes the mesoderm.

Progenesis   Acceleration of gonadal development so that sexual maturity is reached in a small-sized juvenile body with truncation of somatic development (see also *Neoteny,* the other form of paedomorphosis). A category of heterochrony (q.v.).

Prokaryotes   Organisms such as bacteria and blue-green algae that lack a nucleus and binary fission.

Proteoglycan   A large ECM macromolecule made of protein and sugar in which the quantity of sugar far exceeds the quantity of protein. Characteristic sugars are present in proteoglycans, most of which are in the ECM but some of which can be intrinsic.

Protostome and deuterostome   Animal forms named in terms of the site of origin of the larval mouth. In protostomes, this arises from the blastopore or a nearby location. In deuterostomes, the larval mouth arises at a distance (anteriorly) from the blastopore, which is the site of invagination of cells that will form the primitive gut of the embryo.

Reaction-diffusion (RD) models   Hypothetical models, first proposed by Turing, explaining the origin of pattern in development as a result of nonlinear coupling of chemical reactions, diffusion, and flow.

Recapitulation   Acceleration of the appearance of a somatic feature in relation to gonadal maturation so that an adult trait becomes a juvenile trait in a descendant. A category of heterochrony (q.v.).

Regulative development   Development in which induction occurs as a result of morphogenetic movements but which can compensate for or regulate cell fates within certain time frames as a result of cellular interactions. A region that can regulate following the ablation of any of its parts is known as a morphogenetic field. Regulation is a function of time, cell number, and neighborhood. It has been contrasted with mosaic development (q.v.), but in fact all development shows some degree of regulation.

Retinotectal projection   Refers to the mapping of retinal ganglion cell axons to a primary visual area, the tectum (q.v.), in such a way as to provide a map of visual space.

Segment polarity genes   Genes in *Drosophila* that in mutant form lead to an altered pattern within each body segment.

Selector (S) genes   One of the three main kinds of genes postulated by the morphoregulator hypothesis to be important for morphogenesis. Similar to homeotic genes, S genes restrict expression of sequences of cytodifferentiation at certain places and developmental times by affecting certain historegulatory genes. S genes thus control histogenetic pathways.

Somatic selection   Refers to systems such as the immune system in which antibody variation occurs as a result of somatic recombination and mutation of antibody genes followed by selection through enhanced replication of lymphocytes carrying antibodies with binding sites complementary to an antigen. Also used to refer to the selection of combinations of synapses in a single individual's brain as a result of behavior (see *Neuronal group selection, Theory of neuronal group selection*).

Somites Periodically repeated, cephalocaudally disposed epithelial masses surrounding the neural tube. They give rise to the *sclerotome*, a mesenchyme that provides cells for vertebrae, and to the *dermamyotome*, an epithelial structure from which cells will migrate to form dermis and various muscles.

Species The taxonomic category subordinate to genus, the members of which are defined by extensive similarities, including the ability to interbreed.

Spinal ganglion Ganglia containing sensory nerve cell bodies located laterally to each side of the spinal cord in vertebrates; also called sensory ganglion and dorsal root ganglion.

Strict mechanical pattern propagation (SMPP) models The proposal of Oster and colleagues that cells can alter their movements and patterning by long-range effects of stretch and compression propagated through matrix proteins spanning many cell diameters.

Substrate adhesion molecules (SAMs) Molecules found in ECM (both basement membrane and matrix proper) secreted by cells and capable of binding to cell surface receptors (integrins) as well as to each other in a large variety of ways by a large number of sites of different specificity.

SAM modulation network Members of the SAM complex present in different distributions and amounts bind to each other and to cells, forming a network with different properties at different embryonic sites. It has been hypothesized that combinatorial variation in the network leads to different forms of cell surface modulation. Inasmuch as their interactions are more complex than those of CAMs, and some network molecules are extracellular, the control or regulation of SAMs in networks must differ in kinetics and type from that of CAMs.

Synapse The specialized region of interaction between neurons, usually formed between axons and dendrites, but also formed between any pair of these structures (like or unlike) or between any one of these structures and the nerve cell body. Most synapses are chemical, releasing one or more neurotransmitters from the *presynaptic neuron* to bind to receptors on the *postsynaptic neuron*.

Tectum The structure in the central nervous system that first receives axons from retinal ganglion cells.

Theory of neuronal group selection The theory which proposes that the brain functions for perceptual categorization via somatic selection events and reentrant maps. First, developmental selection forms a variant microanatomy as a result of CAM and SAM action. Then, after the brain's anatomy is formed, particular combinations of synapses in populations are selected by changing their strengths during behavior. Selection providing a basis for categorization is made from mapped structures that have reciprocal connections and exchange reentrant signals (see also *Neural Darwinism* and *Neuronal group selection*).

Topobiology The study of the place-dependent regulation of cells resulting from interactions of molecules at cell surfaces with those of other cells or substrates. In the context of this book, such place-dependent molecular interactions can regulate the primary processes of development and lead to changes in morphology by epigenetic means. The fundamental problem of topobiology is to determine how cells of different types are ordered in time or place during development to give species-specific tissue pattern and animal form.

Totipotency   The ability of a cell or group of cells to give rise to a whole organism.

Transformation rules   Referring here to means that relate alterations in phenotype (upon which natural selection acts) to changes in gene frequency (by which population geneticists analyze evolutionary change). The emphasis in this book is on T_1, the set of rules connecting events and morphologic patterning of development to those in the mature animal (conferring selective advantage), and somewhat on T_2, the rules related to ecological interactions of animals in interspecies and intraspecies competition.

Trophectoderm   The outer layer of the mammalian blastula involved in acquiring nutrients from the uterine wall (see *Inner cell mass*).

Vegetal pole   The pole of the egg that is opposite to the animal pole. Structures near the vegetal pole give rise to "vegetal" organs such as the gut (see *Animal pole*).

Von Baer's laws   A set of dicta stating that, while earlier stages of various taxa resemble one another, as development progresses, each species develops in its own particular pattern. Perhaps closer to a descriptive truth than Haeckel's biogenetic law. Present findings, however, suggest that these laws do not apply inexorably even to very early development.

Yolk   Parts of the egg or of its progeny containing nutritional elements in storage form.

Zygote   A fertilized egg.

CREDITS

Figures 3.1 and 7.5 from *Neural Darwinism: The theory of neuronal group selection,* by Gerald M. Edelman. Copyright © 1987 by Basic Books, Inc. Reprinted by permission of the publisher.

Figure 3.2 from "Cell-adhesion molecules: A molecular basis for animal form," by Gerald M. Edelman. Copyright © 1984 by Scientific American, Inc. All rights reserved.

Figure 4.1 reproduced from *The Journal of Cell Biology* 101 (1985):1009–26, by copyright permission of the Rockefeller University Press.

Figures 4.2, 6.2 (*top*), 6.5, and 7.3 reproduced, with permission, from the *Annual Review of Cell Biology,* vol. 2. Copyright © 1986 by Annual Reviews Inc.

Figure 5.1 reproduced from Elliot Sober, 1984, *The nature of selection: Evolutionary theory in philosophical focus,* by copyright permission of the MIT Press.

Figures 6.1*B* and 6.6*A* reproduced from Gerald M. Edelman, "Surface modulation in cell recognition and cell growth," *Science* 192 (16 April 1976):218–26. Copyright © 1976 by the AAAS.

Figure 6.6*B* reprinted by permission from *Nature* 259:406–9. Copyright © 1976 Macmillan Journals Limited.

Figures 7.1, 7.2, 8.1, and 10.4*A, B,* and *C* copyright © 1987 Munksgaard International Publishers Ltd., Copenhagen, Denmark.

Interstitial cell surface proteoglycan and small interstitial proteoglycan in figure 7.7 from V. C. Hascall, 1986, *Functions of the proteoglycans,* Ciba Foundation Symposium 124. Reprinted by permission of John Wiley & Sons, Ltd.

Figure 7.9 reprinted with permission from Gerald M. Edelman, "Morphoregulatory molecules," *Biochemistry* 27:3534–43. Copyright © 1988 American Chemical Society.

Figure 7.10*A, B,* and *D* from *Junctional complexes of epithelial cells,* Ciba Foundation Symposium 125. Reprinted by permission of John Wiley & Sons, Ltd.

INDEX

Page numbers for items in the glossary are not listed; these items should be consulted independently.